THE STORY OF BRITAIN

VOLUME II
FROM 1485 TO 1714

BY

H. A. CLEMENT M.A.

ADULT EDUCATION TUTOR CAMBRIDGE UNIVERSITY
FORMER SENIOR HISTORY MASTER AUDENSHAW GRAMMAR SCHOOL
LATE SENIOR SCHOLAR IN HISTORY TRINITY COLLEGE CAMBRIDGE

AUTHOR OF
"THE STORY OF THE ANCIENT WORLD"
"THE STORY OF MODERN EUROPE"
ETC.

GEORGE G. HARRAP & COMPANY LTD.
LONDON   TORONTO   WELLINGTON   SYDNEY

First published in Great Britain 1941
by GEORGE G. HARRAP & CO. LTD.
182 *High Holborn, London, W.C.*1

Reprinted: February 1944; *January* 1945;
September 1945; *November* 1946; *May* 1948;
August 1951; *January* 1953; *August* 1954;
April 1955; *March* 1957; *June* 1958;
June 1960

MADE IN GREAT BRITAIN. PRINTED AT THE PITMAN PRESS, BATH

PREFACE

THE aim of this book is to cover the main features of British history, in their European setting, from 1485 to 1714.

As with the first volume, the subject-matter has been broadened to include much besides the merely political and military events of history. While these have not been neglected, room has been found for other elements in our national history as well: for economic and social developments, for the growth of the British Empire, for literature, science, and architecture.

A novel feature of the book lies in its treatment of the European background. This is not scattered about in odd snippets amid the sections on British history, although, wherever necessary, reference is made in the British-history sections to the European background. But the main features of European history are described in separate chapters, each dealing with an important topic covering about half a century: namely, the Reformation, the Counter-Reformation, the Thirty Years' War, and the Age of Louis XIV. Each of these chapters has been placed just before the corresponding chapters on British history, so that the pupil can obtain a knowledge of the European setting before he studies the history of his own country.

As in the first volume, there are numerous maps and illustrations, together with questions and exercises to test the pupil's reading. The subject-matter has been made sufficiently full to meet the requirements of the Ordinary Level examinations of the various Boards.

I am indebted to Mr J. Lord and to my father for help in revising the proofs.

H. A. C.

CONTENTS

MAPS AND PLANS

GENEALOGICAL TABLES

ILLUSTRATIONS

THE STORY OF BRITAIN

PART I
THE TUDOR PERIOD (1485-1603)

CHAPTER I
THE BEGINNING OF THE MODERN WORLD

A Turning-point in History

THE year 1400 can be regarded as near the end of the Middle Ages, the year 1600 as soon after the beginning of the modern period. Two questions arise from this statement. When did the change-over occur, and what is it that distinguishes the modern period from the Middle Ages?

The first question cannot be answered very exactly. Dividing-lines in history do not occur in any one particular year; in this respect they are unlike battles, Acts of Parliament, and the births and deaths of famous persons. Rather they are like the divisions in a person's own life: the periods of childhood, boyhood, youth, manhood, middle age, and old age, which merge into one another with very little change that can be seen from one day to another. Still, changes do occur, and we all have some rough idea as to when they take place. In the same way the change from medieval to modern times is regarded by most people as occurring somewhere about the year 1500.

As for the second question, four main changes can be regarded as marking this transition from medieval to modern times:

(1) The decay of feudal power and the growth of united nations under the rule of strong monarchs.

(2) The advancement of human learning, either by the rediscovery of the knowledge of the ancients or by the opening up of altogether new fields of knowledge.

(3) The discovery of new lands and routes. The outstanding events in this connexion were the voyage of Christopher Columbus to America in 1492 and the voyage of Vasco da Gama round the Cape of Good Hope in 1498.

(4) The decline of the Catholic Church. This culminated in the movement known as the Reformation, which resulted in the establishment of Protestant Churches in many countries.

(1) *The New Monarchy and the Decline of Feudalism*

After the fall of the Roman Empire in the fifth century Europe had been thrown into a state of great confusion. This confusion had lasted for about five centuries, and by the year 1000 the so-called Dark Ages were at an end.

Various forces and institutions had by then appeared to give Europe the benefit of law and order. The greatest of these was the Catholic Church, which had become universal throughout western Europe. As a counterpart to the Catholic Church there had been established the Holy Roman Empire; but although the first Holy Roman Emperor, namely, Charlemagne, had ruled over wide territories and wielded vast powers, the later emperors had lost much of this power and territory and had become less powerful than the strong kings of certain other countries. At the other end of the scale to these dreams of universal rule by Pope and Emperor there had grown up the feudal system, which, although more modest in its aims, had been more successful in many ways in carrying them out. The feudal lords soon became extremely powerful. They held large estates, they regulated the lives of their tenants, they held law-courts to settle disputes, they raised armies and built castles, and at times they even waged war against their king.

Kings had existed before the feudal lords appeared; but their power had not been great, as at first they were little more than tribal chiefs. None the less, as the centuries passed the power of the king gradually grew. In England the House of Wessex became supreme; but the real beginning of a strong monarchy in England came with the Norman Conquest. In France the Capetians laid the foundations of a strong royal house; in the fourteenth century they were succeeded by the Valois, who were able in the end to unite France against the English invasions of the Hundred Years' War. In Spain there were at first several Christian kingdoms which engaged in crusades against the Moors, who occupied large parts of the country. In time most of these kingdoms united, and with the marriage of Ferdinand of Aragon and Isabella of Castile in 1469, the Spanish peninsula (with the exception of Portugal and a small part that remained in Moorish hands till 1492) soon came under one royal house.

The feudal barons had strongly resisted the growth of these new monarchies, but in some ways their resistance proved their own undoing. The civil wars that they promoted killed off many of their own number, and often gave the king an opportunity of punishing them by fines or execution or by confiscating their estates. Thus the king became strong and wealthy. As commerce and industry developed, townsmen and merchants lent their support to the king in his struggle against the unruly barons. From the fourteenth century onward gunpowder came into use. Kings were then able to batter down the castles of the barons and deal a further blow at the declining power of feudalism. With his growing wealth the king was able to hire professional soldiers and make himself independent of the soldiers supplied by the barons.

The growth of strong monarchies was closely connected with the growth of national feeling. In the Middle Ages men had thought of themselves as peasants, squires, knights, or priests. Now they began to think of themselves as Englishmen, Frenchmen, or Spaniards. With the growth of nationalism the position of the king increased in importance, as he became the symbol of his nation's desire for fame and prosperity. Nationalism proved beneficial in undermining feudalism, but it has brought to the modern world many other problems, for the wrong sort of nationalism leads to hatred and wars between the peoples of the world. The new outlook found perfect expression in a book called *The Prince*, written by an Italian, Machiavelli, in 1513, wherein it was maintained that a ruler is justified in any means, however dishonest, so long as he increases the power of himself and his state.

In Germany and Italy strong monarchies and united nations failed to appear, and even in those countries where strong monarchies had appeared by 1500, parts of the feudal system still lingered on. In France and most other Continental countries the humble peasant was still no more than a serf, tied to the soil and with many duties to perform for his lord. The *complete* decay of feudalism did not come in many countries till the lapse of another three centuries.

(2) *The Renaissance, or Revival of Learning*

With the decline of the ancient world and its final overthrow by the barbarian tribes in the fifth century A.D., much of the civilization and learning of ancient Greece and Rome was forgotten. From A.D. 1000 a gradual reawakening took place, and the writings of the Greek Aristotle and the Roman Vergil were studied, though often through faulty translations. From about 1400, however, the Renaissance can be said to have begun in earnest. Men began to study the ancient writers in their original languages—in Latin, Greek, and Hebrew. In its broadest sense the movement was not confined to a mere revival of what had gone before. *New* literatures began to grow up. In England Chaucer had written his *Canterbury Tales*, and in Italy Dante had written his *Divine Comedy*. In time the Renaissance came to include every branch of human knowledge, and progress has gone on without interruption ever since.

The Italian city-states were the pioneers of the new learning, and after the fall of Constantinople in 1453 they welcomed many of the Greek scholars who fled with their learning and their manuscripts from the barbarous Turks. In Rome the Vatican Library was founded by Pope Nicholas V (1447–1455), and in Florence the Renaissance was supported by the rich and powerful ruling family of the Medici. The Renaissance in Italy was mainly concerned with beauty and art. Leonardo da Vinci (1452–1519) painted the famous picture of *The Last Supper* and the portrait of *Mona Lisa*; this remarkable painter excelled also as architect, sculptor, engineer, and mathematician. Botticelli (1444–1510) painted his picture of *Spring*; Raphael (1483–1520), probably the greatest of the Italian painters, produced his world-famous paintings of the Madonna. The most famous painter that Venice produced, Titian (1477–1576), excelled as a portrait-painter. The art of sculpture was raised by Michelangelo (1475–1564) to a height that it had not known since the glory of fifth-century Athens. In Italy, too, the new Renaissance style of architecture was evolved to take the place of the medieval Gothic (see Chapter XXI).

In the realm of science men soon outstripped the ancients. The Polish astronomer Copernicus (1473–1543) taught that the sun was the centre of the universe and that the earth and the planets revolved round it. This had only been dimly suspected by a few of the ancients, and in the Middle Ages it had been forgotten in favour of the opposite view held by the Egyptian astronomer, Ptolemy. The new theory of the universe was at first strongly opposed, but it found a worthy champion in the Italian scientist Galileo (1564–1642), often regarded as the inventor of the telescope. He was certainly the first to use it to any great extent for the science

of astronomy, and showed that the sun (regarded in the
Middle Ages as an object of perfection) was actually be-
smirched with spots ! Galileo also experimented with falling
objects from the Leaning Tower of Pisa and showed that a
body weighing 100 lb. did not fall to the earth more quickly
than one weighing only 1 lb.

ERASMUS
After a portrait by Holbein in the Louvre.
Photo Alinari

Perhaps the greatest figure
of the whole Renaissance was
the Dutch scholar Erasmus
(1466–1536). Erasmus was
born at Rotterdam and was
early sent to a monastery. His
mind was too active for the
monastic life, however, and he
left the monastery and spent
much of his life in the Universities of Paris, Oxford, and
Cambridge. He became in
time the foremost Greek scholar
of his age, and in 1516 he published a new Greek version of
the New Testament which corrected many of the errors in
the medieval Vulgate. Erasmus was a devout Catholic, but
he could see that much was wrong with the Church of his
time. In his book *The Praise of Folly* he attacked the lives of
many of the leaders of the Church and the ignorance and
superstition of many of its members. Erasmus was one of
the Oxford Reformers, the pioneers of the new learning in
England, whose work is described in the following chapter.

No account of the Renaissance would be complete which
did not mention the invention of printing. About 1440 a
German, John Gutenberg, of Mainz, discovered how to
print by means of movable type. He was the first European
to print by this method, though the art of printing had
been known for many centuries in the Far East. The new
system spread rapidly. The printers of Italy invented the

italic type of letters to save space. In 1476 William Caxton set up the first printing-press in England, under the shadow of Westminster Abbey. The production of books was increased and cheapened beyond all imagination, and by 1500 there were probably eight millions or more printed books in existence. The Renaissance would have spread much more slowly if it had not been for its new-born ally of printing.

AN ASTROLABE

A nautical instrument for calculating latitudes by observing the height of the sun above the horizon.

(3) *The Geographical Discoveries*

In the Middle Ages precious metals, silks, and spices found their way to Europe from India, China, and Japan. They came either by caravan or across the Indian Ocean and the Red Sea. All these routes reached Europe via the Mediterranean Sea and made the Italian city-states of Venice and Genoa very prosperous. In 1271 a Venetian traveller, Marco Polo, had set out for the east, and the account he wrote of the riches of Cathay (China) and Zipangu (Japan) stimulated men's imaginations and led them to try to find new ways to the east. In the middle of the fifteenth century Constantinople and Egypt passed into the hands of the Turks. This made trade in the eastern Mediterranean more dangerous for Christians, and the need for finding alternative routes to the east became more urgent. It was in attempts to find these routes that the geographical discoveries were made. Fortunately the introduction of the mariner's compass (possibly from China) made long voyages safer.

Under the influence of a Portuguese prince named Henry the Navigator (1394–1460), Portuguese sailors pushed farther and farther down the west coast of Africa. The vast expanse of the Sahara Desert seemed never-ending, until, in 1445, a headland green with vegetation was sighted and named Cape Verde, or the 'Green Cape.' In 1471 the Equator was crossed, and in 1486 Bartholomew Diaz reached the Cape of Good Hope, which he called the Cape of Storms until the Portuguese King altered its name. On June 8, 1497, Vasco da Gama left Portugal with four ships provisioned for three years. The Cape was rounded, and

da Gama came at Christmastide to a country which he named Natal, in honour of the season (Latin *Dies Natalis* means 'the Day of the Nativity'). Proceeding slowly up the east African coast, he was able eventually to hire an Arab pilot who took him across the Indian Ocean to Calicut (1498). A new way to the east was now opened up.

Meanwhile adventurous spirits had been seeking new ways to the east by sailing in a westerly direction. The belief that the earth was round was slowly coming to be held. One of its firmest believers was Christopher Columbus (1451–1506). Columbus was born in the busy Italian trading-city of Genoa, and as a boy he haunted the quays and longed to roam the ocean. His father, however, decided to give him a good education first of all, and sent his son to the University of Pavia. Columbus studied the travels of Marco Polo and the theories of Ptolemy, the Egyptian astronomer who had taught that the world was a globe. But Ptolemy had thought the world smaller than it was, and Marco Polo had over-estimated the distance he had travelled eastward. This led Columbus to imagine that a journey of 2500 miles across the Atlantic would bring him to Zipangu, or Japan. Columbus now tried to obtain support for his scheme. Many countries were tried without success. At last the Queen of Spain, Isabella of Castile, promised him the ships he required and appointed him viceroy of whatever lands he might discover.

In August, 1492, Columbus set sail from Palos with three ships, the *Santa Maria*, the *Pinta*, and the *Niña*. The *Santa Maria* was a ship of 100 tons' burthen and carried a crew of fifty; the other ships were much smaller. The total crews of about ninety men were composed largely of prisoners pressed into service. After leaving the Canaries Columbus promised his men land in three weeks, but on the twenty-first day the limitless ocean still stretched round them. By persuasion, threats, and even deception Columbus managed to keep his men from mutiny, and at length, on October 12—nearly six weeks after they had left the Canaries—the West Indies were reached. Altogether Columbus made four voyages to America, but he believed to the day of

SPANISH CARAVEL IN WHICH COLUMBUS DISCOVERED AMERICA

From a drawing attributed to Columbus.

his death that he had reached the east. Hence the names West Indies and Indians which were given to the new islands and the inhabitants of America.

A few years after the first voyage of Columbus an Italian named John Cabot obtained from the English King, Henry VII, permission to sail from Bristol to discover unknown lands. Together with his son, Sebastian, John Cabot reached Newfoundland in 1497, and the English flag was the first to be hoisted on the mainland of America.

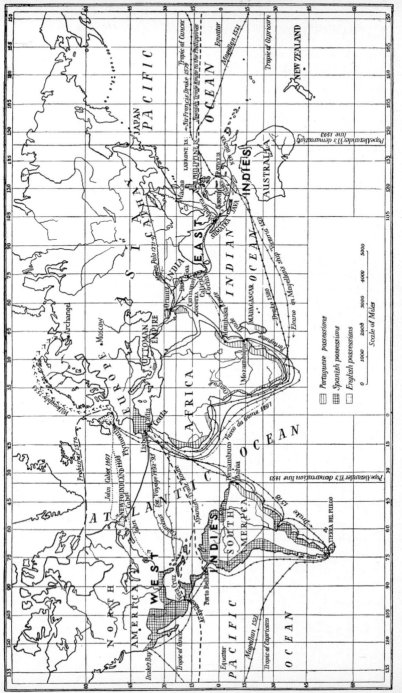

THE VOYAGES OF DISCOVERY

After 1500, numerous voyages of discovery took place. Only two need be mentioned here. An Italian named Amerigo Vespucci sailed to America and wrote a book describing his voyage. The book became popular, and so the new continent came to be called America, after the author's name. Far more important was the voyage of Ferdinand Magellan, a Portuguese sailor in the service of Spain (1519-1522). Magellan sailed down the coast of South America, through the strait which was later named after him, and so across the Pacific to Asia. The Philippine Islands were annexed to Spain, but Magellan himself was slain in a fight with the natives. One ship out of the five which had set out returned round the Cape of Good Hope to Spain, and was the first ship to have sailed round the world.

The geographical discoveries led to the gradual decay of the Italian city-states of Venice and Genoa, and to the increased importance of countries along the Atlantic— Spain and Portugal, followed soon by England, France, and Holland. Soon commercial and colonial rivalries appeared between the chief European nations. Spain built up a large empire in the west, and Portugal did likewise in the east. In 1493 the Pope drew an imaginary line round the world to separate Spanish from Portuguese lands, but this attempt to map out the world by peaceful means did not succeed, as other countries naturally claimed a share. Both east and west were soon pouring their treasures into Europe. The large supplies of precious metals that came to Spain and Portugal gradually filtered through to other European countries. The amount of money increased, and so in time prices rose, and new problems of poverty were produced. Finally, the slave-trade between the west coast of Africa and America developed in the sixteenth century and flourished for three hundred years.

(4) *The Decline of the Catholic Church*

The Catholic Church had done much good in the Middle

Ages, but during the later centuries it had declined, and many of its earlier ideals had grown dim. For nearly seventy years (1309–1378) the Popes had lived at Avignon under the influence of the French kings. This had been followed by a still more distressing spectacle—two rival lines of Popes lasting fifty years, each line claiming to be the only true line. During the Renaissance some Popes thought more of art and learning than of religion and a good life. Among the lower ranks of the Church, the monks and friars in particular had fallen from their earlier ideals. The opponents of the Church exaggerated these short-comings, and it would be a mistake to think that the whole Church was corrupt. But even such devout and sincere Catholics as Erasmus and Sir Thomas More recognized that all was not well.

The Renaissance led many, especially in northern Europe, to question the very authority of the Church. They found a wide gulf separating the teaching of Christ and many of the teachings and practices of the Catholic Church. They even discovered that some of the latter were based upon forgeries, whose origin had been completely forgotten in the course of centuries. None of this proved the Catholic Church in itself to be necessarily wrong, as Erasmus was the first to maintain. But confidence in the Church was shaken and could not easily be repaired.

Lastly, the growth of strong nations and strong monarchies led to a weakening of the Church. The Catholic Church was an *international* body, and the Pope had often interfered in the affairs of all nations. The new nations, under their strong and ambitious rulers, resented this inter-ference, especially as the Popes were usually Italians. No successful attack was made on the Catholic Church till Martin Luther's protest in 1517. This marked the beginning of the Reformation, *i.e.*, the break-up of the Catholic Church and the establishment of Protestant Churches, the details of which are reserved for a later chapter.

QUESTIONS AND EXERCISES

1. Write a few lines about each of the four facts which distinguish the Middle Ages from the modern period.

2. Write an essay on the Renaissance. How did the Renaissance of northern Europe differ from that of Italy?

3. How did the rise of Turkish power in the eastern Mediterranean affect (a) the Renaissance, (b) the geographical discoveries?

4. If you had been a sailor during this period, which voyage would you have liked to take part in most of all? Give your reasons.

5. Explain the origin of the following words: italics, West Indies, Natal, Magellan Strait, America.

CHAPTER II

HENRY VII AND THE NEW MONARCHY IN ENGLAND

Tudor Monarchs

Henry VII	1485–1509
Henry VIII	1509–1547
Edward VI	1547–1553
Mary	1553–1558
Elizabeth	1558–1603

How Henry Tudor became Henry VII

WE have seen in an earlier volume how, on the deposition of Richard II (the last of the Plantagenets) in 1399, the

HENRY VII
From a portrait in the National Portrait Gallery, London.

Lancastrians were able to seize the throne. Half a century later the Lancastrian rule was challenged by the Yorkists, and the Wars of the Roses resulted. The great Yorkist King, Edward IV, ruled from 1461 to 1483, and it seemed as if the Yorkists were firmly seated on the English throne. But it was not to be. Edward IV left behind him two sons, Edward and Richard. The former, twelve years of age, succeeded his father as Edward V. Real power, however, lay with Richard, Duke of Gloucester, who was the late King's brother. The Duke of Gloucester had his two nephews murdered in the Tower of London (1483), and was himself proclaimed king as Richard III (1483–1485). This was too much for many of the Yorkists themselves, who were now ready to support even a Lancastrian if they could

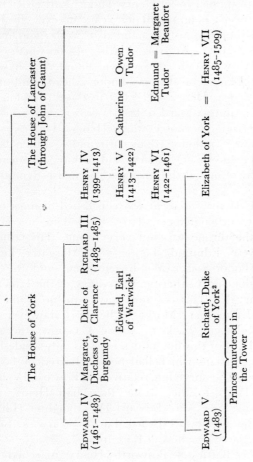

EDWARD III

The House of York

The House of Lancaster
(through John of Gaunt)

EDWARD IV (1461-1483)

Margaret, Duchess of Burgundy

Duke of Clarence

RICHARD III (1483-1485)

HENRY IV (1399-1413)

HENRY V = Catherine = Owen Tudor (1413-1422)

HENRY VI (1422-1461)

Edmund Tudor = Margaret Beaufort

Edward, Earl of Warwick[1]

EDWARD V (1483)

Richard, Duke of York[2]

Princes murdered in the Tower

Elizabeth of York = HENRY VII (1485-1509)

THE DESCENT OF HENRY VII

[1] Impersonated by Lambert Simnel.
[2] Impersonated by Perkin Warbeck.

get rid of the treacherous uncle. A Lancastrian champion appeared in the person of Henry Tudor, Earl of Richmond, who had been spending many years in exile in France. Seizing his opportunity, he landed in Wales and marched against Richard. At the Battle of Bosworth (1485) Richard III was slain. His crown, found in a hawthorn-bush, was placed on Henry Tudor's head, and its new wearer hailed as Henry VII. But in those troublous times it was often quite as hard to keep a crown as to win it, and there was no guarantee that Henry Tudor's sudden rise might not be followed by an equally sudden fall. In actual fact, however, Henry laid before his death the foundations of one of the strongest of English dynasties, the Tudors.

As far as Henry's descent was concerned, it must be confessed that, although he had royal blood in his veins, his claim to the throne was not very strong. His father and mother were Edmund Tudor and Margaret Beaufort. Edmund Tudor was a Welsh gentleman and the son of Owen Tudor and Catherine, the widow of the Lancastrian King Henry V. This certainly gave him no claim to the throne. His mother, Margaret Beaufort, however, could trace her descent back to John of Gaunt, the son of Edward III. But this line of descent was only a side-branch of the Lancastrians which had been debarred by law from the throne. The surviving relatives of Edward IV had far stronger claims to the throne than had Henry Tudor. Chief among these were Edward IV's daughter (Elizabeth of York), his nephew (Edward, Earl of Warwick), and his sister (Margaret, Duchess of Burgundy).

After the Battle of Bosworth Henry marched on to London, where his position was strengthened by his election as King of England by Parliament. Even so, he had sore need to extend the basis of his power. This he did by an advantageous marriage. He had much earlier promised to marry Edward IV's daughter, Elizabeth of York, so as to win Yorkist support in his attack on Richard III. But he had purposely postponed his marriage till after his election to the throne by Parliament, so that it could not be said that he owed his position to his wife's Yorkist blood. In January, 1486, the marriage took place.

Two Rebel Impostors: Lambert Simnel and Perkin Warbeck

Henry VII had to deal with two serious rebellions, both organized by Edward IV's sister, Margaret, Duchess of Burgundy. Unfortunately for the plotters, they had no worthy male candidate to put forward, as Edward IV's two sons had been murdered in the Tower, while Henry VII had, immediately after Bosworth, imprisoned Edward IV's nephew, Edward, Earl of Warwick.

In 1487 an Oxford tradesman's son, Lambert Simnel, claimed that he was the young Earl of Warwick. Margaret of Burgundy accepted him as such and furnished him with men and money. Simnel was sent to Ireland, which, throughout the Wars of the Roses, had always been strongly Yorkist. Henry VII paraded the real Earl of Warwick through the streets of London—but in vain, as far as the extreme Yorkists were concerned. At Dublin Simnel was crowned king as Edward VI. He then crossed the Irish Channel to Lancashire, but as he marched inland his forces grew weaker. While trying to capture the fortress of Newark, in Lincolnshire, he was completely defeated by Henry at Stoke (1487). To show his contempt for the impostor Henry made Simnel a servant in the royal kitchen.

Several years later a more serious and more prolonged rebellion broke out. A young and handsome Fleming, named Perkin Warbeck, who was really only a silk-merchant's assistant, claimed that he was the younger of the two sons of Edward IV who were generally supposed to have been murdered in the Tower. Once more Margaret of Burgundy accepted the impostor, who from 1492 began his wanderings from one country to another in search of support. France, Ireland, Flanders, and Scotland at one time or another lent him aid; but Henry was constantly on the watch, endeavouring by negotiation and treaty to prevent the danger from coming to a head. At length in 1496 the King of Scotland, James IV, invaded England on behalf of Warbeck. The invasion itself was not serious, but it produced a rebellion in Cornwall. Henry had levied a special tax for the Scottish war, and the Cornishmen, whose sympathies were Yorkist, rose in revolt. They marched on London, but at Blackheath, in Kent, were completely defeated (1497). Warbeck now took a desperate chance. He landed in Cornwall, hoping to revive the rebellion; but failing to do so, he lost heart and was easily captured (1497). He made a full confession of his imposture and was imprisoned in the Tower. In 1499 he and the Earl of Warwick were executed on a charge of trying to escape. This act of cruelty removed Henry's most dangerous rival and finally brought the Wars of the Roses to an end.

Henry VII's Character

Henry's ability to keep his crown was now manifest to all, but he never won what should accompany the crown, namely, the affection of his subjects. He was too cold and cautious. Although merciful, according to the standards of his age, he was not swayed by generosity or affection. He was shrewd and cunning, always calculating in a detached way the best course to follow. Realizing that money formed a sound basis on which to build his power, he set himself out to acquire as much as possible and spend as little as possible.

A century later Sir Francis Bacon, in his *History of Henry VII*, observed:

> As for the disposition of his subjects in general toward him, it stood thus with him; that of the three affections which naturally tie the hearts of the subjects to their sovereign, love,

fear, and reverence; he had the last in height, the second in good measure, and so little of the first, as he was beholden to the other two.

He was a Prince, sad, serious, and full of thoughts, and secret observations, and full of notes and memorials of his own hand, especially touching persons. As, whom to employ, whom to reward, whom to inquire of, whom to beware of, what were the dependencies, what were the factions, and the like; keeping, as it were, a journal of his thoughts. There is to this day a merry tale; that his monkey, set on as it was thought by one of his chamber, tore his principal note-book all to pieces, when by chance it lay forth; whereat the court, which liked not those pensive accounts, was almost tickled with sport.

Henry VII and the Barons

In his aim of strengthening the royal power Henry was aided by two very important facts. Firstly, the country desired peace and order, after the anarchy of the previous thirty years. Secondly, the barons were by now considerably reduced in number and importance; many had been killed off in the wars, and their estates were held by minors or else had been confiscated by the King.

Henry began his reign by taking back all lands that the Crown had lost or given away since 1455, when the Wars of the Roses had commenced. He now attacked an evil of long standing, the practice known as livery and maintenance. Many barons had adopted the habit of employing large numbers of armed retainers, who wore the livery or badge of their lord, and supported him on every possible occasion. If any of them got into trouble and were brought before a court, their lord would often fill the court with other armed men and bully the jury into giving a favourable verdict or perhaps prevent the punishment from being carried out. This practice was known as maintenance. Henry passed a law against livery and maintenance, and, what is more, enforced it without fear or favour.

There is a well-known story that the Earl of Oxford, a

favourite of the King, once drew up a large guard of his own retainers to honour the King's leave-taking after Henry had been well entertained by the Earl. Henry noted their excessive number and exclaimed, "My Lord, I thank you for your good cheer, but I cannot endure to have my laws broken in my sight! My attorneys will speak with you." The Earl was fined £10,000.

In 1487 Henry passed his Act for the reorganization of the Court of Star Chamber. The king and his council had always claimed and exercised the power of establishing special courts to deal with cases that, for some reason or other, were unsuitable for the ordinary law-courts. At the Star Chamber in Westminster—so called because of the stars painted on the ceiling—such a court had long been in existence. Henry now strengthened it and used it for cases of rebellion or lawlessness on the part of over-mighty subjects. Sitting in London, composed of royal councillors, and under the general control of the king, it proved eminently suitable for its task. It was not bound by any cumbersome rules of procedure and could act promptly and efficiently. It could use torture if it wished to obtain evidence. It could not inflict the death-penalty, but since it was the King's special policy to enrich himself and impoverish his enemies by heavy fines, this did not diminish the court's usefulness. In its early years the Court of Star Chamber was very popular with all who desired good order and prompt justice. Bacon says of Henry and his policy of fines:

> Justice was well administered in his time, save where the King was party; save also, that the council table intermeddled too much with *meum* and *tuum*.

In his struggle against the barons Henry was aided by the possession of artillery, which by law was forbidden to anyone but the king. With artillery the medieval castle lost its importance, as its walls could now be more easily battered in.

Henry VII and the Middle Classes

Just as Henry aimed at weakening the barons, so his policy was to strengthen the middle classes. This was because both they and the King had the same desire of checking feudal anarchy and establishing law and order. The middle classes and the smaller gentry were employed as royal servants and officials. They were usually more businesslike than the older baronial families and were more dependent upon the King. They owed their promotion to him, and if they displeased him they could be easily dismissed. Examples of such ministers in Henry's reign were Archbishop Morton (who was the King's chief adviser for the first fifteen years of the reign), Bishop Fox, and the lawyers Empson and Dudley.

This policy of Henry VII was followed by his successors. Sir Thomas More, Cardinal Wolsey, and Thomas Cromwell, under Henry VIII, and Lord Burghley and Sir Francis Walsingham, under Elizabeth, were all 'new men' of relatively humble origins. The Tudors also became famous for the extensive use they made of the local gentry by appointing them as Justices of the Peace and heaping loads of duties upon them. These magistrates, who became the 'men of all work' of the Tudors, were usually small landowners, with none of the dangerous ambitions of the powerful barons.

A Money-making King

Henry early set himself to amass a fortune. Enemies were usually fined; estates were confiscated; treaties with foreign rulers often provided for the payment to Henry of sums of money. One of Henry's favourite methods of raising money was by means of forced loans, or benevolences. In this connexion the device known traditionally as 'Morton's Fork' (named after Henry's chief minister) deserves mention. People who lived in an expensive fashion were told that they could obviously afford to lend the King money; those who lived economically were informed that they must be able to lend the King something out of their savings. Thus one prong or other of the fork was bound to prove effective.

In the latter part of his reign Henry employed Sir Richard Empson and Sir Edmund Dudley to raise money. They revived old laws and fined people for having broken them, and soon they became the two most unpopular men in England. At the end of his reign Henry was able to neglect Parliament and leave to his son a treasure equivalent to about £4,500,000 in modern money.

England and Other Nations

At the outset of Henry's reign the King of France was endeavouring to obtain possession of Brittany, the last of the independent provinces of France. In alliance with Spain Henry prepared to make war upon France, and obtained a large grant from Parliament. Henry soon realized that he was powerless to prevent the absorption of Brittany, and, as the French King was busy with a scheme for invading Italy, the two monarchs made peace before the war had begun in earnest. By the Treaty of Étaples (1492) the French King bought off Henry with the payment of a large yearly sum —although Henry had already levied taxes in England for the war! Another clause banished Perkin Warbeck from France and prevented him from obtaining French support.

Soon afterwards Henry took steps to lessen the danger from Ireland, which had been a Yorkist stronghold for half a century. As his Lord Deputy Henry sent over one of his most trusted councillors, Sir Edward Poynings. The latter persuaded the Irish Parliament to pass the celebrated Poynings' Law (1494), under which all laws passed by the Irish Parliament had to receive the assent of the English Government, and all laws passed by the English Parliament were to apply automatically to Ireland. But effective English authority was still confined to the district round Dublin known as 'the Pale.'

Henry's next actions showed his desire to encourage

English industry and commerce. Flanders was the chief market for English cloth, but during the Yorkist rebellions it had championed the impostors and placed heavy duties upon trade with England. In 1496 Henry concluded a commercial treaty with Flanders known as the Intercursus Magnus or Great Treaty; trade with England was freed from all restrictions, and Yorkist claimants (again this meant Perkin Warbeck) were to receive no further support. Ten years later Henry tried to increase English trading-privileges still further by a short-lived treaty which the Flemings christened the Intercursus Malus or Evil Treaty.

Henry also encouraged Cabot's voyage across the Atlantic (see Chapter I); he extended English trading-privileges in the Baltic and the Mediterranean; he passed Navigation Laws to promote the use of English ships in English trade; and he granted a charter to the Merchant Adventurers, who exported English cloth (see Chapter IX).

Important Marriage Alliances

In the pursuit of his policy Henry carried through two important marriage schemes. In 1503 Henry's daughter, Margaret, married James IV of Scotland. This did not produce the peaceful relations between the two countries that were hoped for, but exactly a century later it resulted in the union of the Crowns of England and Scotland, when the great-grandson of this marriage, James VI of Scotland, became James I of England.

The other marriage schemes were concerned with Spain, whose friendship was sought by Henry to strengthen the Tudor Monarchy. In 1501 Henry's elder son, Arthur, married Catherine of Aragon, the daughter of Ferdinand and Isabella of Spain. In the following year Arthur died, but Henry was reluctant to give up the marriage alliance with Spain and return the dowry that had accompanied it. It was therefore arranged that Catherine should marry the King's other son (later Henry VIII). For this purpose a special dispensation had to be obtained from the Pope, as the laws of the Church forbade a man to marry his brother's widow. This dispensation was accepted by all parties at the time, and the marriage took place in 1509. Nearly twenty years later, however, Henry VIII questioned the validity of his marriage with Catherine and broke with the Pope because he refused to dissolve it. In this way Henry VII's marriage schemes with Spain led up to the English Reformation.

The Renaissance in England

Many English scholars visited Italy during the reign of Henry VII. Chief among these were Grocyn, Linacre, and Colet. On returning to England, Grocyn lectured upon Greek literature, Linacre upon Greek medicine, while Colet became the leading spirit of a group of scholars known as the Oxford Reformers, so called from their association with Oxford University. They included, besides Colet, the Dutch scholar Erasmus (who studied and lectured at both Oxford and Cambridge—see Chapter I) and a rising English scholar, Sir Thomas More.

John Colet (1467–1519) attracted attention after his return from the continent by his lectures at Oxford on the Epistles of St Paul. His approach to the subject was very different from that of the medieval theologians. He used the original Greek text and tried to arrive at the real meaning of St Paul's message and apply it to the needs of his own age, instead of worrying about relatively small points of wording or theology. Some years later he was made Dean of St Paul's Cathedral. On the death of his father he inherited a fortune, and in 1510 he used some of the money to found St Paul's School. Here the new methods of study, especially of Greek, were put into practice, and some of the most famous scholars of the time wrote new text-books for the pupils. This famous school still exists, though it has been transferred from its original site under the shadow of St Paul's.

While in London, Colet made the acquaintance of a young and attractive scholar named Thomas More (1478–1535), whose home at Chelsea became the meeting-place of the chief scholars of the time. As a young boy More had served in the household of Cardinal Morton, the minister of Henry VII, and a great future had been prophesied for him by his master. After qualifying as a lawyer More entered Parliament. There he attracted attention by his fearless opposition to Henry VII's demands for taxation. It was in Henry VIII's reign, however, that he reached the height of his fame. In 1516 he published his book *Utopia*, or 'Nowhere,' which describes an ideal country discovered by a traveller to the New World. Many are the reforms

SIR THOMAS MORE
After Holbein

that More advocated; some have since come to pass, but for others, alas, we still wait. In *Utopia* crime was practically abolished, work was reduced to a minimum, religious toleration was observed, and there was no war or private property. Later in Henry VIII's reign, More rose to the highest legal position in the country, the Lord Chancellorship of England. In 1535 he was beheaded for opposing the King's religious policy; More, like the other Oxford Reformers, although realizing that much was wrong with the Catholic Church, desired reform from within and opposed the establishment of new Churches.

The Renaissance period was a time of educational activity. Colet founded St Paul's School early in Henry VIII's reign. Soon afterwards Manchester Grammar School was founded. Henry VII's mother, Lady Margaret Beaufort, founded

B

St John's College, Cambridge, whose boat-club is still named after its royal foundress.

QUESTIONS AND EXERCISES

1. Mention six separate ways in which Henry VII strengthened his position on the throne.

2. In what ways does Henry VII's reign show that the Middle Ages were ending in England?

3. Write notes on: livery and maintenance, Court of Star Chamber, Poynings' Law, *Utopia*.

4. What were the marriage alliances with Scotland and Spain, and why were they important in the later history of England?

5. Write a short essay on the Renaissance in England. How did it differ from the Renaissance in Italy?

CHAPTER III

EUROPEAN SURVEY (I): THE REFORMATION

Chief Rulers

Charles V	(Spain and the Empire)	1519–1556
Francis I	(France)	1515–1547
Henry VIII	(England)	1509–1547
Leo X	(Papacy)	1513–1521
Clement VII	(Papacy)	1523–1534
Suleiman the Magnificent	(Ottoman Empire)	1520–1566

Europe at the Beginning of the Sixteenth Century

DURING the first half of the sixteenth century many of the states of Europe were ruled by monarchs of outstanding ability. In our own country was Henry VIII. In France was the Valois King Francis I, a gay and witty young man intent on raising his country to the chief place of importance in the affairs of Europe. In Spain and the Empire was the Emperor Charles V, a slow but capable ruler whose chief aim was to keep intact his vast and scattered possessions. In the east was the capable Sultan, Suleiman the Magnificent, whose rule threatened to extend beyond the Balkan peninsula into Hungary and the Empire.

CHARLES V
From a painting by Titian.

The huge Empire of Charles V was the outstanding political fact of the time. Charles was a Hapsburg, the grandson of Ferdinand and Isabella of Spain on his mother's side and of the Emperor Maximilian I on his father's side. In 1516, on the death of Ferdinand of Spain, he had succeeded to the throne of Spain and all that accompanied it— the wealthy possessions in the New World, and Naples and Sicily in southern Italy. In 1519, on the death of his other grandfather, the Emperor Maximilian I, he had succeeded to the hereditary Hapsburg possessions in Austria, the Netherlands, and Burgundy. The title of Holy Roman

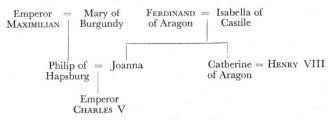

THE DESCENT OF CHARLES V

On his father's side Charles inherited the Hapsburg possessions in Austria, the County of Burgundy, the Netherlands, and the claim to the Imperial title. On his mother's side Charles inherited Spain, possessions in Italy, and the Spanish Empire in America.

Emperor was elective, however, though for several centuries it had been the almost invariable practice of the seven electors to choose a prince of the House of Hapsburg. None the less, in 1519 both Francis I and Henry VIII put themselves forward as candidates. They were unsuccessful, and so from 1519 Charles was able to style himself the Emperor Charles V and include the Holy Roman Empire under his rule. It is doubtful, however, whether this meant any real increase of power, as the princes of the Empire were strong and numerous enough to defy their overlord if they so desired.

The Struggle between Francis I and Charles V

Francis and Charles soon came to blows. Frontier-questions along the Pyrenees and the Rhineland caused enmity between them. More important than these was the question of Italy, over which both monarchs wished to extend their rule. Behind these territorial disputes was the fundamental question as to who was to be the leading ruler in Europe. The part played by England under Henry VIII's minister, Cardinal Wolsey, was to maintain the balance of power between the two rivals, *i.e.*, to prevent either side from becoming so powerful as to crush the other and become a danger to the rest of Europe. After Henry VIII had met Francis I at the Field of the Cloth of Gold in 1520, he met Charles V and decided, despite the show of splendour that had marked his meeting with the French King, to give his support to the Emperor.

When war broke out, the chief centre of operations was northern Italy. Here, in 1525, Francis was utterly defeated and taken prisoner at Pavia. He was forced to sign a treaty renouncing his claims to Italy and other disputed territories; but no sooner was he set free than he repudiated his signature. Charles's success had alarmed the rest of Europe. The Pope feared for his own possessions in central Italy and took the lead in forming an alliance against the Emperor. Wolsey, true to his principle of the balance of power, now deserted Charles, and persuaded Henry VIII to join the new alliance. The imperial troops, an undisciplined and unpaid army of mercenaries, marched upon Rome, which they took and sacked (1527). Charles himself was not with his troops at the time, but the Pope, Clement VII, was now in his power. This had important results upon the course of events in England, where Henry VIII was at this period trying to persuade the Pope to annul his marriage with the Emperor's aunt, Catherine of Aragon.

By the Peace of Cambrai (1529) the war was brought to an end with the honours definitely on the side of the Emperor, whose claims in Italy were recognized by his rival. Although the struggle was renewed at various intervals during the next thirty years, the final result was to confirm Spain in her Italian possessions. But the many wars had prevented Charles from devoting his full attention to the Reformation which had commenced in Germany at the beginning of his reign.

The Revolt of Martin Luther against Rome

Martin Luther (1483–1546) came from Saxon peasant stock; his father was a miner or slate-cutter. Martin was

sent to a university to study law, but soon after taking his degree he became obsessed with a sense of his own sinfulness and entered a monastery. There his superior advised him to study the works of St Augustine, a fifth-century Christian writer. These writings, together with those of St Paul in the New Testament, had an immense influence on Luther's religious outlook. From them he learned his characteristic belief that salvation can only come to men through having faith in Christ. Without this,

MARTIN LUTHER
Louis Cranach.

he taught, any amount of fasts and penances and good acts would avail nothing. In 1508 Luther was moved to another monastery at Wittenberg, in Saxony. Here he became professor of theology in the university that had recently been founded by the Elector of Saxony. In 1510 he visited Rome and was appalled at the wickedness and superstition of much that he saw there.

In 1517 a monk named Tetzel arrived at Wittenberg selling indulgences on behalf of Pope Leo X. Leo X was a typical figure of the Italian Renaissance, more interested in art than in religion, and he desired money to pay for building-schemes in connexion with the new Church of St Peter at Rome. Hence the mission of Tetzel, who regarded his work much like a commercial traveller. According to the laws of the Church a priest who pardoned a repentant sinner had to inflict a penance before the sin was completely wiped out. An indulgence freed a sinner from this penance; but the sinner had first of all to have shown repentance and been pardoned for his sin. Tetzel omitted all such qualifications and preached that by purchasing his indulgences people could obtain pardon for their own sins or release their dead friends from Purgatory. This teaching merely followed the example of many other indulgence-sellers and was only what most simple-minded Catholics believed. But it shocked Luther's sincerity and deep sense of religion, and he decided to protest. On the church-door of Wittenberg he nailed up his famous ninety-five theses, or statements against indulgences (1517).

The Pope and the Church authorities refused to consider Luther's objections and ordered him to remain silent. It was this high-handed obstinacy that caused Luther to move further and further away from the Church. He soon became a national hero, and his writings were in great demand throughout Germany. In 1520 the Pope issued a Bull of excommunication against Luther. The latter led a crowd of university professors and students to a place just outside the city-walls of Wittenberg and there publicly burnt it. The gulf between Luther and the Catholic Church was now unbridgeable.

At this stage the newly elected Emperor Charles V interfered. In 1521 he summoned a Diet, or Imperial Parliament, at Worms, and gave Luther a promise of safety to induce him to attend. A hundred years before, John Hus had been given a safe-conduct to attend the Council of Constance but had been burnt for heresy. Luther, however, was too courageous to be kept back through fear and said afterwards:

> Even had I known that there would be as many devils at Worms as tiles upon the house-roofs, still I should joyfully have plunged in among them!

At Worms Luther was asked if he would retract his opinions. His answer was bold and decisive:

> I must be convinced either by the testimony of the Scriptures or clear arguments. For I believe things contrary to the Pope and councils, because it is as clear as day that they have often erred and said things inconsistent with themselves. I am bound by the Scriptures which I have quoted; my conscience is submissive to the word of God; therefore I may not, and will not, recant, because to act against conscience is unholy and unsafe. So help me God! Amen.

The Emperor regarded Luther as a misguided heretic and declared him an outlaw. But there was a strong current of opinion inside Germany in favour of the 'heretic,' and much relief was felt when it was learned that Luther had been safely lodged in a castle. There he translated the New Testament into German so that the ordinary people could read it. The outlook was very uncertain, however, and would have daunted the bravest heart.

The Principles of the Reformation

Broadly speaking, the principles for which the Protestants fought can be classed under three main heads.

Firstly, Luther taught the doctrine known as 'justification by faith.' This meant that complete faith in the saving grace of Christ was the only way of achieving salvation. This conflicted with the Roman Catholic view, which, although regarding faith as necessary, taught that the intercession of the Church through its priests and services was also necessary.

Luther's second point can be summarized as the priesthood of all believers. According to Luther, every person was in the end his own priest, because he alone could give himself the faith necessary to salvation. Priests and ministers were helpful, but they had no special powers separating them from ordinary men and women.

Thirdly, Luther taught that the final authority in matters of religion was the Bible and that it was permitted to every one to read the Bible and find out things for himself. This led Protestants of all kinds to translate the Scriptures into native tongues and encourage their reading by the common people. This again conflicted with the Roman Catholic view that the real authority in religion was the Church, with the Pope at its head, and that it was the Church's function to teach the people what to believe.

These three central doctrines led to many important corollaries. The Protestants denied transubstantiation, or the power of the priest to change the bread and wine into the body and blood of Christ; this was the central act in the Roman Catholic Mass. They also allowed their ministers to marry, and disapproved of the practice of monasticism. As time went on, the Protestants began to differ among themselves; but they all held fast to the main principles of the Reformation described above.

The Outcome of the German Reformation

Luther's teaching appealed to many Germans, who for long had regarded the Church as too much under Italian influence. It also appealed to those who were convinced that the Catholic Church was hopelessly corrupt and that its doctrines were erroneous. As for the Pope and the Emperor, they could do very little. The Pope was busy governing and protecting his own territories in Italy, and was often at loggerheads with the Emperor. Charles V had too many tasks to perform to allow much time for dealing with a rebellious monk and his supporters. Charles's enemies, Francis I and the Sultan Suleiman the Magnificent, often joined forces against him. Inside Germany Charles found that many of the rulers of his loosely knit Empire were only too ready to support a religious revolt that tended still more to undermine the Emperor's power. Luther's own strongest supporter was the Elector of Saxony.

Hence, for one reason and another, Charles lacked both time and power to attend to German affairs.

In 1525 many of the peasants of Germany thought they found in Luther's teaching an excuse to revolt against their feudal lords. This was a critical event for Luther; if he supported the peasants—and they had plenty of just grievances—his teaching would be classed as dangerous by the German rulers and might be stamped out. But Luther won the favour of the princes by condemning the rebels and callously urging the authorities to suppress them with every possible means.

In the following year (1526), at the height of the quarrel between Charles and the Pope, an imperial Diet at Spires decreed that every ruler inside the Empire could decide for himself whether to adopt Lutheranism or Roman Catholicism as the religion of his state. Three years later (1529), when Charles had settled his quarrel with the Pope, a second Diet of Spires reversed the decision of the first Diet and ordered Luther's teachings to be suppressed. From the princes who *protested* against this decision we have obtained the word 'Protestant.'

For many years Charles was occupied with wars against the Turks, and the Protestant princes took the opportunity to form a league for their mutual defence. In 1546 Luther died. Soon afterwards war broke out between the Emperor and the Protestants, but although the Emperor met with early successes, the forces against him were too strong. After 1550 he gave up his various titles one by one and retired to a monastery, where he died in 1558.

Three years earlier (1555) the Peace of Augsburg ended the religious strife in Germany—for the time being. Every ruler inside the Empire could decide whether to adopt the Catholic or the Lutheran religion, and his subjects had to abide by his choice. This still excluded a new and more extreme form of Protestantism that had been growing up in Switzerland under John Calvin.

Calvin at Geneva

The Reformation in Switzerland was begun by a scholar named Zwingli, but after Zwingli's death on the field of battle in 1531, the movement passed into the hands of John Calvin.

Calvin (1509–1564) was a Frenchman by birth and had studied law at the University of Paris. He became dissatisfied with the condition of the Catholic Church and fled from France to Switzerland. In 1536 he published the *Institutes of the Christian Religion*, wherein his religious views were set forth with great clearness. In 1541 he made himself ruler of the Swiss city-state of Geneva, which had just expelled its bishop. From 1541 till his death in 1564 Calvin was the religious and political dictator of Geneva. His rule was strict and severe, for Calvin had a Puritanical outlook which disapproved of many of the pleasure-seeking habits of his citizens. Nor would he allow any opposition, and he punished, with death if necessary, opponents of his rule. Geneva soon became the headquarters of the Reformation, the 'Rome of Protestantism,' and reformers of all nations went there to take back the message of Calvinism to their own countries.

Calvin's message was similar to Luther's in many respects, but he went much further in his opposition to the Roman Catholic Church. He worked out his doctrine of faith to its logical conclusion and taught that in the last resort an all-powerful God must have predestined certain people to have faith and thus be saved, and others to lack faith and be lost. He denied the need for sacraments and, unlike Luther, disbelieved completely in the doctrine of transubstantiation. In Calvin's Church there were no bishops, and the government of the Church was largely in the hands of the congregation. Calvin also taught that as religion was more important than political affairs, the religious leaders should be obeyed in preference to the political rulers. This again was very different from the teaching of Luther, who was content to allow the political ruler to govern his Church.

Calvinism was thus more extreme, more democratic, and more aggressive than Lutheranism. As such it soon became the fighting-creed of the Reformation, and its influence spread far beyond its original home. Wherever it spread it came into conflict with the political rulers. In France it was the creed of the Huguenots; in Holland it influenced the Dutch to rebel against their Spanish masters; in England it produced the Puritans, who emigrated to America for religion's sake or led the Civil War against the Stuarts; in Scotland it produced the Presbyterians, who, under the name of Covenanters, withstood all attempts at repression. Without Calvinism in its various forms, the revolt from Rome would have been much less thorough and much more peaceful.

The Progress of the Reformation to 1550

Generally speaking, the countries of southern Europe remained true to the Catholic faith. These were Spain, Portugal, France, and Italy. In central and northern Europe the position was very different. Switzerland was divided into Protestant and Catholic cantons. Germany also was divided, the southern part remaining Catholic and the northern part becoming Protestant. The Scandinavian countries of Norway, Sweden, and Denmark became Protestant; being of German race, they found it easier to adopt the Lutheran form of Protestantism. The Netherlands, as yet, were mainly Catholic, but there the seeds of Protestantism were soon to be sown. As for our own islands, while Ireland remained Catholic, England and Scotland became Protestant.

QUESTIONS AND EXERCISES

1. Write a brief essay on Martin Luther.

2. Write short notes on: balance of power, justification by faith, 'Protestant,' the Peace of Augsburg (1555).

3. Why did Charles V oppose the Reformation, and why was he unable to crush it?

4. What were the chief differences between (a) the Catholics and the Protestants, (b) the Lutherans and the Calvinists?

5. Draw a map of Europe, and show upon it the distribution of the Protestant and the Catholic religions about the year 1550.

CHAPTER IV

HENRY VIII AND THE BREACH WITH ROME

A Popular King

IN 1509, on the death of Henry VII, a new King ascended the throne as Henry VIII. As the son of Henry VII and

HENRY VIII
After Holbein.

Elizabeth of York, he united in his own person the claims of both Lancastrians and Yorkists and had nothing to fear from rival claimants to the throne. From his money-hoarding father he inherited a large fortune, which enabled him to lead a life of luxury and display without at first making heavy financial demands upon his subjects.

But it was the young King's character and accomplishments that appealed most to the nation, especially after the cold reign of Henry VII. The new King was in many ways a child of the Renaissance. Among his accomplishments were theology, music, and languages. In person he was handsome and strong, delighting in all kinds of bodily exercise, especially hunting, wrestling, shooting, and dancing. Small wonder that this overgrown boy—for he was only eighteen years of age—became the idol of the nation.

Henry began his reign with a popular act by executing his father's extortioners, Empson and Dudley. But he hung on to the fortune that they had helped his father to amass.

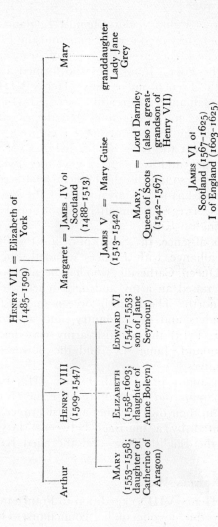

THE TUDOR ROYAL FAMILY

The descent through Henry VII's daughter, Margaret, shows (a) the claim of Mary, Queen of Scots, to the English throne, assuming Elizabeth dead or a usurper, (b) the claim of James VI to the English throne on Elizabeth's death in 1603.

War against France

An opportunity of military glory against England's old enemy, France, soon presented itself. Spain and the Empire were anxious to check the growing power of France, and were helped by the Pope (Julius II), who formed a Holy League to drive the French out of Italy. Henry VIII was invited to join the alliance and readily accepted. In 1512 an English force was sent to Guienne; but the expedition was badly organized and ended in complete failure.

In the following year the King himself led an expedition into northern France and won an easy victory over the French at Guinegate; so fast did the French cavalry retreat that the engagement has been known since as the Battle of the Spurs (August, 1513). Soon afterwards Tournay surrendered to the English King.

During Henry's absence, the Scots, pursuing their traditional policy of alliance with France, invaded England. Henry's Spanish Queen, Catherine, who had been appointed regent, promptly raised an army and despatched the Earl of Surrey to the north. The English force managed to get between the invaders and their country, and at Flodden Field (September, 1513) the Scottish army was defeated. The King of Scotland, James IV, and the flower of his nobility lost their lives.

In 1514 Henry made peace with France. He realized that his allies in Spain and the Empire were merely using him as a catspaw in their own schemes against France. The peace was cemented by a marriage between Mary, the younger sister of the English King, and the aged King of France.

The Rise of Thomas Wolsey

The success of Henry VIII's expedition to France in 1513 had been largely due to one of his councillors, Thomas Wolsey, who had been placed in charge of the arrangements for transporting the troops and provisions.

Thomas Wolsey (c.1471–1530) was, like many Tudor ministers, of middle-class origin. He was the son of a wealthy grazier and cattle-dealer of Ipswich. He was educated at Magdalen College, Oxford, and took his degree at the age of fifteen. He soon entered the Church, not so much because a life of religion appeals to him as because it was still one of the surest avenues to wealth and power. As tutor to the son of Lord Dorset he soon attracted attention, and towards the end of Henry VII's reign he was taken into the service of Bishop Fox, the King's minister. Early in Henry VIII's reign he distinguished himself as a subordinate member of the council. He was given the tasks of arranging for the evacuation of the troops from Guienne in 1512 and organizing a fresh expedition to northern France in 1513. In the following year it was under his influence that Henry VIII concluded peace with France.

CARDINAL WOLSEY
After Holbein.

From now on till his fall in 1528–1529 Wolsey was the most important of Henry's ministers. At times he wielded more power than the King, as Henry, encouraged by the astute Wolsey, was still apt to be keener on his pleasures than on the nation's business. In 1514 Wolsey became Archbishop of York, and in the following year he was made Chancellor of England and a Cardinal of the Catholic Church. In 1517 he was appointed Papal Legate, or the Pope's representative in England. Other positions he held were the bishoprics of Winchester, of Bath and Wells, of Tournay in France, and of two districts in Spain; in addition he was Abbot of St Albans. Wolsey never visited many of the places above mentioned; his offices merely served to give him the wealth and power that his being craved. His mode of living was luxurious in the extreme. His household contained five hundred persons, and for his own use he built the red-brick palace at Hampton Court that later became a royal residence.

Wolsey's Foreign Policy

In 1514 Wolsey had persuaded Henry to make peace with France. In the following year the young and ambitious Francis I ascended the French throne, and the peaceful relations between France and England were threatened by personal jealousies between their two Kings. In 1518, however, Wolsey was able to conclude a general peace among the powers of Europe.

This did not last long, as a new factor was emerging to threaten the peace of Europe. This was the growth of the power of Charles, the grandson of Ferdinand of Spain and the Emperor Maximilian. It has been shown in the previous chapter how Charles succeeded in 1516 to Spain and her possessions in Italy and America, and how, three years later, on the death of Maximilian, he succeeded to Austria and the Netherlands. The position of Holy Roman Emperor also fell vacant through the death of Maximilian, and both the Tudor Henry VIII and the Valois Francis I endeavoured to prevent it from falling into the already full hands of Charles. All three Kings put themselves forward as candidates, but the tradition of electing a Hapsburg was too strong for the German electors, and Charles became Emperor as Charles V (1519). War between Francis and Charles was now certain.

Wolsey had to decide which side to support. His policy is often described as the balance of power. England was to prevent either side from becoming over-powerful, and was to be the deciding factor in the struggle between the two combatants. Undoubtedly this idea often influenced Wolsey's schemes, but it is a mistake to imagine that it was pursued consistently. Important forces pulled England in the direction of a Spanish and imperial alliance, whatever Wolsey himself desired. England was the traditional foe of France, and the English Queen (Catherine of Aragon) naturally used her influence in favour of a Spanish alliance; the Emperor Charles V, who ruled in Spain as Charles I, was her nephew. For the time being this policy suited Wolsey's own schemes as well, as the great Cardinal hoped to become Pope some day and looked to the Emperor to help him.

Henry and Wolsey did not show their real purpose immediately, but flirted first with one side and then with the other. In 1520 Charles V met Henry in England. Later in the same year Henry and Francis met near Calais amid scenes of such pageantry and splendour that their meeting is known as the Field of the Cloth of Gold, and later still, Henry and Charles again met, this time at Gravelines, in the Netherlands. Here an alliance was made, and England once more declared war on France. An English campaign in northern France in 1522 achieved nothing. Wolsey was not keen upon the war; still less so was the English taxpayer, who found the demands upon his purse heavy now that Henry had spent his father's fortune. Wolsey tried to browbeat Parliament into granting money, and, when this failed to raise the necessary amount, tried—with less success still—to raise an 'amicable loan' from the rich.

Events were now conspiring to bring the war to an end. In 1525 Francis was severely defeated at Pavia and taken prisoner by the Emperor. This threatened to change the balance of forces on the continent, and a change of policy on England's part was indicated. Wolsey was not averse, as he now realized that the Emperor would never help him to the Papacy. Peace was therefore made with France, and the alliance with the Emperor was terminated. Another event—the divorce of Henry from his Spanish wife—soon appeared to confirm the new trend in English foreign policy.

Wolsey's Domestic Policy

Little of outstanding importance had happened in England during these years. As Chancellor, Wolsey was head of the legal system of the country. He used the Court of Star Chamber to enforce the laws of Henry VII against livery and maintenance, and also did something to cheapen the processes of law for poorer people. In another way Wolsey showed his sympathy for the poor. During the Tudor period many wealthy landlords enclosed the land for the profitable business of sheep-farming (see Chapter IX). Many were the protests against these enclosures, which not only injured the poor but threatened the country's agriculture and its healthy agricultural population. Wolsey tried, with little success, to limit these enclosures by sending commissioners round the country.

Wolsey was affected by the renewed interest in education that accompanied the Renaissance. In 1524 he suppressed some of the smaller and less useful monasteries to obtain money for two educational foundations that lay near his heart—a college in his native town of Ipswich, and a college at his old University of Oxford. The latter was to have been called Cardinal College, but after Wolsey's fall the King renamed it Christ Church.

Wolsey was unwilling to share his influence over the King with anyone else. He excluded the nobles from all power; they, in return, regarded him as an upstart. Nor did he encourage the wealthy middle classes in their claims to political power; they were suitable for providing the King with money but not for governing the country. Only once did he summon Parliament. This was in 1523, to obtain large supplies for the French war. The proud Cardinal went in person to the House of Commons to demand the money; but the members refused to discuss the question while Wolsey was present, and after his withdrawal they granted him only half his demands. Wolsey had found his match in Sir Thomas More, who, as Speaker of the Commons, voiced their determination not to be thus browbeaten. On other occasions Wolsey raised money by benevolences or forced loans, as, for instance, his 'amicable loan' of 1525; but this method was even less popular than taxation. Wolsey had few friends when the storm broke that swept away his power—and the clouds were already beginning to gather.

The Divorce Question and the Fall of Wolsey

For some time the King had been disturbed by the fact that he had no son to succeed him. Five children had been born, but all except his daughter, Mary, had died. Henry was therefore anxious to marry again—a desire soon strengthened by the fact that he had fallen in love with a young woman named Anne Boleyn who had been a lady-in-waiting at court.

Henry had no difficulty in finding an excuse for his desires. Catherine of Aragon had previously been married to Henry's elder brother, Arthur, who had died soon afterwards. A special dispensation had been obtained from the Pope to enable Henry to marry his brother's widow, as the canon law and the Scriptures forbade this. The King now began to question the validity of this dispensation and thus of his marriage, even suggesting that the death of most of Catherine's children was a sign that the marriage was unlawful. The Pope (Clement VII—a different one from the Pope who had granted the original dispensation) was therefore asked to declare that Henry's marriage with Catherine was invalid and that Henry was really a bachelor.

It was left to Wolsey, the King's right-hand man and the representative of the Pope in England, to obtain the required declaration from Rome. The Cardinal was quite anxious to please his master in England, but soon found that his master in Rome was unwilling to grant his request. Catherine of Aragon was the aunt of the Emperor Charles V, whose troops had sacked Rome in 1527. Charles was at the height of his power and was strongly opposed to any declaration that his aunt had been unlawfully married for twenty years. The Pope took refuge in the common device of wasting time in the hope that something might turn up to ease the situation. He sent Cardinal Campeggio to England to try the case in conjunction with Wolsey. Campeggio's instructions were to dissuade Henry from his course, or, failing that, to waste as much time as possible. After much delay the Pope recalled the case to Rome for his own decision (July, 1529).

By this time Henry had completely lost patience, and prepared to vent his wrath on Wolsey. The dismissal of the proud Cardinal would be a popular act and would help to reinstate Henry in the eyes of the nation, as popular sympathy in general was on the side of the unfortunate Queen. Wolsey was accused of breaking the Statute of Praemunire by having accepted the office of Papal Legate and was deprived of all his offices except the Archbishopric of York. For twelve years the King had known of his minister's 'illegal' action! In the same year the King summoned Parliament—the Reformation Parliament, as it has since been called. Wolsey retired to York, where for the first time he devoted himself to his duties as Archbishop. But his enemies, who now included the Boleyns, persuaded the King to summon the disgraced minister to London to answer charges of high treason. At Leicester Abbey, on his way south, Wolsey died (1530).

Henry's treatment of his faithful servant for fifteen years was an act of ingratitude; but it is well to recall what one who knew the Cardinal wrote of his fall:

> Here is the end and fall of pride and arrogance of such men, exalted by fortune to honours and high dignities; for I assure you, in his time of authority and glory, he was the haughtiest man in all his proceedings that ever lived, having

more respect to the worldly honour of his person than he had to his spiritual profession; wherein should be meekness, humility, and charity.[1]

New Ministers

Sir Thomas More succeeded Wolsey as Lord Chancellor. More and the King had been close friends, and Henry had often visited More in his house at Chelsea to enjoy his friend's companionship and conversation. But More was already experiencing misgivings about the King's policy, and the friendship was beginning to cool.

A more sympathetic adviser for Henry was Thomas Cranmer, a priest who lectured in theology at Cambridge University. Cranmer suggested that the question of the King's divorce should be submitted to the universities of Europe and that the Archbishop of Canterbury should then give a decision based upon the answers received. This way out of the difficulty appealed to Henry. Cranmer soon became the King's religious adviser, and in 1533 he was made Archbishop of Canterbury.

Lastly, Henry lent his ear to the suggestions of Thomas Cromwell. The son of a blacksmith at Putney, Cromwell had risen after a life of adventure abroad to the position of servant to Cardinal Wolsey. He had avoided all evil consequences to himself at the time of his master's fall, and he now suggested to the King that he should make the royal will supreme in Church and State. Cromwell was a student of Machiavelli's *The Prince* and a firm believer in the doctrine that the state was all-important and that the ruler's authority knew no bounds. For the next ten years (1530–1540) Cromwell was the King's chief minister.

The Reformation Parliament (1529–1536)

Henry was no Protestant and had no desire to follow the example of Luther in Germany. In 1521 he had written a

---

[1] *Life of Cardinal Wolsey*, by George Cavendish (1555).

book against Luther's doctrines and had received from the Pope the title of *Fidei Defensor*, or Defender of the Faith. Nevertheless, the King was determined to have his own way over the question of the divorce. The power of the Pope and the pretensions of the clergy were unpopular in England, and Henry decided to use Parliament as the instrument of his desires.

In 1529 the fees that the clergy could charge for administering the sacraments were reduced, and pluralism (or the holding of more than one office) was restricted.

In 1531 the clergy were fined £118,000 for having broken the Statute of Praemunire by recognizing Wolsey as Papal Legate. In the same year they were forced to recognize Henry as "Supreme Head of the Church, as far as the law of Christ will allow." In 1532 Convocation (the governing body of the Church) agreed to submit all existing and future canons of the Church to the King's approval.

In 1533 Henry appointed Cranmer Archbishop of Canterbury, and by hinting to Rome that some of the anti-Papal acts might not be put into force, he obtained full Papal sanction for his new appointment. Soon afterwards Cranmer, selecting the replies from the universities that were favourable, declared Henry's marriage with Catherine invalid. Thus Anne Boleyn became Henry's lawful wife, and any children she might have were declared heirs to the throne; but popular sympathy lay with the ill-used Catherine, who lived for another three years.

Henry now persuaded Parliament to complete its attack on the Papacy. In 1533 the Act of Appeals prevented Catherine or anyone else from appealing from the English Church Courts to Rome. In 1534 the Annates Act forbade bishops to pay the customary first year's revenue of their sees to Rome; instead it was to go to the King. The breach between Henry and the Pope was completed by the Act of Supremacy (1534) which enacted "that the King, our sovereign lord, his heirs and successors, kings of this realm, shall be taken, accepted, and reputed the only supreme head in earth of the Church of England." This completely abolished the Pope's power in England, and, instead of the Pope as its master, the English Church now had the King.

In 1535 executions took place of those who refused to take the oath of supremacy recognizing Henry's headship of the Church; they included four Carthusian monks, the aged and saintly Bishop of Rochester (John Fisher), and Henry's old friend, Sir Thomas More. Three years earlier More had resigned the Chancellorship

CARTHUSIANS IN PRISON

The Carthusians, or monks of the Charterhouse, were imprisoned and their Prior put to death for refusing to acknowledge Henry VIII's religious supremacy.

owing to his misgivings about Henry's policy. He was now brought from his retirement to the scaffold, where he met his end with serenity and even with a touch of quiet humour. "I pray you, master lieutenant," he said as he mounted the rickety scaffold, "see me safely up, and for my coming down let me shift for myself."

The last Act of the Reformation Parliament authorized Henry, now more than ever under the influence of Thomas Cromwell, to suppress the smaller monasteries (1536).

The Dissolution of the Monasteries

The King had made Cromwell his vicar-general to help him exercise his new authority as head of the Church. It was Cromwell who pointed out to Henry the desirability of attacking the monasteries. They did not form part of the

English Church in the usual sense, but were often under the control of the Pope or of foreign superiors. Then, again, they were very wealthy, and finally it was alleged that the monks had become corrupt and were no longer serving any useful purpose. Henry succumbed to these arguments and gave Cromwell the authority to organize a visitation or inspection of the monasteries. Commissioners were sent round the country to collect the necessary evidence against the monks. They reported—as they knew they were expected to report—that the monks were leading idle and, in many cases, vicious lives. There will always be controversy as to how far these charges were justified, but it can be safely maintained that although the monasteries had in some cases outlived their usefulness, the evidence brought against them of vice and immorality was largely exaggerated.

In 1536 the Reformation Parliament authorized the suppression of the smaller monasteries, *i.e.*, those with an income of less than £200 a year. This affected nearly four hundred religious houses.

The monks were not popular among many classes, but in the north especially they still enjoyed much respect and affection. They helped the sick and the poor, gave hospitality to travellers, and were, in general, kind landlords. Hence a widespread rising, known as the Pilgrimage of Grace, took place in Lincolnshire and Yorkshire (1536). Social as well as religious motives influenced the rebels, who demanded a cessation of enclosures and sheep-farming, a return to Rome, the restoration of the monasteries, and the dismissal of the upstart Cromwell. The Lincolnshire rising was quickly and cruelly suppressed. The rising in Yorkshire (where over fifty monasteries had recently been dissolved) was more serious. It was led by an able and moderate lawyer named Robert Aske. The rebels numbered nearly 40,000 men of all classes: nobles, gentry, abbots, tenants—all, in fact, who were attached to the old order. For a time Henry was powerless and pretended to listen to the rebels' demands. But he was merely biding his time, and when the rebels had dispersed he exacted a cruel vengeance, many, including Aske, being executed.

In 1537 Henry established a committee of the Privy Council, called the Council of the North, to keep order in the remote northern counties. It is convenient to notice here that in 1534 he had already established a similar council for Wales, and had followed this up in 1536 by allowing Wales to send members of Parliament to Westminster. Both the Council of Wales and the Council of the North resembled the Star Chamber in the way they were empowered to enforce the royal will.

In 1539 Cromwell's policy was carried to its logical conclusion when the remaining monasteries were dissolved and their property vested in the Crown. Thereafter monasticism ceased to exist in England for several centuries.

The suppression of about 550 monasteries and the transference of all their property into other hands could not fail to have important results upon the life of the country. Some of the more obstinate (or rather, more conscientious) monks who refused to yield to Henry's demands were put to death; most of them, to the number of 7000, were turned loose upon the world with little or nothing to support them. This, together with the disappearance of the monasteries which had themselves helped to relieve the poor, aggravated the problem of poverty which played such a large part in Tudor social history (see Chapter IX). Henry used his newly acquired money and land in various ways. He built a few castles round the coast, some dockyards and warships, and established Trinity House in London to supervise lighthouses and pilots. A little money was devoted to education; Wolsey's college (Christ Church) at Oxford was completed, and Trinity College at Cambridge was founded by grouping several old foundations together. New bishoprics were established at Gloucester, Chester, Oxford, Peterborough, and Bristol. In most cases, however, the old monastic buildings were allowed to fall into ruins, and their lands were either given or sold cheaply to royal favourites. Thus there grew up a new landed aristocracy, composed largely of self-made men with quite a different outlook from the monks. They regarded the land as a source of profit, and the fact that the Reformation had brought them new wealth made them once for all staunch opponents of any return to Rome.

Henry VIII—a Conservative Reformer

Henry was no Protestant in the Lutheran sense of the term. Generally speaking, he wished the old services to be held, and the old faith to be clung to—always providing that the Pope's authority was denied. In 1536 as head of the Church he issued Ten Articles, which, although warning the nation against the superstition of images, ordered most of the old Catholic doctrines to be observed. In 1539 Henry persuaded Parliament to pass the famous Act of Six Articles, which laid down six of the most characteristic doctrines of the Catholic Church which it was forbidden to deny. These were transubstantiation, the denial of the clergy's right to marry, the usefulness of private masses and of confessions to the clergy, the binding nature of monastic vows, and the right to deny wine to the laity at communion. This Act, more than anything else, shows Henry's determination to avoid all suspicion of Lutheranism. The penalties were very severe, and people were put to death for denying the doctrine of transubstantiation. The Protestants called the Act 'the Whip with Six Strings.' The gentle Cranmer, who was himself married and moving towards certain Lutheran doctrines, persuaded Henry not to enforce the Act too rigorously. None the less, it remained law for the rest of Henry's reign.

In another respect, however, the latter part of Henry's reign saw a fresh move in the direction of Protestantism. In 1525 an Englishman named William Tyndale published an English translation of the New Testament. Tyndale was a Protestant who lived abroad, and later suffered death for his faith, and his translation, which contained notes strongly attacking the Roman Catholic Church, was printed secretly in Flanders and smuggled into England. Henry disapproved of Tyndale's advanced views and forbade people to read his writings. In 1539, however, Henry ordered a new translation, known as the Great Bible, to be placed in every church; this version, made by Miles Coverdale, was influenced by Tyndale's translation. Before his reign ended Henry allowed Cranmer to issue certain prayers in the English language.

We can perhaps summarize the religious changes made by Henry VIII by saying that he established an *English* Catholic Church, *i.e.*, one in which the authority of Rome was replaced by that of the King, while retaining most of the old Catholic doctrines and ways of worship. Although this naturally did not please everyone, it was acceptable to the majority of the nation, which distrusted foreign interference whether from the Pope or from the Protestants.

Henry's Matrimonial Affairs and the Fall of Cromwell

Henry's second wife, Anne Boleyn, did not have the son that Henry desired, but only one daughter, the future Queen Elizabeth. In 1536 Anne was executed on a charge of unfaithfulness and plotting against her husband. Soon afterwards Henry married his third wife, Jane Seymour, who in 1537 gave birth to a son, Edward. The queen died shortly afterwards, but Henry had his son, albeit a sickly baby.

A few years later Henry planned to marry again, and Cromwell seized the opportunity to further his own ends by arranging a marriage between Henry and a north German princess, Anne of Cleves. The marriage was to be part of an alliance between England and the Lutheran States of Germany to counter a possible joint attack upon England by the Emperor and Francis I. But when Anne of Cleves arrived in England Henry was disappointed with her plain looks and lack of charm. He married her and pensioned her off almost in the same action, and then wreaked his anger upon

Cromwell. The King's minister had long been unpopular as an upstart and an extreme Protestant, and Henry sacrificed him to his enemies as he had sacrificed Wolsey ten years before. In 1540 an Act of Attainder was passed against Cromwell, and he was executed.

Henry did not seek another minister, but he still sought a wife. After the Lutheran Anne of Cleves he married Catherine Howard, a member of the powerful Catholic family of the Norfolks; but she proved unfaithful and was executed in 1542. His sixth and last wife, Catherine Parr, was middle-aged and had been twice widowed. She tended her husband in his declining years, looked after his children, and managed to survive him.

Henry's Last Years

Henry's reign ended, as it had begun, on a warlike note. In 1541 he proclaimed himself 'King of Ireland.' Hitherto English kings had been merely 'Lords of Ireland,' with the Pope in theory as their overlord. The new King of Ireland placated many of the turbulent Irish nobles by allowing them to plunder the Irish monasteries and seize their lands; but Ireland still remained a Catholic country at heart.

Henry next turned his attention to Scotland, which, under its King, James V, and his minister, Cardinal Beaton, remained officially Catholic, although Protestant opinions were steadily gaining ground. Henry had dreams of uniting the two countries, but his methods merely aroused greater hostility on the part of the Scots. After a few border skirmishes an English army severely defeated the Scots at Solway Moss (1542). James V died soon afterwards, leaving his week-old daughter, Mary, to succeed him. Henry now tried to arrange a marriage between his son, Edward, and the Queen of Scots, but the Scots strongly resented his proposal. Henry sacked Edinburgh and instigated the murder of Cardinal Beaton; but the Scots, finding English methods of wooing distasteful, invoked their 'auld alliance' with France.

This led to a French war (1544–1546), in which the English captured Boulogne (1544). A French naval attack upon England was defeated, as Henry had organized our coastal defences and built up a strong navy. In some ways Henry was the creator of our modern navy, being the first

THE "HENRI GRÂCE À DIEU"
Notice the lofty superstructures, which are a characteristic of the galleon type of ship.

to mount rows of cannon below deck with their gaping muzzles peering out through portholes. His famous warship, the *Great Harry*, or the *Henri Grâce à Dieu*, was the pride of our fleet. The French had to admit defeat and leave Boulogne in our hands for the time being. The chief result of the war for England was that Henry debased the coinage, *i.e.*, put less precious metal in it to make both ends meet. This produced confusion among merchants and customers and raised prices.

In January, 1547, the King died. His many faults are

apparent; but 'bluff King Hal,' who broke the bonds connecting England with Rome, yet refused to forge fresh ones with the Wittenberg of Luther or the Geneva of Calvin, interpreted the instincts and the thoughts of the majority of his countrymen. He ranks as one of our strongest and most popular sovereigns.

QUESTIONS AND EXERCISES

1. What do you associate with the following places: Guinegate, Flodden Field, Ipswich, Hampton Court, Leicester Abbey, Christ Church (Oxford), Solway Moss, Boulogne?

2. Give as many examples as you can to show Henry VIII's ingratitude to those who had served him.

3. Write a brief life of Thomas Wolsey.

4. Who do you think deserved his death the more, Wolsey or Cromwell? Give your reasons.

5. Summarize the work of the Reformation Parliament (1529–1536).

6. Show how Henry's matrimonial affairs affected English history. Do you think the English Reformation would have occurred without the divorce question?

7. Write a life of Sir Thomas More.

8. Write down any evidence you can think of to show (a) how Henry moved away from the Catholic Church, (b) how he kept to it.

9. Which do you think influenced Henry's foreign policy more, the balance of power or hostility towards France?

CHAPTER V

EDWARD VI AND EXTREME PROTESTANTISM

The Opening of the New Reign

HENRY VIII had arranged to be succeeded by Edward (the nine-year-old son of Jane Seymour); then, if Edward died without heirs, by Mary (the daughter of Catherine of Aragon); and finally by Elizabeth (the daughter of Anne Boleyn). He had also appointed a Council of Regency of sixteen members of varied shades of religious opinion.

Many difficulties faced the new government. In religion the extreme Catholics and the extreme Protestants were dissatisfied; the latter were increasing in number owing to the return of Englishmen from abroad, where they had imbibed the new doctrines. Moreover, Edward VI was, despite his youth, keenly interested in religious matters and was sympathetic towards Lutheranism. Within a few weeks the Protestant members of the Council

EDWARD VI
After a portrait by a French painter.

of Regency gained the upper hand, and the King's uncle, Edward Seymour, became the real ruler of England with the titles of Duke of Somerset and Lord Protector.

Important social and economic problems also demanded attention (see Chapter IX). The enclosure of common land and the eviction of tenants for the purpose of sheep-farming were still proceeding. To this cause of poverty were now added others: the dissolution of the monasteries, the vagrancy of many ejected monks, Henry VIII's debasement of the coinage, and the rise in prices following the influx of precious metals from the New World.

Finally, there were the legacies of the Scottish and French wars. The Protector Somerset was anxious to carry out Henry VIII's plan of marrying Edward VI to Mary, Queen of Scots, and in 1547 an English army invaded Scotland, won a victory at Pinkie, and sacked Edinburgh. Again the Scots failed to appreciate such rough methods of making love. They sent their young Queen to France, where she later married the Dauphin. The French were also able to recapture Henry's conquest of Boulogne (1550).

The Progress of the Reformation

Under Edward VI England became for the first time a Protestant country. The boy King was an ardent Protestant; Archbishop Cranmer had moved far from Henry VIII's Anglo-Catholicism; while the nobles and the Council of Regency hoped for further chances of attacking Church property. The Duke of Somerset was an advanced Protestant, although inspired by higher religious ideals than most of the other nobles. He soon persuaded Parliament to repeal Henry VIII's Act of Six Articles, and to proclaim a measure of toleration. In this Somerset was far in advance of his age; but the wisdom of his policy can be doubted. It resulted in Calvinistic ideas from Geneva being introduced into the country, where they soon came into conflict with the older Catholic and the more moderate Lutheran views. Religious strife resulted, and brawls, fights, and noisy demonstrations soon showed that the people were not really ready for religious toleration as we know it.

The government added to the discontent and confusion by launching an attack upon all so-called superstitions. Extreme Protestants were given full rein to destroy images, statues, paintings, frescoes, stained-glass windows—in fact every adornment that had beautified the churches of the Middle Ages. No doubt some of these had encouraged superstitious beliefs, but the loss inflicted upon the English churches was irreparable, and the common people were aghast.

A further attack was then made upon religious property. Many gilds devoted part of their wealth to religious purposes; such wealth was seized. A similar fate befell the chantries. These were small chapels, which had been endowed to enable priests to say masses for the dead and, in some cases, to act as schoolmasters. All such chantries now disappeared. The confiscated wealth went mainly into the pockets of the greedy Protestant nobility; only a small proportion of it went to found the King Edward VI Grammar Schools, many of

THOMAS CRANMER
Fliccius

which still exist. The Protector himself scandalized the Catholic-minded folk by pulling down churches and using the materials to build the first Somerset House in London.

Happily these destructive years did succeed in producing one thing of beauty, namely, the first English Prayer Book (1549). This was the work of Archbishop Cranmer, who took as his basis the Latin prayers of the Middle Ages and translated them into perfect English. The old Latin Mass was abolished, and the new English Communion took its place. Protestant feeling was placated by communion being allowed in both kinds (bread and wine) for the laity and by substituting a general and public confession in place of private confessions to a priest. The Act of Uniformity (1549) made the use of the new prayer book compulsory in all churches, but did not compel people to attend them.

The religious changes were most acceptable in the 'advanced' south-east district round London. In the remoter districts they aroused opposition. In 1549 a rebellion broke out in Devon and Cornwall against the new prayer book. The rebels seized Exeter, but the Protector took strong measures and suppressed them.

Ket's Rebellion and the Fall of Somerset (1549)

In the same year a rebellion of an economic and social character broke out in Norfolk under the leadership of a landowner named Robert Ket. Ket's followers protested against the continuance of enclosures and sheep-farming and, to show their opposition to the latter, slew and devoured thousands of sheep. They encamped on Mousehold Heath, outside Norwich, and soon took the city.

Somerset really sympathized with the rebels. He had tried to stop enclosures by sending round Commissioners and establishing a Court of Requests to hear complaints against encroaching landlords. But when he began to negotiate with the rebels, the other nobles on the council authorized Somerset's chief rival, the Earl of Warwick, to put down the rebellion. This he did with much energy, and Robert Ket was executed.

This heralded the downfall of Somerset. A well-meaning and moderate man, he was not strong enough to solve the problems of his age. He had also aroused opposition by executing his own brother, Lord Seymour of Sudeley, for plotting to marry the Princess Elizabeth and overthrow the Government (1549). Somerset was imprisoned in the Tower, but was soon released and allowed to take his seat again on the council. But for the rest of the reign (1549–1553) power lay with his enemy, the Earl of Warwick. The new government soon succeeded in still further alienating the people.

The Rule of Northumberland

The Earl of Warwick was the son of Dudley, Henry VII's extortioner, who had been put to death on Henry VIII's accession. In 1551 he was made the Duke of Northumberland, the title by which he is usually known. He differed from Somerset in many respects. He possessed no sympathy for the poor, and was out entirely for his own ends. In religion he was an advanced Protestant; but this was mainly because of the prospect of power and plunder that Protestantism offered, rather than because of any deep conviction. He managed to obtain complete hold over the mind of the young King, and, although he never took the title of Protector, his was the hand that guided English policy for the rest of the reign.

To overcome the government's financial difficulties the coinage was still further debased. Somerset's social policy was completely reversed, and an act was passed making it a crime to oppose enclosures. The former Protector was still a member of the council, and his popularity revived as the country realized the character of the new Government. Northumberland decided to strike his rival down, and in January, 1552, Somerset was executed. He was mourned by many as a friend of the people, but his own nephew, the King, showed no grief.

In 1552 the second Prayer Book was issued. It was based upon Cranmer's Prayer Book of 1549, but was altered by extremists like Bishop Ridley to make it more distinctively Protestant. Transubstantiation was more strongly denied, the services made simpler, and the minister's vestments made plainer. An Act of Uniformity (1552) made the use of the new book compulsory and forced everyone to attend a church. Northumberland now despoiled the churches of still more of their precious articles—candlesticks, bells, chalices, censers, and vestments. In the same year (1552) Cranmer and Ridley drew up the Forty-two Articles of Religion for the Church of England. These were based largely upon the Lutheran faith and, owing to Cranmer's moderation, were not too strongly worded. They form the basis of the present-day Thirty-nine Articles of the English Church.

The extreme Protestantism of Edward VI's reign gave great displeasure to many. Bishops Bonner and Gardiner opposed the changes and were deprived of their sees; their places were taken by Ridley and Hooper. Many advanced reformers from the Continent came to England; but the mass of the people wished for a return to the old ways. Northumberland's position, and perhaps his very life, depended entirely upon the King, and early in 1553 it became apparent that Edward VI, whose health had never been good, was dying of consumption.

The Nine Days' Queen

The next heir to the throne was the devout Catholic Mary, the daughter of Catherine of Aragon. Northumberland therefore persuaded the dying King that the succession of a Queen, and a fanatical Catholic at that, was a danger to the state. Edward VI made a new will leaving the Crown to the male heirs of Lady Jane Grey, the grand-daughter of Henry VIII's youngest sister, Mary; she was sixteen years of age and a Protestant. Northumberland then secured his own position (as he thought) by marrying his own son, Lord Guildford Dudley, to Lady Jane. He also altered the will to make the Crown go to Lady Jane herself. Cranmer and Ridley gave their support to Northumberland's scheme.

In July, 1553, Edward VI died, and Northumberland proclaimed Lady Jane Queen. But the mass of the people supported Mary. They had no wish for Northumberland's government of plunder to continue, and they hoped that the daughter of 'bluff King Hal' would restore the religion of her father. Mary fled to Norfolk, where the memory of Ket's rebellion made Northumberland doubly unpopular. She soon had 30,000 men to support her, and when Northumberland marched against her his own army dwindled away. When he reached Cambridge he realized that the game was up. He acclaimed Mary as Queen and declared himself a Catholic! Mary had him executed and placed the unfortunate Jane—the Nine Days' Queen—together with her husband in the Tower. The country looked forward with high hopes to the reign of Mary Tudor.

QUESTIONS AND EXERCISES

1. Describe the policy of the Duke of Somerset. Do you think he deserved his fate?

2. In what ways did England become a Protestant country under Edward VI?

3. Why do you think the mass of the people opposed the extreme Protestantism of Edward VI's reign?

4. Illustrate from his actions the character of the Duke of Northumberland.

CHAPTER VI

MARY TUDOR AND THE RETURN TO ROME

The Queen's Marriage

MARY TUDOR began her reign with the sympathy and support of the majority of the nation. It was felt that her accession to the throne atoned in some degree for the treatment of her mother, Catherine of Aragon. Her Catholic faith was well known, and after the excesses of the reign of Edward VI a return in the direction of Catholicism was hoped for, though few people wished for a complete return to Rome.

MARY TUDOR AT THE TIME OF HER MARRIAGE
From the painting by Antonio Moro in the Prado Museum.

She began her reign by undoing much of Edward VI's work. The English Prayer Book was abolished and the Latin Mass restored; but Parliament enacted this only after a certain amount of opposition. Bishops Bonner of London and Gardiner of Winchester were restored to their sees, and the latter became Lord Chancellor. The most important question awaiting solution was the Queen's marriage. When Parliament requested the Queen to marry an English nobleman, Mary coldly replied: "Your desire to dictate to us the consort whom we shall choose, we consider somewhat superfluous." Mary intended to marry her cousin, Philip, the son of the aged Emperor Charles V. Philip would soon be King of Spain, and although by marrying Mary he would not become King of England, he would naturally exercise an influence over his wife's policy, and if a son were born of the marriage England might eventually become part of the Spanish Empire.

Such considerations produced widespread opposition to the proposed marriage, especially in the south-east, which was strongly Protestant. In 1554 Sir Thomas Wyatt raised a force of five thousand and marched from Kent upon London. Mary went to the Guildhall and appealed to the citizens of her capital. They responded loyally and barred the advance of the rebels across London Bridge. Wyatt then marched up the Thames and approached London from the west. But as he drew near the capital his numbers diminished, and realizing the hopelessness of his cause, he surrendered. His execution followed as a matter of course; but the government made efforts to implicate Mary's half-sister, Elizabeth, in the plot. Wyatt's intention had been to place Elizabeth and an English nobleman, Edward Courtenay, Earl of Devon, on the throne; but Wyatt declared on the scaffold that Elizabeth had known nothing of the scheme. Elizabeth was placed in the Tower for two months, but otherwise she escaped punishment. Mary took the opportunity of executing the unfortunate Lady Jane Grey and her husband, whom she now regarded as too dangerous to live.

In July, 1554, Philip of Spain arrived at Southampton and was married to Mary a few days later in Winchester Cathedral. The marriage treaty drawn up by Parliament safeguarded the independence of England, but it could not prevent Mary from allowing her husband, for whom she had a real affection, a large measure of control over the government's policy.

The Return to Rome

In the autumn of 1554 Mary persuaded Parliament to repeal all the anti-Papal legislation of Henry VIII; but

Parliament refused to restore the monastic lands that had been seized, and Mary realized that on this point she would have to give way. She none the less surrendered the stolen goods that were still in royal hands, declaring that she set more by the salvation of her soul than by ten kingdoms acquired by robbing the Church.

On November 30, 1554, a solemn ceremony of reconciliation with Rome took place at Whitehall Palace. The Pope was represented by an Englishman, Cardinal Pole, who had left England at the time of Henry VIII's quarrel with Rome. The two Houses of Parliament presented a petition to the Papal legate begging that the country might be taken back to the bosom of Mother Church. Cardinal Pole granted the request and absolved the country from its sin. Thus—for the last time in its history—England became part of the Roman Catholic Church.

The Marian Persecution

At the request of Philip and Mary, Parliament now re-enacted the old laws against the Lollards, such as *De Heretico Comburendo*, which had authorized the burning of heretics. The bishops were ordered to inquire closely into the religion of the clergy and their flocks, and early in 1555 the persecution began which resulted in the burning of nearly three hundred Protestants.

The first victims were Canon Rogers and Bishop Hooper, who were soon followed by others of less standing. Later in the same year Philip left England to take over the government of the Netherlands. He had never felt at home in England and did not feel the love for his wife that she felt for him. Mary sought consolation in pushing on more vigorously with the burnings. In October, 1555, Latimer and Ridley (the ex-bishops of Worcester and London) were burnt together at Oxford. Latimer's words to his fellow-sufferer as the ordeal began are memorable and prophetic: "Be of good cheer, Master Ridley, we shall this day light such a candle, by God's grace, in England as I trust shall never be put out."

The burning of the arch-heretic Cranmer, who, as Archbishop of Canterbury, had pronounced the marriage of Catherine of Aragon invalid and had drawn up the First Prayer Book of Edward VI, took place in 1556. Mary wished first to obtain the Pope's consent to his deposition and, if possible, to persuade the ex-Archbishop to renounce his Protestant views. Under continual pressure and with the fear of burning ever before him, Cranmer, who was not made of such stern stuff as the others, gave way and signed a recantation. He found, however, that he was to be burned despite his recantation. On the day of his execution his courage returned. He publicly renounced what he had in his weakness signed, and that he might show his detestation of his "unworthy right hand" he held it in the flames to be consumed first of all.

> And when the wood kindled, and the fire began to burn near him, stretching out his arm, he put his right hand into the flame, which he held so stedfast that all men might see his hand burned before his body was touched.[1]

The burnings continued at Oxford, Smithfield, and elsewhere for the remainder of the reign, and in all, nearly three hundred Protestants suffered martyrdom for their faith. Most of them were humble folk unknown to history, such as "William Pigot, Stephen Knight, Thomas Tomkins, Thomas Hawkes, John Laurence a priest, and William Hunter," to pick a few at random from the pages of Foxe. Mary had undertaken the persecutions, not out of cruelty, but with the desire to save the souls of her countrymen. Both Protestants and Catholics believed it right to persecute their opponents, and on the Continent thousands suffered death for their faith. But Mary failed completely in her object. The persecutions served to purify Protestantism and to gain for it a

---

[1] Foxe, *Book of Martyrs.*

respect that it had lacked under Edward VI. They also burnt into men's minds a passionate hatred of the Roman Catholic religion, and distrust of Rome remained one of the key-notes of English history for several centuries. Early in the next reign, in 1563, Foxe's *Book of Martyrs* was published. This vivid account of the Marian persecutions soon became, next to the Bible, one of the most widely read books in England and served to perpetuate the national hatred of Rome. Mary had indeed converted England—but to Protestantism.

The Loss of Calais

Philip became King of Spain in 1556 and continued to live abroad. He continued his father's policy of war against France, and looked to his wife's kingdom for support. Englishmen were distrustful of fighting on behalf of Spain, but the Spanish envoys bullied the English Council into declaring war. The result was a bitter disappointment to England, for the French were able to capture Calais (1558), the last of our French possessions. In actual fact, its loss deprived England of an embarrassing possession which would only have produced continual strife with France.

In November, 1558, the Queen died. Her short reign had been full of tragedy, and as her end drew near she learned that her cold-hearted husband was already trying to arrange a marriage of policy with her half-sister and successor, the Princess Elizabeth.

QUESTIONS AND EXERCISES

1. Explain and illustrate the English dislike of Spain during Mary's reign.

2. Summarize the chief stages by which Mary lost the popularity she enjoyed at the beginning of her reign.

3. What do you think were the permanent results of Mary's reign?

4. Outline the life and character of Thomas Cranmer.

CHAPTER VII

EUROPEAN SURVEY (II): THE COUNTER-REFORMATION

Chief Rulers

Philip II	(Spanish Empire)	1556–1598
Elizabeth	(England)	1558–1603
Charles IX	(France)	1560–1574
Henry III	(France)	1574–1589
Henry IV	(France)	1589–1610

The Counter-Reformation

THE second half of the sixteenth century, corresponding roughly with the reign of Elizabeth (1558—1603), is the period of the Counter-Reformation. Till about 1550 the Protestant Reformers had been on the offensive, and the Catholic Church had been too weak and disorganized to put up much resistance. But after 1550 the Catholic Church gathered fresh strength and began to assume the offensive itself. The Catholic Church stemmed the flowing tide of Protestantism in many countries, and France, Poland, the southern Netherlands, and south Germany, where Protestantism had begun to gain a foot-hold, were won back to Mother Church. But the victories, as we shall see, were not all on one side.

The main forces behind the Catholic revival were the new religious order of the Jesuits, the closer definition of the Catholic faith by the Council of Trent, the extended use of the Inquisition to stamp out heresy, and the reformation in the lives of the Popes and of the lower ranks of the Church.

Forces behind the Catholic Revival

The leading Catholic country during the Counter-Reformation period was Spain, and the Spanish King, Philip II (the former husband of Mary Tudor), was the foremost sovereign of his age. Spain also produced Ignatius Loyola, the founder of the Jesuits.

Ignatius Loyola (1491–1556) was a Spanish knight who took up soldiering as a profession, but a severe wound prevented him from continuing his military career. He resolved instead to become a soldier of Christ. Finding his education insufficient, he attended first a Spanish university and then the University of Paris. While there, he made the acquaintance of other serious-minded students, and in 1534 a small band, with Loyola as their leader, set out on a pilgrimage to Palestine. A war between Venice and Turkey interfered with their plans, and Loyola and his friends decided instead to do mission work in Italy, and to call themselves simply members of the Society of Jesus. In 1540 the Pope gave his consent to the new religious order, which soon took the lead in the struggle against Protestantism.

The Jesuits were organized, as befitted their founder, on military lines, with unquestioning obedience as their outstanding characteristic. They mixed freely with the outside world, and, as upholders of absolutism, became acceptable confessors and councillors to kings and princes. They realized that the correct training of the young was the surest foundation for rebuilding the Church, and they became the schoolmasters of a large part of Europe. The order spread so rapidly that when Loyola died in 1556 it possessed two thousand members, and although they concentrated upon the work of combating the Reformation in Europe, we must not forget that they also sent out missionaries, like Francis Xavier, among the heathens of America and Asia.

During the Reformation period there had been many demands inside the Catholic Church for the summoning of a council. The Papacy, however, opposed this demand, as it feared that a council might once more, as in the fifteenth century, try to diminish the power of the Pope. By 1545, however, the Emperor Charles V was strong enough to force the Pope to summon a council at Trent. This council lasted with many interruptions, some of them very long, till 1563. The Catholic doctrines of the Middle Ages were reaffirmed, and all hope of a compromise with Protestantism was gone. The Catholic Church now had a well-defined and coherent body of doctrine, which it could oppose to the beliefs of Protestantism. On the question of reform, the Papacy was clever enough to see that nothing was done to impair its own privileges, but as the Papacy had by this time done much to reform itself, the Catholic Church accepted the new situation.

PHILIP II
Juan Pantoja

In 1542 the Papacy introduced the Inquisition into Italy. The Court of the Inquisition had been established in the Middle Ages to put down heresy, and in Spain it had been used against Jews and Moors. The new Italian Inquisition was modelled on the Spanish.

Philip II of Spain

On Charles V's retirement in 1556 his brother Ferdinand inherited the Austrian lands and became Holy Roman Emperor; and his son Philip inherited Spain, the Netherlands, the Italian possessions (Milan, Naples, and Sicily), and the Spanish Empire in America. Henceforward, till the year 1700, there remained these two branches of the House of Hapsburg, the Imperial and the Spanish.

Philip II of Spain (1556–1598) was the most powerful sovereign of his age, and he soon became the leader of the Counter-Reformation. His vast possessions, his devotion to his religion, and his untiring capacity for hard work fitted him for his task. But he was a man of narrow and fixed ideas, with little sympathy for other people's views or understanding of his fellow-men. He tried to rule his empire from his palace in Spain and was unwilling to delegate authority to others on the spot. In Spain his rule was successful. The Inquisition was used to stamp out heresy, and a revolt on

THE ESCORIAL

This remarkable building, at once a convent, a church, a palace, and a royal mausoleum, was erected by Philip II. It stands about twenty-seven miles from Madrid and contains the remains of Charles V, Philip II, and many later Spanish kings. Its domes and rounded windows show the influence of Renaissance ideas on the architecture of the time.

the part of the Moors was suppressed. Elsewhere, however, he was not so successful.

The Rise of the Dutch Republic

The Hapsburg possessions that had descended to Philip included the Netherlands. These consisted of seventeen provinces, roughly the equivalent of present-day Holland and Belgium. They were dissimilar in their institutions and methods of government, each province having its own separate history and tradition. Furthermore, the northerly provinces were inhabited by a Teutonic people speaking a language akin to German, while the southern provinces were more French in their language and population.

The Emperor Charles V had been born in the Netherlands and understood the people well enough to govern them without much friction. But Philip did not understand them at all and thought to govern them from Madrid by Spanish rulers and soldiers, and to stamp out Protestantism by stern measures. He offended both the local nobility and the growing body of Calvinists by ordering the decrees of the Council of Trent to be strictly enforced. In 1567 the Duke of Alva was sent from Spain as Philip's Regent. Alva was determined to use ruthless methods. "I have tamed men of iron," he boasted. "Shall I not overcome these men of butter?" During the six years of his Regency, his Council of Blood put to death over eighteen thousand political and religious offenders. But the "men of butter" refused to yield. They found an able leader in one of their nobility named William, Prince of Orange (Orange was a small possession of his family in southern France)—also called William the Silent, from his taciturn habits.

Under Alva the revolt of the Netherlands began in earnest. It sprang from mixed motives: hatred of Spanish rule, love of liberty, opposition to the heavy taxation imposed by the foreigners, and the hatred of Catholicism felt by the Calvinists. In 1572 a body of privateers, known as the 'Sea-beggars,' who for long had been preying on Spanish commerce, surprised and seized Brille. As the struggle developed, it seemed as if the whole seventeen provinces would fight for their independence. The situation was saved for Philip by two factors: the arrival in 1578 of the capable Duke of Parma as Regent, and the differences between the Catholics in the south and the Protestants in the north. Parma was able to win back the southern provinces for Spain, but the seven northern provinces, under the leadership of the province of Holland, remained firm. In 1584 the indomitable William of Orange was shot dead by an assassin's bullet, but Philip reaped no advantage from this dastardly act. Elizabeth of England sent help to the struggling Dutch; so, too, did Catholic France, out of hatred for Spain. In 1588 the defeat of the Spanish Armada gave the Dutch fresh hope and afforded them a breathing-space. The struggle dragged on, but the issue was not really now in doubt. In 1609 the Dutch secured practical independence by a Twelve Years' Truce. In 1648 their independence was legally recognized. No sooner was it born than the Dutch Republic attained the stature of a giant (see Chapter X).

Philip's Relations with Other Countries

In 1571 Philip, whose Mediterranean interests included his Italian possessions as well as Spain, decided to check the growing danger of Turkish expansion. A powerful fleet, composed of Spanish, Genoese, and Venetian vessels, was placed under the command of Philip's half-brother, Don John of Austria, and sent against the infidel. At Lepanto (1571), just off the coast of Greece, the Turks were decisively beaten, two hundred and fifty of their warships being destroyed. One of the Spaniards who served under Don John was a young man named Cervantes, who, being badly wounded, decided to take up writing. He produced the world-famous book *Don Quixote*.

Nine years later Philip achieved another triumph. The old royal house of Portugal died out in 1580. By diplomacy and arms Philip forced the unwilling Portuguese to accept him as king. This brought disastrous results to Portugal, as the enemies of Spain (England and Holland) now attacked the Portuguese as well as the Spanish Empire, and the Dutch built up an empire in the east, much of which they still possess. The union of Spain and Portugal lasted till 1640, when the Portuguese threw off the Spanish yoke and founded a new royal house of their own, the House of Braganza.

Elsewhere Philip's foreign policy met with little success. He failed to prevent Elizabeth of England from adopting Protestantism, from encouraging English sea-dogs to attack Spanish commerce, and from helping the Dutch. The disaster of the Spanish Armada (1588) is described in the following chapter. In France, also, his policy failed, as we shall presently see.

The French Wars of Religion

Protestantism had obtained a stronger hold in France than in Spain. John Calvin was a Frenchman, and it was his ideas that were taken up by the Huguenots, as the Protestants in France were called. They never formed more than about one-tenth of the population, but they included many of the wealthy middle-class merchants and tradesmen of the south-west.

Soon after 1560 civil war broke out between Catholics and Huguenots and lasted, on and off, for nearly forty years. In 1560 a boy of ten had ascended the throne as Charles IX (1560–1574), but the real ruler of France was his Italian mother, Catherine de Medici. The Huguenots under the leadership of the House of Navarre, a branch of the royal family, demanded religious toleration. The extreme Catholics, led by the Guise family, looked with dismay at the prospect of the Huguenot House of Navarre succeeding to the French throne, if, as seemed quite possible, the existing Valois line died out. At first Catherine tried a policy of conciliation, but when this failed she turned against the Huguenots. She obtained the King's consent to a massacre of the Huguenots who had flocked to Paris for the wedding of their leader, Henry of Navarre, to the King's sister, Margaret of Valois. The massacre of St Bartholomew's Day (August 24, 1572) spread from Paris to the provinces and resulted in the slaughter of over 10,000 Huguenots. It sent a wave of horror through Protestant Europe.

Two years later Charles IX was succeeded by his worthless brother, Henry III (1574–1589). Under him the confusion grew worse. When the King's brother died, and Henry of Navarre, the Huguenot leader, became heir to the throne, the Catholic League, under Henry of Guise, called in the aid of Philip of Spain, who was only too willing to profit from the weakness of France. In 1588 the King, fearing the growing power of Henry of Guise, had him treacherously murdered. In the following year the King himself was stabbed to death by a fanatical Dominican friar. This left Henry of Navarre King of France as Henry IV, and in 1590 he defeated the Catholic League at Ivry. But France, and particularly Paris, still refused to accept a Huguenot king. At length, in 1593, Henry allowed himself to be converted to the Catholic faith. "Paris is worth a Mass," he is reported to have said. Thereafter, to the dismay of Philip of Spain, whose reign was nearing its end, Henry IV became King of France in fact as well as in name. Henry was the first of the new line of Bourbon kings which ruled in France till the French Revolution of 1789. Henry did not forget his previous co-religionists, and in 1598 he issued the celebrated Edict of Nantes. Huguenots were allowed complete freedom of worship in most districts, and their religion was not to bar them from careers in the state or the army. To make their position secure they were allowed to garrison many towns, including the famous port of La Rochelle in western France. The Edict of Nantes was a praiseworthy attempt at religious toleration in an age of intolerance; but the Huguenot garrisons created misgivings in the minds of most Frenchmen and led to more trouble later on.

QUESTIONS AND EXERCISES

1. Explain clearly what you understand by the term 'Counter-Reformation.'

2. Mention briefly the ways in which the reign of Philip of Spain was (a) successful, (b) unsuccessful.

3. Write notes on: Jesuits, Council of Trent, Lepanto, Massacre of St Bartholomew, Edict of Nantes.

4. "Paris is worth a mass." Explain what Henry of Navarre meant by this. Was he justified in his action?

CHAPTER VIII

THE TRIUMPH OF ELIZABETH

Elizabeth's Difficulties

IT was no easy task that faced Elizabeth when she succeeded Mary in 1558. Commerce was disorganized owing to the debasement of the coinage; the royal treasury was empty; the country had just suffered the loss of Calais owing to its dependence upon Spanish foreign policy; Philip of Spain was hoping to marry Elizabeth and thus continue this state of dependence; and in religion the governments of the three previous reigns had thrown off the authority of the Pope, then established an extreme and unpopular form of Protestantism, and finally re-established the still less popular connexion with Rome. Moreover, the Queen's position itself was disputed by extreme Catholics, who refused to recognize the daughter of Anne Boleyn as rightful heir to the throne. In their view the true Queen of England was Elizabeth's cousin, Mary Stuart, who was descended from Henry VII's daughter, Margaret, and who was married to the Dauphin of France (see genealogical table on p. 51).

ELIZABETH
Crispin van de Passe, after Isaac Oliver

In the event, however, Elizabeth's reign proved to be one of the most glorious in English history. This was undoubtedly due in part to Elizabeth's character, which had been formed in adversity. Her mother had been executed by Henry VIII, and during the reign of Mary, whose mother had been deprived by Anne Boleyn of the royal title, the slightest indiscretion on Elizabeth's part might have cost her her life. But adversity had only strengthened Elizabeth's character and developed her powers of judgment. Above all she had been taught the value of caution, of waiting for her enemies to make mistakes while she herself consolidated her own position.

Elizabeth also possessed her father's faculty of interpreting the wishes of the nation. She called herself in one of her first speeches a "mere English" queen, with no drop of foreign blood in her veins. Her feeling for what was "English" led her to reject Philip of Spain's offer of marriage, to the astonishment of that proud sovereign, but to the delight of the nation. Elizabeth was fortunate, too, in the choice of her chief counsellor. This was Sir William Cecil (later Lord Burghley), who remained at her side till his death in 1598. Cecil had for long acted as Elizabeth's secretary, and she knew his worth. Like most Tudor statesmen, he sprang from the middle classes.

Elizabeth's Religious Settlement

Elizabeth herself was not fanatically religious, as her half-sister Mary had been, and was ready to take a *political* view of religion. The authority of the Pope had become so unpopular as a result of Mary's tragic reign that its abolition was desired by most Englishmen. This agreed with Elizabeth's personal position, for the daughter of Anne Boleyn could hardly recognize the authority of one who regarded her as the daughter of an invalid marriage and looked upon Mary Stuart as the true Queen of England. Elizabeth, however, had no liking for the extreme form of Protestantism that had existed under Edward VI. In particular she had a fondness for much of the old Catholic ritual and elaborate ceremony.

The year 1559 saw the essentials of Elizabeth's religious

settlement carried out. The Roman Catholic legislation of Mary's reign was repealed, and the anti-Papal laws of Henry VIII were re-enacted. In 1559 the Elizabethan Act of Supremacy was passed, by which the sovereign became 'Supreme Governor' of all religious as well as political affairs affecting the kingdom. This title, it was hoped, would prove less offensive than Henry VIII's title of 'Supreme Head.' In the same year was issued another English Prayer Book whose use by the clergy was enforced by an Act of Uniformity. Elizabeth's Prayer Book was based upon the second and more Protestant Prayer Book of Edward VI's reign (1552), but with certain important alterations. The wording of the communion service was made vague, so that the worshipper could choose for himself whether it implied a belief in transubstantiation or not. In addition certain harsh phrases about the 'detestable enormities' of the Pope, as well as prayers for the conversion of Papists, were excluded. A new ornaments rubric also modified the severe rubric of 1552, which had forbidden even the use of the surplice; Elizabeth's rubric took up the less extreme position of the *first* Prayer Book of Edward VI. The new Prayer Book was rejected by all save one of Mary's Catholic bishops and by about 200 clergy—a very small minority. They were expelled from their positions, but otherwise not harshly treated. Elizabeth established in 1559 a Court of High Commission to inflict fines for recusancy, *i.e.*, failure to attend the parish church; but these fines were not always regularly exacted. The majority of the nation willingly accepted the new Prayer Book, which, with few alterations, is the one still in use in the Church of England. Thus Cranmer's work, which was the basis of Elizabeth's book, has become a permanent part of our national life.

At the end of the same year (1559) Matthew Parker, who had already been consulted over much of the new religious settlement, was consecrated Archbishop of Canterbury. Parker was a learned and moderate man whose influence upon our national church till his death in 1575 was very salutary. As a married man he opposed the views of the Queen herself, who was still inclined to hold to the Catholic view of the celibacy of the clergy. Parker issued a new version of the Bible, known as the Bishops' Bible, but its bulky size prevented it from passing into general circulation. The most popular version among the growing body of Puritans was a revision of Tyndale's Bible. In 1571 Parker, with the help of others, issued the Thirty-nine Articles of the English Church, a statement of belief based upon the Forty-two Articles drawn up by Cranmer under Edward VI.

The new Church of England proved permanent because it suited the majority of Englishmen. It was a 'middle way,' or *via media*, between the extremes of Roman Catholicism and Genevan Calvinism. Owing to its intentional vagueness on certain points it satisfied all those who did not hold strong opinions on either side. Its comprehensive nature brought the majority of Englishmen within its fold and was the best policy that Elizabeth could have pursued; but difficult problems arose later on, owing to the inclusion of different parties within the same Church.

The Reformation in Scotland (1559–1560)

The Scottish Queen since 1542 had been Mary Stuart, or Mary, Queen of Scots, who in 1558 had married the Dauphin of France. In the following year her husband became King of France as Francis II, and Mary was now Queen of France as well as of Scotland. She also claimed the throne of England, being next in succession to the 'heretical' Elizabeth. Francis died in 1560, and in 1561 Mary returned to Scotland.

During Mary's absence from Scotland her French mother, Mary of Guise, had acted as Regent, but had been unable to prevent the spread of Protestantism. The Catholic Church in Scotland was badly in need of reform, and its great wealth was a temptation to greedy nobles. The leader of the Reformation in Scotland was John Knox (1505–1572), who had visited Calvin at Geneva and had learnt at first hand the doctrines of extreme Protestantism. On his return to Scotland Knox, who was a powerful and eloquent preacher, converted the masses to Protestantism. Abbeys were sacked, monks were expelled, and churches were robbed of their ornaments. Knox found allies among the Scottish nobles, who, partly from religious conviction but partly also from the desire of plunder, formed a Protestant association called the 'Lords of the Congregation of Jesus Christ' to attack the 'Congregation of Satan,' as they called the Catholics.

In 1559 Mary of Guise and her French soldiers attempted to put down the Protestants by force, but the French soon found themselves besieged at Leith. The Lords of the Congregation appealed to Elizabeth to send help (1560). Elizabeth saw her opportunity. She was willing to risk the enmity of France in order to win the friendship of Protestant Scotland. An English fleet was sent to the Firth of Forth, and the French were defeated. Mary of Guise soon died, and by the Treaty of Edinburgh or Leith (1560) the French troops had to leave Scotland, and Elizabeth was recognized by the Scots as lawful Queen of England.

John Knox now proceeded to organize the Scottish Church on the principles he had imbibed at Geneva. Each parish elected its own minister, or presbyter, who was helped by a number of lay 'elders.' The governing body of the whole Church consisted not of bishops, as in the English and the Catholic Churches, but of representatives sent by each parish to form a General Assembly. The Scottish Presbyterian Church was thus democratic in its organization. It taught the Calvinistic doctrine of predestination and took a genuine interest in educating the Scottish peasantry. It soon became the most influential body in Scotland.

Such was the Scotland to which the Catholic Mary returned in 1561.

Mary in Scotland (1561–1568)

For the next twenty-six years the rivalry between Mary and Elizabeth fills the pages of history with plots, assassinations, and romantic adventures. The two women were very different in many respects. Mary was womanly, charming, and gay; she was the more adventurous and the readier to take risks; but she was also more inclined to let her heart overrule her head. The English Queen was the cooler and the more patient of the two; but she lacked (to her regret) the graces of Mary. Both were women of exceptional ability and ready to stoop to any deceit or trickery to further their plans. Mary, however, pursued an unpopular policy and failed to win the devotion of her countrymen. With Elizabeth the exact opposite was the case.

Despite the wishes of her nobles and the eloquence of John Knox, Mary refused to give up her Catholic faith. For several years she ruled cautiously, and then came to grief over her love-affairs. In 1565 she married a Scottish nobleman, her own cousin, Lord Darnley. Darnley was a prominent Catholic and, like Mary herself, was descended from the marriage between James IV of Scotland and Margaret, the daughter of Henry VII (see p. 51). Mary's marriage therefore strengthened her claim to the English throne and made her more dangerous to Elizabeth. In other respects, however, it weakened her position, as Darnley was worthless and brainless, and sulked when Mary refused to allow him any real authority. Husband and wife soon quarrelled, and Darnley grew jealous of Mary's Italian secretary, David Rizzio. The Lords of the Congregation persuaded the dissatisfied Darnley to join forces with them. On the night of March 9, 1566, while Mary was talking to her attendants after supper in her room at Holyrood Palace, Darnley and others burst into her presence, and while Darnley held his wife the unfortunate Rizzio was dragged out and stabbed to death.

Mary was determined on vengeance, though for some time she feigned forgiveness. In June, 1566, she gave birth to a son (afterwards James VI of Scotland and James I of England). She then plotted to get rid of her husband, for she had fallen in love with a rough border baron, the Earl of Bothwell. While Darnley was recovering from smallpox, the house in which he was sleeping (it was Mary's own

LOCHLEVEN CASTLE
Photo Hardie

house, Kirk o' Field, near Edinburgh), was blown up, and Darnley was found strangled in the garden (February, 1567). The crime was undoubtedly the work of Bothwell, and the evidence points to Mary being implicated. The infatuated Queen protected her lover, and, as soon as he had divorced his own wife, married him (May, 1567). This was too much for her subjects, who rose in rebellion against her. She was defeated at Carberry Hill (June, 1567), was forced to abdicate, and was imprisoned in Lochleven Castle. Bothwell had fled to the Continent. In the following year she escaped by winning over her gaoler and raised a fresh army. She was easily defeated at Langside, and to escape further imprisonment at the hands of her own countrymen, fled across the border to England (1568).

Catholic Plots against Elizabeth

Elizabeth was placed in a difficult position by the flight of Mary to England. As a Queen herself she had no desire to encourage rebels by handing Mary back as a prisoner to the Scottish nobles. She could hardly, however, force them to accept Mary as their Queen, especially as this would mean breaking the alliance between herself and the Scottish Protestants. An inquiry into Darnley's murder was held in England, and the Scottish nobles produced the famous Casket Letters to prove their case against their Queen. These letters were supposed to consist of correspondence between Mary and Bothwell, but their authenticity has been much doubted. In the end Elizabeth decided to allow Mary to remain in England, half guest and half prisoner. Very soon plots were formed to place Mary on the English throne, and Elizabeth had to face the attacks of the Counter-Reformation.

In 1569 occurred the Rising of the Northern Earls. It was partly a feudal rising against the growing power of the monarchy, partly an aristocratic protest against the influence of Sir William Cecil, and partly a revolt of Catholicism (which was still strong in the north) against the Queen's religious policy. Its leaders were the Duke of Norfolk and the Earls of Westmorland and Northumberland. The rebels seized Durham, where they tore up the English Prayer Book and Bible and celebrated High Mass. They then marched south to rescue Mary, perhaps with the intention of declaring her Queen of England. Elizabeth and Cecil removed Mary farther south and sent forces against the rebels. Northumberland and Westmorland escaped, and Norfolk was imprisoned for a year; but several hundred peasants who had joined in the rebellion were hanged. Cecil's position was now stronger than ever, and in 1571 he was created Lord Burghley.

In 1570 Pope Pius V, who had encouraged the northern rebellion, issued a Bull excommunicating and deposing "the heretic, pretended Queen of England, servant of iniquity." Henceforth extreme Catholicism was identified with disloyalty. The effects were to strengthen the penal laws against Catholics and to encourage further plots.

In 1571 an Italian banker, Ridolfi, plotted to dethrone Elizabeth (by murder, if necessary) and place Mary on the throne. He was supported by Philip of Spain, the Duke of Alva in the Netherlands, the Pope, and a number of discontented English peers, including the treacherous Duke of Norfolk. Burghley, however, scented the conspiracy and in September, 1571, laid it bare. After some hesitation Elizabeth consented to the execution of Norfolk, but she refused to proceed to extreme measures against Mary, who had undoubtedly been implicated in the scheme.

For some years there was a lull in the English plots, and the scene shifted to the Continent. In 1572 the Dutch 'Seabeggars' seized Brille; the revolt of the Netherlands had begun and was henceforth secretly helped by Elizabeth. In the same year the Massacre of St Bartholomew took place. For a time this interrupted the peaceful relations between England and France, but not for long. Elizabeth had cultivated friendly relations with France so as to counteract the influence of Spain, and had even entered into marriage negotiations with the Duke of Anjou (the brother of Charles IX, who later became King Henry III of France). About 1580 she encouraged the Duke of Alençon, another brother of Henry III; but nothing came of these marriage schemes, which were diplomatic moves rather than affairs of the heart.

In 1568 an English Catholic, William Allen, had founded a seminary or training-college at Douai, in Flanders, to train young Englishmen as Catholic missionaries. From

1574 Allen's seminarists began to arrive in England, and in 1580 they were reinforced by a regular Jesuit mission under Campion and Parsons. Elizabeth soon struck back. In 1581 the fines against recusants (*i.e.*, non-attenders at English churches) were increased from one shilling to £20 a month, and the penalties of treason were imposed upon anyone who tried to convert the Queen's subjects to the Catholic faith. Campion was captured and executed, but Parsons escaped. During the rest of the reign about 200 Catholics suffered death, on account, the Government alleged, not of their religion, but of their treasonable activities.

The Plots thicken—the End of Mary

In 1583 a Cheshire Catholic, Francis Throgmorton, plotted to murder Elizabeth and place Mary on the throne. Elizabeth's secretary, Francis Walsingham (a younger and more bitterly anti-Catholic minister than Burghley), laid bare the scheme in December, 1583, and sent Throgmorton to the block (1584). The Spanish ambassador, Mendoza, who had also been concerned, was expelled from the country.

The assassination of William the Silent in 1584 revealed the danger to Elizabeth. In 1584 a Protestant Association was formed to protect the Queen, and an Act of Parliament excluded from the throne anyone who benefited from the Queen's death. The Babington Plot, in 1586, hatched by Anthony Babington, who had once been Mary's page, was the last straw. A commission found that Mary was implicated, and the country demanded her execution. After much hesitation Elizabeth signed Mary's death-warrant, later declaring that she had not meant it to be dispatched. In February, 1587, after nineteen years' captivity, Mary was executed at Fotheringay Castle in Northamptonshire. She bequeathed her claims to the English throne to Philip of Spain, who was already contemplating an invasion of England.

England enters the Maritime Race

Henry VII and Henry VIII had encouraged commerce and navigation, but it was not till the reign of Elizabeth that England really began to press home the advantage she possessed in being an island-state on the fringe of the Atlantic. England was inevitably brought into conflict with Spain and, to a less extent, with Portugal, whose Empire was united with that of Spain in 1580. The Spanish Empire had been built up by Hernando Cortés, who in 1520 overthrew the old Aztec civilization of Mexico, and by Francisco Pizarro, who in 1532 conquered the Incas of Peru. Spanish America included most of the continent south of Mexico with the exception of Brazil, which belonged to Portugal.

When Elizabeth refused to marry Philip of Spain, and England emerged as the leader of Protestantism, the enmity between the two countries grew. English sailors were soon tempted by the desire for gain and the love of adventure to intrude into the preserves of the most Catholic King of Spain. The tortures of the Spanish Inquisition only served to inflame passions. Elizabeth saw that sooner or later open war would result; but her policy was to postpone the outbreak of hostilities as long as possible.

Certain English sailors tried to find routes to the east which would not cross the paths of Spain and Portugal. In 1553 Willoughby and Chancellor tried to find a north-east passage round the north of Europe. They reached Archangel, on the White Sea, and Chancellor found his way home via Moscow. This voyage resulted in the formation of the Muscovy Company to trade with Russia (see p. 134). From 1576 to 1578 Frobisher attempted to find a north-west passage round the north of America, and ten years later further attempts were made by Davis. But most English sailors unhesitatingly attacked Spain in its two most vulnerable spots —the English Channel, which was the highway between Spain and the Spanish Netherlands, and the coasts of Central and South America, which were too long to be adequately defended.

The English Channel—'Sea-cradle of the Reformation'

The English Channel has been aptly described as the 'sea-cradle of the Reformation.' The coasts of Cornwall, Dorset, and, more particularly, Devon bred a race of alert and hardy men whose delight and profit it was to attack the Spanish galleons on their way to the Netherlands. The Spanish ships were mostly large vessels with square sails, built not for quick manœuvring, but for laying alongside the enemy's ships for boarding. Such ships proved successful in the calm waters of the Mediterranean, as when they destroyed the Turkish fleet at Lepanto in 1571; but they were often helpless against the English ships, whose sails were designed for speed and rapid turning and whose portholes bristled with guns to sink the enemy ships before they could draw close.

Philip protested to Elizabeth against these attacks, which were really nothing less than piracy. Elizabeth professed her inability to check them, but in reality she approved—provided they did not lead to open war. In 1568 a Spanish fleet, laden with borrowed gold to pay the Spanish troops in the Netherlands, was driven into English ports, and Elizabeth re-borrowed the money for her own purposes.

John Hawkins and Francis Drake

The two most famous Elizabethan seamen were the cousins, Sir John Hawkins and Francis Drake.

Hawkins was the first Englishman to engage in the slave-trade. The Spaniards ill-treated the natives of America so much that they began to die off like flies, and, to provide fresh labour, the Spaniards began to use kidnapped negroes from Africa. Despite the opposition of the Spanish Government, Hawkins joined in the profitable slave-trade himself.

On his third voyage, in 1568, he was treacherously attacked at San Juan de Ulloa by a Spanish fleet which he had allowed to shelter in the harbour from a gale. The profits of the expedition were lost, and Hawkins, together with his young cousin, Francis Drake, barely escaped with their lives. On his return Hawkins remained ashore to reorganize the Royal Navy; but Drake vowed—and soon exacted—revenge.

Francis Drake (1540–1596) was the embodiment of the

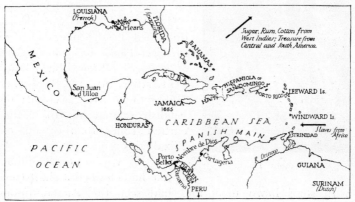

CENTRAL AMERICA AND THE SPANISH MAIN

spirit that animated the Elizabethan sea-dogs. Born in Devon, he served his apprenticeship with the Channel pirates and with his elder cousin, Hawkins. He determined to apply the methods of the Channel pirates to the larger and more profitable sphere of the Spanish Main—the region bounded by the West Indies and the American coast from Darien to the Orinoco. In 1572–1573 he sailed to the Isthmus of Panama and tried unsuccessfully to capture the town of Nombre de Dios.

But he being discontented with the repulse which he had received there, came to the sound of Darien, and having conference with certain negroes which were fled from their

D

masters of Panama and Nombre de Dios, the negroes did tell
him that certain mules came laden with gold and silver from
Panama to Nombre de Dios, who in company of these negroes
went thereupon on land and stayed in the way where the
treasure should come with an hundred shot, and so took two
companies of mules, which came only with their drivers

mistrusting nothing, and he
carried away the gold only, for
they were not able to carry the
silver through the mountains.

Thus is Drake's exploit
described in the pages of the
*Principal Voyages and Navigations
of the English Nation*, in which an
Oxford scholar, Richard
Hakluyt, gathered accounts of
English seamanship from the
earliest times to the end of
Elizabeth's reign.

On his voyage to Panama,
Drake had climbed a giant tree

SIR FRANCIS DRAKE

with steps hewn in it and had seen the Pacific, upon
which no Englishman had hitherto sailed. Drake thereupon
prayed God "to give him life and leave to sail once in an
English ship upon that sea." Several years later his wish was
fulfilled. In November, 1577, Drake sailed from Plymouth
with five ships, of which the *Golden Hind* of 100 tons was the
largest. He sailed across the Atlantic, threaded the Straits
of Magellan, and plundered the undefended coasts of Chile
and Peru. By this time Drake had only one ship, and he
realized that a Spanish fleet would probably block his return
home. He therefore pushed on up the west coast of America
hoping to find a north-west passage back. Finding none, he
decided to follow Magellan's route and return by way of
Java, the Indian Ocean, and the Cape of Good Hope. At
the end of 1580 Drake reached England with a treasure of

£800,000. He was the first Englishman to sail round the world. The Queen showed her approbation by knighting Drake on board the quarter-deck of the *Golden Hind* as it lay in harbour at Greenwich.

Attempts at Colonization

Although these buccaneering expeditions brought profit and adventure to their participants, Hakluyt and others urged that England's best policy in the long run was to establish colonies of her own.

In 1583 Gilbert made the first attempt to found an English colony. Unfortunately he chose a difficult region for his experiment, namely, Newfoundland, and the colonists he took with him were unfitted for their task. The venture failed, and Gilbert was drowned on his return journey.

The next attempts were made in a more hospitable region farther south, which was named Virginia in honour of the Queen. In 1585 Sir Walter Raleigh sent out over one hundred colonists, but once more conditions proved too hard, and in the following year Drake brought back the starving colonists. In 1587 Raleigh promoted another attempt to colonize Virginia, but this met with no more success than the first. The end of Elizabeth's reign saw England a strong maritime power, but still without any empire of her own.

Open War with Spain

Open war with Spain could not be long delayed. Following the assassination of William the Silent, Elizabeth sent a small army to the Netherlands under her favourite, the Earl of Leicester (1585). The expedition proved a complete failure and is remembered chiefly for the death of Leicester's nephew, Sir Philip Sidney, at Zutphen (1586). Having received a mortal wound, Sidney handed his water-bottle to a dying soldier in the ranks with the words, "Thy necessity is yet greater than mine."

In 1585 Elizabeth sent Drake to the West Indies to plunder the Spanish colonies. He was given a fleet of nearly thirty vessels, with over 2000 men—the biggest expedition that had been sent so far against Spanish America. Drake attacked Vigo in Spain, and plundered San Domingo and Cartagena in the Spanish Main, capturing much booty. On his return he brought back Raleigh's first colonists from Virginia.

THE "ARK ROYAL"
This was the flagship of Lord Howard of Effingham.

These open attacks, together with the execution of Mary, Queen of Scots, in 1587, led Philip to prepare a fleet for the invasion of England. But Drake sailed to Cadiz and destroyed many of the Spanish ships while they lay in harbour. This exploit, described by Drake as his "singeing of the King of Spain's beard," delayed the Armada for a year and gave England time to make her own preparations.

The Spanish Armada (1588)

In 1588 the Armada was at last ready. Its original admiral, the Marquis of Santa Cruz, was now dead, and the chief command was given to a less experienced Spanish nobleman, the Duke of Medina Sidonia.

The Spanish fleet consisted of 132 vessels and carried about 10,000 mariners and 20,000 soldiers. It was instructed by Philip to sail in close formation up the English Channel, avoiding naval battles as far as possible, and to join forces with the Duke of Parma in the Netherlands. It would then help to transport a further 30,000 picked Spanish troops

THE GREAT ARMADA IN THE CHANNEL
From an engraving after a tapestry made for Lord Howard of Effingham.

across to England. The English fleet consisted of 34 vessels of the Royal Navy together with about 150 merchant and private ships converted into men-of-war for the occasion. It was under the supreme command of Lord Howard of Effingham, assisted by men like Drake, Frobisher, and Hawkins, and was divided into two squadrons, one to guard the western part of the Channel and the other the eastern, where Parma's troops were assembled. The English aimed at preventing the union of the Armada and Parma at all costs.

The English fleet was manned by much more experienced sailors than the Spanish and was not crammed with the many soldiers that in some ways hampered the movements of the Spaniards. The English vessels were lower in the water and much quicker at manœuvring than the tall, top-heavy Spanish vessels, with their high castles fore and aft. Further, the English guns had a longer range than the Spanish, and could pour their shot into the tall sides of the enemy ships while remaining themselves comparatively safe. On the other hand, owing to Elizabeth's economy, the English were short of ammunition and powder, and England was very deficient in military forces in case Parma and his Spaniards effected a landing. A hastily trained army had been gathered at Tilbury, where the Queen went down and addressed them; training was also proceeding throughout the English counties. English superiority thus lay in the sea and in a type of naval fighting that avoided close engagements; Spanish superiority lay in her armed men, whether used for boarding enemy ships or for invasion.

The Armada left Lisbon on May 20, 1588, but put again into Corunna to replenish its stores. On July 12 it sailed from Corunna and was sighted off the Lizard on July 19. By July 21 it had reached Plymouth, where the English western squadron was bottled up by a south-westerly gale. Drake skilfully warped out most of his ships, manœuvred windward of the Armada, and attacked with his guns. The Spaniards were driven along the Channel, where a running-fight took place for the next seven days. On July 27 the Spaniards dropped anchor in Calais Roads, hoping for a breathing-space. On the next day the wind and tide bore eight English fire-ships down upon them. The Spaniards cut their cables in haste and escaped with the loss of only one ship. But they were now in rout and sadly deficient in anchors and cables. On July 29 a strong north-west wind hemmed them in off the coast at Gravelines and placed them at the mercy of the English, who were in the open sea to windward. The battle raged from nine o'clock in the morning to late in the evening, the English ships by their quicker manœuvring and stronger artillery gaining a complete victory. The English lost not a single ship, and although the Spaniards lost only four or five in the actual engagement, their ships were so battered, their supplies so low, and their soldiers and sailors so exhausted that they had no further fight in them. On the following day the Spaniards took advantage of a south-west wind to escape from the coast. They dared not run the gauntlet down the Channel again, and decided to sail round northern Scotland and Ireland. The English chased them till their own supplies of powder ran out and then left them to the mercy of the weather. *Flavit Deus et dissipati sunt* ("God blew with his winds, and they were scattered") was the inscription placed by Elizabeth on her Armada medal. The coasts of Scotland and Ireland were strewn with wreckage, and only 53 vessels struggled back out of the original 132.

The rout of the Armada saved England from invasion; it also aided the Dutch in their struggle for independence and Henry of Navarre in his fight for the French crown. It ensured the victory of the Reformation over the Counter-Reformation in northern Europe, and although Spain remained for many years a mighty power, it marked an important step in her decline. It demonstrated also the naval supremacy of England and the superiority of the new naval warfare over the old. From English naval supremacy the British Empire later sprang.

Closing Events of the War

The war with Spain continued to the end of the reign, with successes scored on both sides. In 1591 Lord Thomas Howard, who had hoped to capture the Spanish treasure-fleet in the Azores, retreated before a superior Spanish fleet. The *Revenge*, under Sir Richard Grenville, stayed to fight 53 Spanish ships. Grenville held them at bay for fifteen hours until, with his ship sinking and himself mortally wounded, he surrendered. In 1595 Drake and Hawkins set out upon what proved to be their last expedition to the Spanish Main. Nombre de Dios was taken and burnt, but an expedition against Panama had to be abandoned. Hawkins died at the end of 1595, and early in 1596 Drake caught a fever and followed his cousin to the grave. His body was buried in Nombre de Dios Bay, in those waters that had witnessed his gallant, if not always honourable, exploits.

In 1596 Cadiz was sacked, and many Spanish ships were destroyed. In the following year an expedition to the Azores under the Earl of Essex ended in complete failure. Philip II died in 1598, and Elizabeth in 1603; but the tradition of Anglo-Spanish enmity remained to poison the relations between the two countries for several generations to come.

England and Ireland under the Tudors

Ireland had been Yorkist during the Wars of the Roses and had supported the various attempts to dethrone Henry VII. In 1494 Henry VII's Lord Deputy in Ireland, Sir Edward Poynings, persuaded the Parliament held at Drogheda to pass the famous Poynings' Laws, which obliged the Irish Parliament to submit its measures to the English government for their approval.

Henry VII and Henry VIII tried for long to govern Ireland through the powerful Anglo-Norman family of the Fitzgeralds, or Geraldines. The head of the family, the Earl of Kildare, was chosen as Lord Deputy. But the Geraldines proved unworthy of their trust and used their position to wage their own family feuds. In 1534-1535 the Geraldines revolted against the authority of Henry VIII; the rebellion was put down, and the leaders were executed.

The Reformation provided a fresh source of trouble. Henry VIII made himself head of the Irish as well as the English Church. The Irish Church was in a particularly corrupt condition, and Henry dissolved the monasteries. He gave the lands to the Irish chiefs to win them to his side and made himself King, instead of Lord, of Ireland (see p. 66). Spasmodic efforts were made under Henry VIII and Edward VI to introduce a more Protestant ritual, but

Ireland remained a Catholic country, and religious discontent was now added to political and social grievances. Although

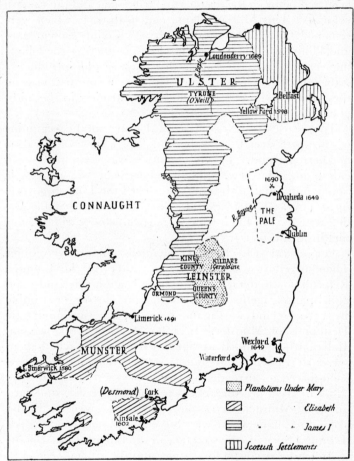

IRELAND UNDER THE TUDORS AND STUARTS

Mary re-established the Catholic religion, she began a policy that proved more powerful than religious differences in embittering relations between the two countries. Irish land was confiscated from rebellious chiefs and given to English settlers; the rights of the tribes were ignored, and warfare occurred between the disinherited tribesmen and the English colonists. This Marian plantation, in districts which were renamed Queen's County and King's County, after Mary and Philip, was the forerunner of many others in the following century. It was hoped that they would introduce a stable and loyal element into the turbulent country. Instead they placed a Protestant minority of intruders in the midst of a Catholic peasantry.

The death of O'Neill, Earl of Tyrone, at the beginning of Elizabeth's reign gave the signal for a fresh outbreak in northern Ireland. Tyrone's position was contested by his eldest son, Matthew, and a younger son, Shane O'Neill. Shane murdered his brother and defied the English government (1561). After several years of civil war Shane was defeated by the English Governor, Sir Henry Sidney, and met his death in 1567.

For several years Ireland remained comparatively quiet. Then an effort was made by the forces of the Counter-Reformation to detach Ireland from English rule, and Papal and Spanish agents toured the country to stir up trouble. By 1579 Ireland was again in revolt, this time under the Desmonds of Munster. In 1580 about 800 Spanish and Italian troops landed at Smerwick and entrenched themselves at Limerick, in south-western Ireland. They were soon forced to surrender and were massacred in cold blood (1580). By 1583 the rebellion was suppressed, and large parts of Munster were confiscated and given to English colonists, among whom were Sir Walter Raleigh and the poet Edmund Spenser, the secretary to the English Lord Deputy.

Ireland was cowed for a time, and the critical year of the Spanish Armada passed without disturbance. But the country was far from pacified, and the closing years of Elizabeth's reign saw another serious outbreak—once more under the O'Neills of Ulster. Papal and Spanish agents, together with Jesuits and seminarists, had prepared the ground by working up hatred against Elizabeth's religious settlement. In 1598 a new Earl of Tyrone, the nephew of Shane O'Neill, defeated the English forces at Yellow Ford. This was the signal for a general outbreak. Elizabeth sent over her favourite, the Earl of Essex, with 20,000 men; but Essex foolishly wasted his time in the south of Ireland, and when eventually, under the Queen's orders, he marched north he made terms with Tyrone which the English government refused to accept. Essex deserted his post and hurried home, hoping that his influence over the Queen would save his reputation. "By God's son," Elizabeth angrily exclaimed, "I am no queen; this man is above me." Essex was dismissed from his position, and smarting with jealousy at the growing influence of Burghley's son, Robert Cecil, he combined with the enemies of the government. A foolish revolt in London in 1601 led to his execution.

The capable and energetic Lord Mountjoy now took charge in Ireland, and in 1602 he compelled a Spanish force to surrender at Kinsale. By 1603 Tyrone realized that further resistance was useless. He renounced his foreign allies, submitted to the government, and was pardoned. Ireland was indeed conquered, but at a terrible cost. Large districts had been laid waste, while confiscations, religious animosity, and acts of cruelty embittered the relations between the two countries for centuries to come.

The Growth of Puritanism

Elizabeth's attempt to establish a national Church on the basis of the 'middle way' had met with success as far as the majority of the nation was concerned. But it was attacked on two sides—by those who regarded Elizabeth as a heretic and wished for a return to Rome, and by those who wished to introduce the more extreme views of the Continental reformers into England.

The early Puritans, as the extreme Protestants came to be

called, objected to certain points of ritual in the Church of
England: the use of the surplice and other vestments by the
minister, the ring in marriage, the sign of the cross in baptism, and the practice of kneeling at Holy Communion.
These questions led to what was called the Vestiarian Controversy. Parker, who was Archbishop of Canterbury from
1559 to 1576, was a moderate-minded man, anxious not to
create trouble. Neither he nor the Queen sympathized with
Puritanism, however, and in 1566 he issued his *Advertisements*
in an attempt to enforce uniformity upon the Church.
Ministers had to agree to certain doctrines and practices or
else leave the Church.

The next Puritan attack struck deeper, and was led by
Thomas Cartwright, a Cambridge professor of divinity who
had studied at Geneva. Cartwright attacked the government of the Church by means of bishops and advocated the
Presbyterian system, as recently established in Scotland.
This would have made the Church much too democratic
and powerful for the government's liking. The new Archbishop of Canterbury, Grindal (1576–1583), had Puritan
leanings and was suspended by the Queen. His successor,
Whitgift (1583–1604), was a determined opponent of
Puritanism. He reorganized the Court of High Commission,
drew up searching questions for suspected ministers, and
deprived Puritans of their posts. His vigorous measures provoked a corresponding opposition. In 1588–1589 some of
the leading Puritans issued the *Martin Marprelate Tracts*,
which abused the Archbishop and other officials of the
Church with such names as "Anti-Christ," "incarnate
devils," and "forlorn atheists."

Towards the end of the reign a new sect appeared—the
Brownists—who taught that each congregation should elect
its own minister and determine its own form of worship.
They were the forerunners of the Independents of the Stuart
period and the Congregationalists of our own day. Unlike
the other Puritans, they refused to stay inside the Church of

England in the hope of altering it, but left it to form independent Churches of their own. In 1593 Parliament passed an Act against Seditious Sectaries, which threatened those who refused to attend church with banishment or even death. This Act was aimed in particular against the Brownists, many of whom fled to Holland. But the last years of Elizabeth's reign were in the main years of religious peace. They saw the publication of Richard Hooker's *Laws of Ecclesiastical Polity*—a learned defence of the Church of England against the attacks of its opponents.

Elizabeth and Parliament

Elizabeth was proud of ruling with the affection of her subjects, but she only summoned Parliament for thirteen sessions during her reign of forty-five years. It passed many important laws relating to religion, the relief of poverty, and the general economic condition of the country (see the following chapter). But the Queen was angry when it discussed the question of the succession or suggested that she should marry. Likewise she opposed the demand of the Puritans, who were already making their voice heard in Parliament, for a revision of the Prayer Book. Such questions, she maintained, touched her royal prerogative.

Parliament's chief strength lay in its control over the nation's purse-strings. The old idea still held that the sovereign should 'live of his own,' *i.e.*, should provide for his own needs and for the government of the country out of his own revenues. These consisted of the income from the royal lands and of certain taxes like tunnage and poundage (duties on wine, wool, and other goods) granted to the sovereign for life. But the cost of government was becoming more expensive, owing to the growth of its activities and to the rise in prices that followed the influx of precious metals from the New World into Europe. Elizabeth had to economize in many directions, even to the point of niggardliness; for she had a dictator's dread of applying to Parliament for money and placing herself at its mercy. Towards the end of her reign she began to grant patents of monopoly to her favourites to allow them the sole right of dealing in certain articles. This enabled them to raise prices and make large profits, of which the Queen claimed a share. In 1597 Parliament protested against what was really an indirect method of taxing the nation, and in 1601 Elizabeth bowed to the storm and withdrew the monopolies, protesting with characteristic dishonesty her anger that the monopolists should have abused their trust. The struggle between Crown and Parliament was already being foreshadowed.

Elizabeth's Ministers and Favourites

Elizabeth's chief minister for forty years was William Cecil, Lord Burghley. Cecil had served his political apprenticeship under the Protectors of Edward VI's reign, and during the dangerous years of Mary Tudor's reign he had attached himself to the Princess Elizabeth. On Elizabeth's accession she immediately appointed him a member of her council, and he remained at her side till his death in 1598. His advice was characterized by its moderation and common sense, and next to Elizabeth he deserves chief credit for having guided the country safely through the dangers of the Counter-Reformation. He was a staunch opponent of Spain and sometimes went further than the Queen in advocating an active policy. Usually, however, he counselled caution. As one of the Tudor 'new men,' he was a loyal supporter of the monarchy. He aimed at making the state powerful not only through its armed defences, but also through its industry, commerce, and agriculture; he carried through a recoinage of the currency, passed the Statute of Apprentices (1563), and encouraged useful immigrants like the Flemish woolweavers (see the next chapter for a fuller treatment of economic matters).

In the middle years of the reign Burghley was aided by the eager and enthusiastic Sir Francis Walsingham, who favoured a more active policy against Spain and the Catholics. Although his views were not always adopted by the cautious Queen, he performed a useful service in organizing the spy-system that checked the activities of Mary Stuart and Philip of Spain. The very letters of Babington's conspiracy, which were concealed in beer-barrels, were entrusted to one of Walsingham's spies, who took a copy of every one. Walsingham died in 1590, and thereafter Elizabeth increasingly employed the services of Burghley's son, Robert Cecil.

The Queen's employment of 'new men' naturally produced intrigues at court and led to jealousy on the part of her courtiers. Elizabeth herself was fond of the lighter moments of life, when she could forget (in part, at any rate) the cares of state and could yield to the flatteries of the courtiers whom she gathered around her. Chief of her favourites till his death in 1588 was the Earl of Leicester, the son of the Protector Northumberland. Leicester was ambitious and unscrupulous and is reputed to have murdered his wife to be free to win the Queen's hand. Elizabeth refused his advances, and when Leicester married the Countess of Essex, the Queen, quite illogically, was so angry that she threatened to imprison him in the Tower. It was Leicester who entertained the Queen with great extravagance at his castle of Kenilworth, and who in 1585 led the expedition to the Netherlands, which proved a miserable failure (see p. 103).

Other favourites of Elizabeth were the dashing and gallant Sir Walter Raleigh, whom she refused to spare from her court to lead his own colonizing expeditions to Virginia, and the spoilt Earl of Essex, the stepson of the Earl of Leicester. The rivalry of Essex with the younger Cecil, his expedition to Ireland, and his subsequent execution have already been told.

After the death of Essex in 1601 the court lost much of its gaiety. The Queen was growing old, although she tried hard to conceal it, and on March 24, 1603, 'good Queen Bess' passed away.

QUESTIONS AND EXERCISES

1. Write notes on: Lord Burghley, John Knox, Matthew Parker, Sir Walter Raleigh, the Earl of Leicester.

2. In what ways was Elizabeth's religious settlement a *via media*? State briefly (*a*) why it was acceptable to the majority of Englishmen, (*b*) why it was attacked by a minority.

3. Describe and illustrate the danger to Elizabeth from Mary, Queen of Scots.

4. Consider the exploits of Sir Francis Drake as typical of those of the Elizabethan sea-dogs.

5. Write an essay on the Armada.

6. What problems in the relations between England and Ireland arose under the Tudors?

7. Who were the Puritans? Explain clearly why they were dissatisfied with the Church of England.

8. What can you learn of the character of Elizabeth from the preceding chapter?

CHAPTER IX

ECONOMIC AND SOCIAL LIFE UNDER THE TUDORS

The People and their Occupations

BEFORE the first census of 1801 estimates of population are necessarily vague, but the following figures show fairly accurately the population of England and Wales at different periods:

1066	1½ millions
1348 (before the Black Death) . .	4 millions
1350 (after the Black Death) . .	2½ millions
1500	4 millions
1600	5 millions
1700	5½ millions
1801 (the first census) . . .	9 millions
1931 census	40 millions

Of the four or five millions in Tudor and Stuart times the bulk lived in the villages and small towns of the countryside and earned their livelihood on the land. The largest town was London, whose population in 1600 is estimated at less than 200,000, but which, under the Stuarts, increased to half a million. The next largest towns were, in order, Bristol and Norwich, with populations in the seventeenth century of about 30,000 each. Only two other towns, Exeter and York, had more than 10,000 inhabitants by the end of the seventeenth century.

Regulation of Economic Life by the State: Mercantilism

In the Middle Ages economic life had been largely organized on a local basis—by the manorial officials in the countryside and the gilds in the towns. By the opening of the

Tudor period, as a result of the expansion of trade and the welding of the nation into one political unit, economic life

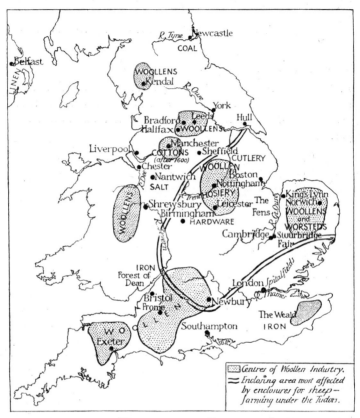

ENGLAND AND WALES UNDER THE TUDORS AND STUARTS:
ECONOMIC MAP

N.B. It must be remembered (a) that inside the area affected by enclosures for sheep-farming the greater part of the land was still cultivated in open fields, and (b) that much land outside this area had for long been enclosed mainly for arable farming.

was fast breaking its medieval bonds and becoming national in its scope and outlook. Both the manorial structure and the gild-system were breaking up. The gilds were too narrow in their outlook for the new conditions of industry and trade, and the attempts on the part of gildsmen to perpetuate their privileges led to charges of exclusiveness being brought against them. Parliament tried to control the gilds by enacting that gild-rules should receive the approval of the Justices of the Peace, and later, when this proved insufficient, of the Judges of Assize. But the gildsmen often controlled the town-government as well as its economic life, and enterprising craftsmen and merchants who found themselves shut out from gild privileges began to move out of the old corporate towns and establish new centres of trade and industry where conditions were freer. In this way Manchester began its history as a textile town (woollens and linen under the Tudors), and Birmingham and Sheffield developed as hardware and cutlery centres. In 1547 the Protestant Protector Somerset ordered the confiscation of all gild-property devoted to so-called superstitious practices. His commissioners interpreted their instructions freely, and the gilds lost much valuable property both of a religious and a non-religious nature. Thereafter the gilds fast declined, retaining in most towns only ceremonial functions to remind observers of their previous importance. Only in London were the gilds powerful enough to repel attacks upon their property, and there they survive as the London City Companies, performing useful philanthropic and educational work.

With the decay of manor and gild, the state stepped in to regulate the nation's economic life, and the mercantile system grew up under the Tudors and continued under the Stuarts. The nation was regarded as an economic as well as a political unit, and its economic life was regulated so as to increase the national power. Hence self-sufficiency was aimed at by the encouragement of tillage and the passing of Corn Laws. Shipping was stimulated by the observance of fish-days, by Navigation Acts, and by ensuring a sufficiency of timber and other naval requisites. Precious metals were regarded as valuable 'sinews of war,' and attempts were made by regulations and by seeking a favourable balance of trade to increase their supply. The peasants in their fields producing the nation's food-supply and providing a useful source of man-power, the craftsmen in their workshops fashioning the articles that were essential for domestic comfort or foreign trade, and the merchants selling English wares abroad and bringing back gold for our coffers or raw materials for our industries—all these were essential parts of the nation's economic edifice. Those who refused to mould themselves to fit the national structure—such as the lord who enclosed his land for sheep-farming, the craftsman who made unworthy goods, or the merchant who ignored the regulations of the trading-companies—these were to be knocked into shape as far as the government could do so, and as for the idle and unemployed, they were to be driven underground, or, where this was not possible, to be supported by the stronger parts of the national edifice.

The reign of Elizabeth represents the high-water mark of Tudor mercantilism. Lord Burghley took a prominent interest in economic matters, and Elizabeth's reign saw the recoinage (1560), the Statute of Apprentices (1563), and, after Burghley's death in 1598, the foundation of the East India Company (1600) and the Poor Law (1601). In addition, the Royal Exchange was founded, fish-days were established, and new industries were encouraged through the protection afforded to immigrant artisans or through the granting of monopolies.

(A) AGRICULTURE

Agricultural England in 1500

During the last two centuries of the Middle Ages important changes had been taking place to undermine the manorial structure of agricultural England. Many villeins had commuted their labour-services for a money-rent, and lords had begun to lease out their demesne lands and stock to farmers who paid the lord a 'ferm,' or rent, out of their agricultural profits. The Black Death of 1348–1349, which nearly halved the population, checked commutation for the time being, and the discontented villeins rose in the Peasants' Revolt of 1381. But this was suppressed, and villein services were, wherever possible, strictly enforced. The fifteenth century saw the beginning of the enclosure movement for sheep-farming. This solved the labour-problem (as fewer labourers were needed to look after sheep than to till the soil) and brought in huge profits owing to the growth of the English woollen-industry. Enclosures completed the break-up of the manorial system, as they rendered labour-services unnecessary. Furthermore, where they occurred they destroyed the medieval open-field system of cultivation.

By 1500 new classes of tenants had appeared to replace those of the Middle Ages. These were (1) copy-holders, (2) free-holders, (3) lease-holders, and (4) small cottagers. The copy-holders were really the medieval villeins with a new name to denote their changed position. When the villeins' labour-services had been commuted, a copy of their new rents had often been entered on the court roll of the manor; hence the villeins became copy-holders. They formed the bulk of English rural society, accounting for perhaps three-fifths of the whole tenantry. Their rents consisted mainly of money-payments, with sometimes a few relics of the old payments in produce or labour. Their position was by no means strong legally, as they often held their lands only for a number of lives and could be subjected to arbitrary fines when one copy-holder succeeded another. But villeinage, in the sense of personal serfdom, had died out by about 1500 without any specific law to this effect. The free-holders were in a more fortunate position; their right of succession was undisputed, their rents were fixed, and they were not subject to arbitrary fines. They were fewer in number than the copy-holders, except in East Anglia. The lease-holders were the ancestors of the modern farmer; they rented their lands for a period of years from the lord, and at the end of their lease they had to make a new one, perhaps with their rents raised. They were as yet few in number, although they increased considerably under the Tudors. Lastly, there was a class of cottagers with little or no land, who worked as labourers for the lease-holders and other large tenants and were paid a money-wage. Few of these labourers were completely landless, however, as most are at the present day.

Despite these changes in the medieval *structure* of rural society, the old agricultural *methods* still continued. Enclosures had made little headway, and open fields divided into strips were still the commonest feature of the English countryside.

Tudor Enclosures: the Motives

Under the Tudors the practice of enclosing, or 'making a close' by consolidating strips and surrounding them with a hedge, fence, or wall, continued. Fundamentally enclosures sprang from the desire to obtain a greater profit from the soil. With the growth of commerce and of town-life the possibilities of selling surplus agricultural produce increased. Farming became a source of profit instead of merely an occupation to supply one's own needs. In this connexion the dissolution of the monasteries may be noted. Large tracts of monastic property passed from the conservative-minded monks into the hands of commercial-minded land-owners, who constituted the new rich of their generation. The desire for larger profits was also stimulated by the rising prices of the period, which increased the cost of living and the 'overhead' charges of land-owners and tenants.

Enclosures were an almost indispensable preliminary to more profitable farming. If tillage were considered, the open-field system, with its scattered strips and its communal methods and time-table, was obviously wasteful. For cattle-breeding the old system of common waste and pasturage resulted in poor grass and the easy spread of diseases. As for sheep-farming, which the high price of wool made the most profitable of all kinds of farming, large enclosed tracts were necessary to give the sheep enough room and yet keep them from straying. Finally, with the growth of a wealthy aristocracy the habit of enclosing to lay out deer-parks became more widespread.

Tudor Enclosures: Types and Methods

Broadly speaking, enclosures were of two kinds: those carried through by the tenants themselves, and those by the lord of the manor.

Both before and under the Tudors the more enterprising tenants saw the advantages of exchanging their strips among themselves, and of thus consolidating and enclosing their holdings. It was usually to the advantage of everyone, as it resulted in better arable farming. Evictions, unemployment, and depopulation—the accompanying evils of enclosures for sheep-farming—were not present in this case to goad the peasantry into revolt or to attract the attention of social reformers. By this means much land in the south and south-east was enclosed.

The second type of enclosure was that promoted by the lord of the manor, usually with a view to sheep-farming. The lord would generally consolidate and enclose his demesne lands first of all. Then he would cast greedy eyes on the common waste and pasture, and even on the arable strips of his tenants. By the Statute of Merton (1236) he was bound to leave sufficient waste land for his tenants. But this, strictly speaking, applied only to the free-hold tenants; the rights of copy-holders over the waste and pasture were only customary, and the lord really held the whip-hand. The arable strips presented a more difficult problem. The free-holder was indeed secure unless he were willing to be bought out; but the copy-holder was more at the mercy of his lord. In extreme cases he could be evicted, in others he could be bullied into giving up some of his rights. A common practice among lords was to raise the fine for inheritance, called a relief, when one copy-holder succeeded another. "These extortioners made of a 40s. fine, £40 !" exclaimed one unfortunate tenant. A petition presented by certain tenants to the judges in 1553 gives us an insight into the times. Before the dissolution of the monasteries these tenants had held their lands under the monastery of Whitby. Afterwards the ownership changed hands several times, and their new lord was systematically raising rents and fines against them. The first four of nearly thirty cases quoted read:

	The Old Rent	The New Rent	The Fine
First John Coward . . .	24s.	£3 1s. 4d.	33s. 4d.
From Henry Russell . . .	42s. 11½d.	£4 7s. 3d.	£3 6s. 8d.
From Elizabeth Postgate, widow.	18s. 10d.	41s. 5d.	18s.
From Thomas Robynson . .	12s. 11½d.	40s. 7d.	33s. 4d.

When, by one means or another, the lord had enclosed sufficient land, he either managed it himself or leased it to a farmer—and the result in both cases was often a conversion to sheep-farming. This type of enclosure was commonest in the Midlands (see map on p. 118).

Tudor Enclosures: the Attitude of the Authorities

Enclosures for sheep-farming were opposed by the government and by many social reformers. It was feared that the production of corn would diminish and that the country would become dependent on foreign countries for its food. In some districts depopulation occurred owing to the loss of employment or of holdings. This helped to increase the unemployment and vagabondage problem that faced Tudor statesmen, and diminished the rural population which was regarded as the backbone of the country. Insurrections occurred to embarrass successive governments partly or mainly as a result of the enclosures. Among these were the Pilgrimage of Grace (1536–1537), which was occasioned also by the religious changes of Henry VIII's reign, and Ket's Rebellion in the eastern counties (1549).

Sir Thomas More, in *Utopia* (1516), voiced the general discontent against enclosures for sheep-farming in the following picturesque words:

> Your sheep that were wont to be so meek and tame, and so small eaters, now, as I hear say, be become so great devourers and so wild, that they eat up and swallow down the very men themselves. They consume, destroy, and devour whole fields, houses, and cities.

Beginning in 1489, Tudor governments passed many Acts to check enclosures for sheep-farming. One such Act ordered that newly converted pasture should be put under the plough once more; another that no one should possess more than 2000 sheep. In 1517 Wolsey sent commissioners round the country to report on enclosures. This was repeated by Somerset in 1548, whose sympathy with Ket's rebels was one of the causes of his undoing. Little was really accomplished by these well-meant efforts to limit enclosures. Sometimes the law was evaded by the driving of a single furrow across a field, while more than the stated number of sheep could be kept if the holder pretended that some of the flocks were owned by other members of the family ! The fact is that the Tudors had no means of enforcing these laws. As usual, they relied on the local Justices of the Peace— the very men, often, who were themselves guilty of enclosures. It was economic forces (*e.g.*, the high price of wool) that had stimulated sheep-farming, and it was economic forces that eventually caused the pace to slacken. Towards the end of the Tudor period the price of corn rose sufficiently high to make it worth while to till the land once more, and by the end of Elizabeth's reign England had a surplus of corn for export.

Tudor Enclosures: their Results

The amount of enclosure by 1600 was much less than might be imagined from the outcry it produced. Over the whole country not more than one-fortieth of the total acreage had been enclosed for sheep-farming. Such enclosures had proceeded farthest in the Midlands and eastern counties, but even here less than 10 per cent. of the total acreage had been enclosed for pasturage. The bulk of the land was still being cultivated in open fields. In some districts outside the Midlands enclosures had proceeded farther; but as these had been mainly by agreement for arable farming they had attracted little attention. The new profit-making spirit was more apparent in 1600 than in 1500. Rents had been raised in many cases, and the number of leasehold farmers, renting their land like a modern farmer on a purely economic basis, had grown. All this bespoke the new spirit, which, although it led to a hardening of economic relations, also led to greater productivity. Connected with the agrarian changes was the growth of the problem of poverty, occasioned by the loss of holdings, common rights, or employment. But for those who still possessed their land—and they included the bulk of the peasantry—the end of Elizabeth's reign saw the dawn of a new era of prosperity, a veritable golden age, which lasted well into the Stuart period.

(B) INDUSTRY

The Woollen-industry

The woollen-industry continued under Tudors and Stuarts to be England's chief industry. It supplied the expanding markets both at home and abroad. In 1354 England exported 5000 pieces of cloth; in 1509, 80,000 pieces; in 1547, 120,000 pieces. The industry was scattered throughout the length and breadth of the country, and many a peasant and his family added to their livelihood by part-time spinning and weaving. Certain areas, however, had become important centres for the industry, of which the three chief were East Anglia (with Norwich as its centre), the south-western counties (with Exeter as its main port of export), and the West Riding of Yorkshire (with Leeds and Halifax as important markets). Specialization had pro-

FAIRFORD CHURCH

This beautiful church is one of many in Gloucestershire that were built wholly or in part by wool and cloth merchants. The size and beauty of these churches is a testimony to the flourishing state of the industry in the Cotswolds in the fifteenth and sixteenth centuries. Fairford Church, which possesses a wonderful set of stained-glass windows, was begun by John Tane, a clothier, who died in 1500, and was completed by his son. The style of architecture is perpendicular Gothic. Many such churches, built by woollen cloth merchants, exist in East Anglia.

Photo B. C. Clayton

ceeded so far that each district was famed for its particular kinds of cloth: the east for its fine-quality cloths, including worsted, the south-west for its broad-cloths and serges, and the north for coarser cloths.

It was in the woollen-industry that capitalism made its biggest strides. Many workers spun yarn or wove cloth for a wealthy clothier who supplied them with the raw material, took the finished product off their hands, and paid them a wage for the amount of work done. But the workers still worked with their own tools in their own houses, and for this reason this intermediate stage between the medieval gild-system and the modern factory-system is usually called the domestic system. Capitalism made its biggest advances in the south and east, and in a very few cases employers collected their workers all under one roof, as at the present day. Most famous of such employers was John Winchcombe ('Jack of New-bury'), who is said to have led one hundred of his workmen to Flodden Field. In the remote northern districts the large wealthy clothier was slower in appearing (though he was by no means absent as time went on), and hundreds of small independent clothiers drove their pack-horses across the hill-tops to Leeds or Halifax, where they marketed their own productions.

A WEAVER, SIXTEENTH CENTURY

Weaving was usually done by men, spinning by women (hence the word 'spinster'). In this illustration the woman is bringing a fresh supply of yarn to the weaver, who holds the shuttle in his right hand.

Under Elizabeth the woollen-industry received an impetus from the immigration of thousands of Dutch and Flemings who fled from the religious persecution of Philip II of Spain. They settled mainly in East Anglia, and although they were often regarded with disfavour by the native workers, they brought with them valuable secrets in the manufacture of the finer cloths. They introduced the so-called 'new draperies,' which increased the trade of Norwich and Colchester and eventually brought prosperity to natives as well as immigrants. Their advent can be compared with that of the Flemish weavers under Edward III (see Vol. I, p. 152).

Other Industries

Scattered throughout the country were to be
smaller industries—the puny beginnings of t
giant counterparts. The smelting of iron-ore ...
means of charcoal. The Weald district of Sussex had for
long been famous in this respect, but as its supply of timber
dwindled, other districts grew up to supplement it; the
Forest of Dean was the most important of these. The supply
of timber was a problem that exercised the minds of statesmen, and Elizabeth's government restricted its use for other
purposes to leave sufficient for ship-building. Native iron
was insufficient for our needs, and foreign iron had to be imported to feed the growing hardware-industry of Birmingham and the cutlery-industry of Sheffield. In Cornwall the
age-old tin-mining industry still existed; in Derbyshire lead
was mined. Only one of England's valuable coalfields
was as yet much tapped; this was the Tyneside area,
whence the coal was taken to Newcastle and shipped to
London.

Elizabeth encouraged both natives and foreigners to start
new industries. It was Germans who started the copper-
mines at Keswick and an ordnance-factory at Woolwich.
The manufacture of salt, glass, and paper owed much to
foreign immigrants. Government support was often necessary to protect these newcomers from the jealousy of the
English, who regarded them as intruders. It was largely to
encourage industry that Elizabeth granted patents of monopoly, *i.e.*, the sole right of making or trading in certain
articles. In practice, however, monopolies often resulted in
the public being overcharged, and Parliament, in this and
the succeeding reign, protested strongly against them.

The Statute of Apprentices (1563)

In the regulation of industry by the state the Statute of
Apprentices or Artificers stands supreme. It was occasioned

⨍ the desire on the part of Elizabeth's government to control the unregulated industry that was growing up outside the corporate towns and to check the economic ills of the time, such as the increasing disparity between prices and wages, the neglect of agriculture, and the growth of vagabondage.

The Act declared that all youths entering industry should serve an apprenticeship of seven years; this made nationwide the practice that the gilds had enforced in the corporate towns, and was a praiseworthy attempt to improve the quality of workmanship. The choice of occupation was limited, and the corporate towns were to be favoured by reserving the better occupations for the sons of forty-shilling free-holders in those towns and for the sons of sixty-shilling free-holders outside. To provide reasonable opportunities for employment it was enacted that a certain number of journeymen had to be employed according to the number of youths apprenticed. All workers in agriculture and in industry had to be hired for a year, and those seeking fresh employment had to possess a certificate from their previous employer. By these means it was hoped to check vagabondage. Agriculture was encouraged, and vagabondage once more discouraged, by the provision that all those without a proper trade should be compelled to 'labour in husbandry.' Finally, the Justices of the Peace were to meet every year at Easter to fix rates of wages throughout their county according to the scarcity or plenty of commodities and their general price-level.

The exact degree to which this great Act was enforced is controversial; but it seems certain that most of its provisions were adhered to for a century or more and that they acted as a useful stabilizing factor in a period of slow change. In the eighteenth century mercantile regulations fell into disrepute, and at the beginning of the nineteenth century the Act was repealed, despite the desire of many of the workers for its continuance.

(C) TRADE

Internal Trade

Markets and fairs (like the great Stourbridge Fair, near Cambridge) were held as in the Middle Ages, and pedlars wandered from village to village selling their trinkets and small wares. As towns developed, so merchants multiplied to supply them with their needs. The domestic trade in corn was the most important in this respect, and many were the regulations to prevent corn-merchants from manipulating the market to their own advantage.

The means of communication were no different from those of the Middle Ages. River and coastwise traffic was important owing to the bad state of the roads. But the latter were much used by pack-horse trains and wagons, and efforts were made to improve them. In 1555 it was enacted that each parish, through its two surveyors of highways, should repair and maintain its own roads, and every parishioner had to give four (soon altered to six) days' labour a year on the roads. But compulsory parish labour was no solution, and the roads remained bad till the Industrial Revolution. Under the Tudors, however, the system of post-horses at fixed places was developed for the royal letters. It proved so successful that it was soon extended to travel in general.

A LONDON
MERCHANT
End of the sixteenth
century.

The Expansion of Overseas Trade

The Tudor period saw many changes in the conditions of overseas trade. With the geographical discoveries the chief trading-routes left the inland seas for the oceans; the Italian cities declined, and the countries bordering the Atlantic

(Spain, Portugal, France, England, and Holland) took their place. The Tudor sovereigns encouraged the development of overseas trade. Henry VII restored the wholesale-cloth trade with the Netherlands by his Intercursus Magnus (Great Treaty) of 1496, and for a time he even secured the right of English merchants to engage in the retail trade by the short-lived Intercursus Malus (Bad Treaty) of 1506–1507. Henry VIII established Trinity House to look after the harbours and aids to navigation round the coast. Under Elizabeth many trading-companies were established.

With the development of overseas trade by our own merchants, the activities of foreigners in English trade declined. The last visit of the Flanders galleys of Venice to England was in 1587. The Hanseatic League lost its privileges and was obliged to close its London depôt towards the end of Elizabeth's reign.

Company-trading

From the sixteenth to the eighteenth centuries trade was conducted mostly by means of trading-companies, as, indeed, much of it had been in the Middle Ages. The usual arrangement was for the Crown to grant a charter to a group of merchants conferring upon them the monopoly of trade with a certain region. This had many advantages. The government could collect its taxes more easily and could fix responsibility if anything went wrong. The merchants as a body, with the government behind them, were in a strong position for bargaining with foreign rulers. They could also regulate the activities of their own merchants to see that no trickery or unfair dealing was practised, which, though it might bring in large immediate profits, would spoil the market for future traders. Companies were also in a better position to protect their fleets of ships on the high seas or their agents and members in foreign parts. Two kinds of companies grew up, the regulated and the joint-stock. In the regulated company the merchant paid his admission fee and then traded on his own account within the general regulations of the company. In the joint-stock company it was the company as a whole that traded, and the profits and losses were then balanced and shared among all the members according to the amount of their stock.

Despite the efforts of the companies to monopolize trade, private merchants, called interlopers, often succeeded in trading on their own account. They were much resented, as they often reaped the advantages that others had obtained by their sacrifices and sometimes brought their countrymen into disrepute by unfair methods. But these interlopers sometimes prevented the companies from becoming too exclusive, and they opened up trading-channels neglected by the companies.

Most important of all English trading-companies in Tudor times was the regulated company known as the Merchant Adventurers. This had originated in the Middle Ages, when all the most important sea-ports had their own 'Venturers' who conducted the sale of English cloth abroad. In the fifteenth century the Merchant Adventurers surpassed their rivals, the Merchants of the Staple, who exported only the wool in its raw state. The Merchant Adventurers of London were by far the most important in the kingdom; at Blackwell Hall, in Basinghall Street, clothiers from far and wide marketed their wares, which then passed to English retailers for sale at home or to Merchant Adventurers for sale abroad. In 1505 Henry VII granted a new charter, which established the Merchant Adventurers as a national company, in which, of course, the London merchants were predominant. Most of their trade was with northern Europe, and for long their continental headquarters were at Antwerp. In the Dutch War of Independence they moved to Hamburg, but were driven thence by the Hanseatic merchants. As a reprisal Elizabeth in 1578 withdrew the privileges of the Hanseatic League in London, and in 1597 the League closed its London headquarters, the Steelyard, and brought its long connexion

E

with England to an end. Several years later the Merchant
Adventurers settled once more in Hamburg, which remained
their headquarters till they were expelled by Napoleon at
the beginning of the nineteenth century.

In 1555 the Muscovy Company was established to trade
with Russia; this was a direct result of the voyage of
Willoughby and Chancellor to discover the north-east pas-

HALL OF THE MERCHANT ADVENTURERS, YORK

sage and of the overland journey of Chancellor to Moscow.
It traded in timber, hemp, oil, tallow, and furs, but was
never very successful and declined in the seventeenth century.
In 1579 Elizabeth granted a charter to the Eastland Company to wrest the important Baltic trade in naval stores from
the Hanseatic merchants. This again declined in the following century in face of the growing competition of our North
American colonies. In 1592 the Levant Company was
formed to trade with the lands of the Eastern Mediterranean;
this was more successful, and for long it imported such useful
articles as spices, currants, and cotton-wool.

The most famous of all companies, the East India

Company, was granted its charter on the last day of the year 1600. It arose from the natural desire on the part of English merchants to oust the Dutch middlemen by engaging directly in the valuable trade with the east and thus reducing the "unchristian price of pepper" and other commodities. Its detailed history, however, really begins with the Stuarts and is related in Chapter XX.

(D) THE PROBLEM OF POVERTY

Poverty and Unemployment under the Tudors

The sixteenth century saw the emergence of a definite poverty and unemployment problem. The close of the Wars of the Roses and Henry VII's laws against retainers set free numbers of men who could not, or would not, settle down to peaceful occupations; they became the first of the 'sturdy beggars' of the Tudor period. The agrarian changes added to the problem by depriving many tenants of their rights and holdings, and perhaps even of their employment. When Henry VIII dissolved the monasteries he not only turned adrift several thousand monks to find places for themselves in a hostile world, but he also ended the very institutions that had helped relieve the poor in their neighbourhood and give food and lodging to beggars and pilgrims. The decline of the gilds and the attack upon their property in 1547 aggravated the situation, as the gilds had performed useful 'friendly society' functions for their members and dependants. Finally, the end of the sixteenth century and the beginning of the seventeenth witnessed a rise in prices which made it more difficult for those with small or fixed incomes to make both ends meet. At first prices rose mainly owing to the debasement of the coinage by Henry VIII and Edward VI. In 1560 Elizabeth, with the help of Sir Thomas Gresham (who later founded the Royal Exchange in London), successfully carried through a recoinage; but by this time the influx of precious metals, mainly silver, from the New World was operating to continue the upward trend of prices.

The Government's Policy: Elizabeth's Poor Law of 1601

Tudor governments were alarmed at the growth of begging and vagabondage and passed harsh laws to repress it. In 1547 the severest of these laws prescribed whipping

WHIPPING A BEGGAR THROUGH THE STREETS

and branding with a 'V' (for 'vagabond') for the first offence, enslavement and branding with an 'S' (for 'slave') for the second offence, and the death-penalty for the third offence. It was soon repealed, and Tudor governments began to realize that the problem of poverty was the result of many factors besides mere vagabondage. The poor included the aged, the sick, the orphaned, and those able-bodied who desired work but could not find it. A solution was first sought in private charity, and various Acts were passed enjoining the clergy to exhort their parishioners to make voluntary subscriptions. When these proved insufficient Parliament in 1572 sanctioned the levying of a compulsory rate—the first in our history.

In 1601 the many laws on the subject were summed up and made permanent in the great Poor Law of Elizabeth.

Henceforth each parish was definitely responsible for its own poor, and two overseers were to be appointed to relieve the poverty within their area. They were empowered to levy rates for the purpose, but were to be superintended by the Justices of the Peace. Orphans or other destitute children were to be apprenticed to the humbler trades; the aged or disabled were to be maintained by the parish in houses provided for them; the able-bodied were to be set to work in houses of correction on wool, flax, thread, iron, or other materials provided by the overseers. As for idlers and vagabonds, severe punishments were still their lot if they refused to enter a house of correction.

The Elizabethan Poor Law sufficed for its age and coped successfully with the problem of poverty for nearly two centuries. In the nineteenth and twentieth centuries, however, changing conditions necessitated its abandonment.

(E) Social Life

'Merrie England'

Tudor England, like most countries in all ages, was a land of contrasts. If the sturdy beggar was the dark shadow of the period, the Elizabethan courtier was its high-light. Between these lay the bulk of the nation: merchants, squires, artisans, yeomen-farmers, copy-holders, and so on.

The growth of the middle class as a result of the expansion of trade and industry was one of the distinctive features of the age. Larger and more substantial houses were erected in consequence, built perhaps of timber and plaster or of the more enduring brick or stonework that was becoming popular. But the general appearance of the Tudor town remained much the same as it had been in the Middle Ages. Streets were narrow, and houses were draughty and insanitary. Disease, fire, and robbery with violence were ever-present dangers. Every important town had its grammar school, such as that at Stratford-on-Avon where Shakespeare studied. Altogether about two hundred such schools are known; but many of them suffered as a result of the attack upon gild-property under Edward VI. Later some new ones were founded.

In town and country the old customs of 'merrie England' continued. The whipping-post for beggars, the stocks for drunkards and brawlers, and the pillory for fraudulent tradesmen were common sights. Women who gossiped were muzzled with the brank or, more often, ducked in the nearest pond. Amusements were many, and of a healthier nature than some of our present-day pastimes. While the rich engaged in deer-hunting or hawking, the poor amused themselves with fowling-nets or by coursing rabbits and hares. Bull- and bear-baiting entertained the callous, and at the appropriate seasons the maypole was erected on the village green, and flushed faces betokened the joys of country and Morris dancing. Archery-contests were common among all classes; Henry VIII was fond of them and, judging from the fact that he sometimes had to 'pay up,' did not always win. Football in the streets was often so rowdy that it had to be forbidden by law. A writer of 1531 described it as "nothing but beastly fury and extreme violence, whereof proceedeth hurt, and consequently rancour and malice do remain with them that be wounded." Life in those days made up in zest what it lacked in refinement.

QUESTIONS AND EXERCISES

1. Explain the underlying ideas of the mercantile system. In what ways have some of these ideas been revived at the present day?

2. Explain carefully the different meanings attaching to the word 'enclosure' in Tudor times.

3. Write an essay on the causes and results of the enclosure movement.

4. Show how the Statute of Apprentices and the Elizabethan

Poor Law attempted to solve the economic problems of the Tudor Period.

5. Describe and account for the parallel growth of (a) poverty, and (b) wealth, under the Tudors.

6. What were the advantages and disadvantages of company trading in the sixteenth and seventeenth centuries? Illustrate your answer by reference to any one company.

7. What can be said for and against living in 'merrie England' in the sixteenth century?

PART II
THE STUART PERIOD 1603-1714)

CHAPTER X

EUROPEAN SURVEY (III): THE THIRTY YEARS' WAR

Chief Rulers

Henry IV	(France)	1589–1610
Louis XIII	(France)	1610–1643
Ferdinand II	(the Empire)	1619–1637
Ferdinand III	(the Empire)	1637–1657
Philip III	(Spain)	1598–1621
Philip IV	(Spain)	1621–1665
Gustavus Adolphus	(Sweden)	1611–1632

Trends in European History (1600-1650)

THE first half of the seventeenth century saw in England the establishment and the fall of the Stuart dynasty; while on the Continent Holland and France rose to positions of first-class importance, Spain entered upon its gradual decline, and Germany was rent by the last and greatest of the religious wars, the Thirty Years' War (1618–1648).

The Heyday of Holland

By about 1600 the seven northern provinces of the Netherlands had established their independence. The ten Catholic provinces of the south remained in Spanish hands till 1713; their history, during the seventeenth century, is completely overshadowed by the brilliant achievements of their northern neighbours, who seemed inspired as a result of their long struggle with Spain and their newly won independence.

The first half of the seventeenth century was the most glorious in the history of Holland. The Dutch school of painting produced such well-known pictures as the *Laughing Cavalier* of Franz Hals, the *View of Delft* of Vermeer, and the numerous portraits by the greatest of all Dutch painters, Rembrandt. In 1625 a Dutch writer, Hugo Grotius, published his *De Jure Belli et Pacis* ('Concerning the Law of Peace and War'), the first important attempt to lay down rules of international law in the hope of improving the relations between the different nations of the world.

The Dutch had won their independence largely as a result of their sea-power. During the years 1600 to 1650 England was absorbed in the struggle between King and Parliament, and the Dutch were able to forge ahead in commerce and colonization. They developed a merchant fleet larger than that of any other nation and became the world's chief carriers. Amsterdam, wittily said to have been founded on herrings, became the chief commercial and banking-centre of northern Europe. It was not till the second half of the century that England attempted, by Navigation Acts and war, to undermine the proud position to which Holland had attained.

Nor were the Dutch idle in the sphere of colonization. In South America they colonized Guiana; in North America they founded, on the banks of the River Hudson, New Amsterdam, whose name was later changed to New York. In particular they raided the Portuguese Empire in the Far East; Ceylon and a number of East Indian islands became theirs. To provide a place of call between Europe and the east they sent out farmers, or 'boers,' to colonize Cape Colony in South Africa. Much of this widely scattered empire has since been lost, but the Dutch still retain Guiana and their East Indian islands to remind us of the enterprising vigour of their seventeenth-century ancestors.

France under the Early Bourbons

We have seen in Chapter VII how the Huguenot leader, Henry of Navarre, embraced the Catholic faith and became

King of France as Henry IV. This was the beginning of a new royal line, the Bourbons, which lasted till the French Revolution of 1789. In 1598 the famous Edict of Nantes gave the Huguenots freedom of worship and the right of holding offices under the state. It also allowed them, as a guarantee of their liberties, to garrison certain towns. Henry IV proved a capable ruler and with the help of his finance minister, Sully, helped France to recover from the civil wars that had preceded his accession. In 1610 the first Bourbon was stabbed to death by a fanatical madman while sitting in his coach in a street in Paris.

CARDINAL RICHELIEU
Philippe de Champaign.

Henry's son, Louis XIII (1610–1643), was only a boy of nine at his accession, and during his minority the country threatened once more to relapse into a state of anarchy. It was eventually saved by the energy and ability of Cardinal Richelieu, who ruled France for eighteen years (1624–1642). Richelieu's aims can be given in his own words—"to ruin the Huguenot party, to lower the pride of the nobility, and to restore the country's name among the nations."

In common with most of his countrymen Richelieu regarded the Huguenot garrisons as an infringement of the royal power, which, in his view, should extend equally over the whole of France. When the Huguenots refused to surrender their strongholds, Richelieu in person led an army against their strongest garrison, La Rochelle, in 1628. Charles I of England sent his favourite, the Duke of Buckingham, to try to help the Huguenots, but the expedition was mismanaged (see p. 168) and in October, 1628, La Rochelle fell, and Huguenot resistance was at an end. Richelieu continued to allow the Huguenots freedom of worship and other civil rights; but they were henceforth deprived of their fortresses.

Richelieu's second aim was to strengthen the power of the Crown. He robbed the nobles of their ancient feudal rights, dismantled their castles, and dispersed their armed retainers. Duelling was forbidden because it led to private war. Richelieu created a new class of officials, called *intendants*, to act as provincial governors. Like the Tudor servants, these were drawn from the middle class and entirely dependent upon the Crown for their careers. The ruthless Cardinal struck down his opponents without respect of person, and established a royal despotism, unchecked by the nobility or by Parliament. The French Parliament, or States-General, had last met in 1614. Richelieu refused to summon it, and there was no further meeting for one hundred and seventy-five years—till the Revolution of 1789.

Richelieu's third aim was to make France a first-class power in the affairs of Europe. The Thirty Years' War in Germany gave him the opportunity he sought.

The Beginning of the Thirty Years' War

The Peace of Augsburg (1555), which had attempted to settle the religious question in Germany (see p. 46), had proved deficient in several respects. It allowed no individual toleration, but gave to the prince the right of determining the religion of his subjects. Then again, it allowed only two religions, the Roman Catholic and Lutheran, and forbade even a prince to embrace the Calvinist faith. Finally it had not settled the land question permanently, and under various pretexts Protestant rulers continued to seize lands formerly belonging to the Catholic Church. Behind these religious questions lay, as always, the political opposition of the German princes to all attempts of the Hapsburg Emperors to enforce their authority throughout Germany.

The immediate cause of the war was concerned with the

Crown of Bohemia, which, strictly speaking, was elective, but which had for long been held by the Hapsburg Emperors. The reigning Emperor schemed to keep the Bohemian Crown in his family, but in 1618 some Bohemian nobles broke into the palace at Prague, seized the Emperor's two

Regents and their secretary, and threw them from one of the windows. They dropped seventy feet, but escaped unhurt. The Bohemians then chose as their King, Frederick, the Calvinist Elector Palatine. Contrary to the advice of many of his counsellors and of James I of England (whose daughter, Elizabeth, was Frederick's wife), Frederick decided to accept the Crown.

GUSTAVUS ADOLPHUS
OF SWEDEN

The Thirty Years' War (1618–1648)

The Emperor defeated Frederick at the Battle of the White Mountain (1620), and the 'winter King,' as he was called, on account of his reign of a single season, was expelled from Bohemia. The imperial forces then attacked Frederick's hereditary possessions in the Palatinate, and Denmark and Holland took up arms to help Frederick. But England gave practically no help at all, for Frederick's father-in-law, James I, was intent upon his schemes for a Spanish alliance (see Chapter XI), and Spain had joined forces with the Emperor to crush Protestantism in Germany. For several years the imperial generals, Tilly and Wallenstein, carried all before them and devastated Germany.

In 1630 a new figure appeared on the scene when Gustavus Adolphus, the Swedish warrior King, landed in north Germany to save Protestantism from extinction and, if possible, to win new territories for himself. Marching into the heart of Germany, the 'Lion of the North' won victory after victory. In his armies were many Scotsmen, gaining valuable experience for the English Civil War that broke out ten years later. In 1632 Gustavus defeated Wallenstein at Lutzen, but was himself killed in battle. The cause of Protestantism suffered a great loss, as Gustavus had sought to raise the war to a higher level than the mere butchery into which it had sunk.

In 1635 the Catholic Richelieu, to further French interests and prevent the Hapsburgs of either Germany or Spain from becoming too powerful, entered the war in support of the German Protestants. For thirteen more years the war continued, and Germany suffered a long agony. The French troops were mostly victorious, and in 1648 the Emperor was obliged to sue for peace.

The Peace of Westphalia (1648)

This treaty is one of the landmarks in European history. The religious question in Germany was settled by placing Calvinism on the same footing as Lutheranism and Roman Catholicism, but religious toleration for the people, as distinct from their rulers, was not mentioned. The land question was also satisfactorily settled. In addition France received most of Alsace along the Rhine, Sweden obtained part of Pomerania in north Germany, and the independence of Switzerland and the Dutch Netherlands was formally recognized. Inside Germany the power of the Emperor was reduced to a shadow, and the German princes, numbering over 300, became practically independent.

Germany was exhausted as a result of the war. The population was reduced to about one-third of its previous number, and agriculture and industry had in many places disappeared. It took Germany a century or more to recover, and along with the gradual decline of Spain, the leadership of Europe was fast passing into the hands of France.

QUESTIONS AND EXERCISES

1. Write an account of Holland's greatness in the seventeenth century under the headings (a) art, (b) commerce, (c) colonization.

2. What were Richelieu's three aims, and how did he seek to carry them out?

3. What do you associate with the following places: Nantes, La Rochelle, Lutzen, Westphalia?

4. Why did England not interfere much in European affairs 1600–1650?

CHAPTER XI

JAMES I: THE CLOUDS GATHER

Stuart Monarchs

James I	1603–1625
Charles I	1625–1649
Commonwealth	1649–1660
Charles II	1660–1685
James II	1685–1688
William III	1689–1702
Anne	1702–1714

A New Royal House—the Stuarts

ON the death of Elizabeth in 1603 the Tudor dynasty came to an end, and the English Crown passed to James VI of Scotland, who became James I of England. James was the son of Mary, Queen of Scots, and Lord Darnley, and could trace his descent on both sides back to Margaret, the daughter of Henry VII (see table on p. 51). He had been King of Scotland since 1567 (the year after his birth) and came to England full of confidence in his ability to govern his new Kingdom. Despite the fact that Englishmen and Scotsmen still regarded one another with hostility, the accession of James took place with practically no opposition. The Catholics formed the Bye Plot to compel the King to grant them toleration, while another group of malcontents formed the Main Plot, to place James's cousin, Arabella Stuart, on the throne. Neither of these plots gave the government much trouble, and in connexion with the latter Sir Walter Raleigh was found guilty of treason and condemned to death. He had done little more than talk vaguely against a Scottish King who was making peace with our national enemy, Spain, and his penalty was changed to one of imprisonment in the Tower.

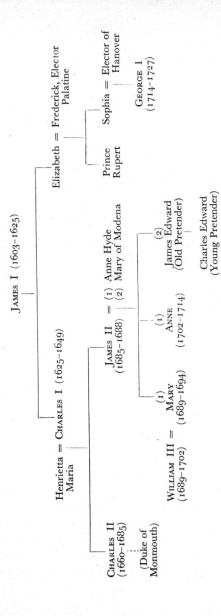

THE STUART ROYAL FAMILY

The descent through James I's daughter, Elizabeth, shows the Hanoverian claim to the English throne as recognized by the Act of Settlement (1701).

The Character of James I

Henry IV of France called James "the wisest fool in Christendom," and we shall see how James's character and views combined the two ingredients of wisdom and folly.

In personal appearance James was very unlike the popular conception of a king. He was fat, slobbering, awkward, and weak-kneed and is said to have trembled at the sight of cold steel. He had, however, many excellent ideas. He wished to unite England and Scotland more closely by combining their Parliaments, Churches, and laws, and by establishing free trade between the two countries. He believed that the persecution of religious opinions was unjust and began his reign imbued with ideas of toleration. He also regarded it as cruel and wicked that nations should 'settle' their differences by means of war, and he was full of schemes for bringing peace to England and the rest of Europe.

Unfortunately James possessed many foolish ideas as well, and even his good ideas did not appeal to the majority of his subjects. Englishmen and Scotsmen refused to sink their differences and combine their governments; the English also feared Scottish commercial competition too much to establish free trade between the two countries. The utmost that James could obtain was a decision of the judges in 1604 that children born after his accession to the English throne were to be citizens of both countries. As for religious toleration, even James found this impracticable in an age of religious animosity; most Englishmen distrusted the Roman Catholics too much to grant them their freedom, while James himself persecuted the Puritans for their opinions. Equally impracticable—sad to relate—was James's idea of establishing European peace. In 1604 he made a peace treaty with Spain which omitted all reference to the vexed question of English trade with Spanish America. The treaty was unpopular in England, as the Spaniards were regarded as our national enemy and the Spanish war had been

profitable to the English sea-dogs. In pursuance of the
same ideas James formed plans to link his own family
with both the Catholic House of Spain and the Calvinist
ruler of the Palatinate in Germany; but these plans, as
we shall see later, only led to further trouble at home and
abroad.

JAMES I HAWKING
The use of hawks for the chase had been a
common sport among the upper classes for
centuries.

In other respects James
was ill-suited for his new
position. He was too fond
of theories and books to
make a successful ruler.
He was learned in theology
and history, but lacked
the practical common
sense that would enable
him to adapt his know-
ledge to the difficult circumstances of his time. He
had also little knowledge
of English ways and was
too proud to learn. He was a poor judge of men, and in the
second part of his reign he allowed himself to fall under the
influence of favourites who won his affection by their worthless flatteries and attentions. He was fortunate in inheriting
from Elizabeth a worthy minister in the person of Robert
Cecil, the son of Lord Burghley. James wisely confirmed
Cecil in his position of Lord Treasurer and made him Earl
of Salisbury. Till his death in 1612 Cecil guided the policy
of the government and saved James from many blunders.

James was a firm believer in the theory of the Divine
Right of Kings, and wrote a book to expound it—*The True
Law of Free Monarchies.* According to this theory kings were
appointed by God, like the patriarchs of the Old Testament.
They were answerable to God alone for their actions. A
good king would study the welfare of his subjects, but a bad
king was a sign of God's displeasure with the people, and it

was sinful to question God's will by criticizing or opposing the king's wishes. "Although I have said a good king will frame all his actions to be according to the law, yet is he not bound thereto but of his good will, and for good example-giving to his subjects." This theory, it is true, was held by many kings besides James; but James was tactless enough to parade it whenever his actions were called in question, and he thought that appeal to it was a sufficient answer to any criticism. As he informed his first Parliament, "They derived all matters of privilege from him," *i.e.*, if they had any powers, it was merely because the king, in his graciousness, allowed them to have them.

Problems facing the Stuarts

James and his successors soon found themselves faced with so many difficulties that it is useful to review them all briefly and see them in their right perspective. Broadly speaking, they were of two kinds, religious and political, though in actual practice they were all often closely related.

In the religious sphere the Elizabethan Church settlement was still being attacked from two directions. The Puritans wished for plainer services and a more democratic system of church government, the Catholics for more elaborate services and a closer union with Rome. The Catholics were strongest among the gentry of the North and Midlands, and they hoped for favours from the son of Mary, Queen of Scots; their numbers were, however, gradually declining, and since the Marian persecution they were regarded with distrust by the majority of the nation. The Puritans constituted a much more difficult problem. Puritanism was strong among the merchants of the towns and the yeoman farmers of the countryside. These men were conscious of their growing wealth and power, and many of them had acquired experience of government as local Justices of the Peace. They were also being increasingly elected as members of Parliament. They supported their arguments by frequent reference to the

Bible, which was the only book in common use. They were themselves divided into various groups: a moderate section, which wished to keep the Church of England in its main essentials but to make the services less ceremonial; the Brownists (later Independents), who wished each congregation to arrange its own form of worship; and lastly, the most numerous section of all, the Presbyterians, who wished to abolish bishops and introduce the Scottish system of Church government by a democratic assembly of presbyters and laymen. The Presbyterians hoped that James, who had been brought up in a Presbyterian country, would grant their requests. They were to be sadly disillusioned, as James had unhappy memories of Scottish Presbyterianism and much preferred the system of government by bishops, which gave the king greater control over the Church.

Political questions raised even more difficult problems. James's theory of Divine Right led him to exalt his own position and to reject outright the claims of his subjects to a share in matters of government. Parliament naturally took quite a different view of the situation. Under the Tudors Parliament had grown in power and status, and already towards the end of Elizabeth's reign it had begun to assert its independence, as over the vexed question of monopolies. Out of deference to the age, sex, and ability of Elizabeth it had refrained from pushing things to extremes. With a new and foreign monarch on the throne, who pursued unpopular policies, the situation soon became quite different. Parliament began to lay more stress upon its alleged ancient privileges—the right to control elections, the right to discuss whatsoever subjects it chose, and the freedom of members from arrest during its sessions. Backed up by many of the lawyers and some of the judges, it also asserted that the laws passed by Parliament were binding upon everyone, even the king himself. Hence Parliament began to oppose the continuance of the Courts of Star Chamber, High Commission, and the Councils of Wales and the North—all courts closely under the king's control. The King replied by asserting his royal 'prerogative,' *i.e.*, the special powers possessed by the king as the fountain of law and justice. He regarded the judges as his own servants, or, as the great lawyer, Sir Francis Bacon, described them, as "lions under the throne," whose duty it was to carry out the royal will. As the judges were appointed by the king and could be dismissed by him, their position was very difficult in cases that concerned the royal power.

In pursuit of its aims Parliament claimed the right to criticize and influence the royal policy on all matters, domestic or foreign. If it did not as yet claim the right of appointing the king's ministers, it certainly claimed the power of removing them by one means or another if they were distasteful. For this purpose Parliament revived the old practice of impeachment, under which the House of Commons prosecuted and the House of Lords acted as judges.

Parliament suffered from the disadvantage of not being summoned regularly, and sometimes many years passed between its meetings. But Parliament had the advantage of holding the purse-strings of the nation, although its hold was not always as strong as it would have liked. The old theory of government was that the king should 'live of his own,' *i.e.*, provide for the needs of government as well as for his own personal needs out of the royal purse. This was made up of revenues from the royal lands, of certain feudal dues that dated back to the Middle Ages, and of tunnage and poundage which were usually granted by Parliament to the king for life. These latter were originally taxes upon wine and wool coming into or going out of the country, but they now included many other articles as well. It was becoming increasingly difficult for the monarch to 'make both ends meet,' and Elizabeth had been obliged to practise many economies. On the one hand the work of government was gradually expanding, and on the other hand prices were rising owing to the influx of precious metals from the New

World. But the royal revenues were fairly stationary. The King, therefore, had to find new ways of raising money. If he applied to Parliament, he was often met with the reply, "Redress precedes supply," *i.e.*, no grants of money will be given till certain grievances have been remedied. This led the King to raise money without resort to Parliament, and to do this he revived old laws and ways of obtaining money that English monarchs had once used. This, in its turn, gave further offence to Parliament when it was summoned, and' so the dispute went on.

It is impossible to say which side was in the right. The King undoubtedly possessed many of the powers he claimed, and he was ultimately responsible for the government of the country. But the characters and policies of the early Stuarts led Parliament to distrust monarchical government. Parliament was really fighting for its very existence and for the principle that the Crown should seek the consent of the nation in carrying on the work of government. In support of its claims Parliament, too, appealed to the past, though with less justification. In particular it sought to base its claims upon Magna Carta, but could only do so by misreading that ancient document. It is perhaps best to regard the dispute between Crown and Parliament under the Stuarts as the 'growing-pains' of the country.

The Hampton Court Conference (1604)

As James was on his way from Scotland to London he was presented with a petition, alleged to have been signed by a thousand ministers of the Church of England, and hence called the Millenary Petition. It asked that the Church should be made more Puritan by the abolition of certain practices, such as the cross in baptism, the ring in marriage, the wearing of vestments by the clergy, and the bowing at the name of Jesus.

James decided to summon a conference at Hampton Court (1604), where he hoped to be able to air his knowledge of theology. Both the Puritans and the High Church party were represented, but James, in his capacity of chairman, openly sided with the latter. When one of the Puritans referred to a presbytery James gave vent to an angry outburst. "If you aim at a Scottish presbytery," he exclaimed, "it agreeth as well with a monarchy as God with the Devil. . . . How they used the poor lady, my mother, is not unknown, and how they dealt with me in my minority. I thus apply it: no Bishop, no King"—by which he meant that if bishops were abolished the royal authority would be diminished, perhaps to the point of nothingness. James refused to grant the Puritan demands, and soon afterwards 300 Puritan clergy were expelled from their livings for refusing to conform in every particular with the English Prayer Book.

The conference had one very important result, however; James agreed with the request that a new translation of the Bible should be prepared and appointed commissions of learned divines for the purpose. In 1611 the Authorized Version appeared—the best and noblest translation of all books into the English language. Thereafter it was widely read and had an immense influence upon later thought and literature. It is still the favourite version of the Bible, being more widely used than the Revised Version, which was brought out nearly three centuries later.

The Gunpowder Plot (1605)

The Catholics, in their turn, hoped for favours from the son of Mary, Queen of Scots. James was not a Catholic, but he believed in religious toleration, and at the outset of his reign he relaxed the recusancy laws against the Catholics, provided they promised loyalty to the government. The result was to show the existence of far more Catholics, especially in the North and Midlands, than the government had imagined. In alarm, the government re-imposed the recusancy laws.

Some of the Catholics, urged on by Jesuits, then formed the most famous plot in English history. Led by Robert Catesby, a Warwickshire gentleman, they plotted to blow up the King and both Houses of Parliament when they reassembled on November 5, 1605. In the resulting confusion the Catholics were to rise and obtain their freedom. The actual blowing up of Parliament was entrusted to a Yorkshireman named Guy Fawkes, who had served with the

CATESBY AND HIS FELLOW-CONSPIRATORS
From a Dutch engraving.

Spanish army in the Netherlands, where he had learnt the practical details of mining. Cecil, however, discovered the plot in time, partly through an anonymous letter sent by one of the conspirators to his brother-in-law, Lord Monteagle, warning him to keep away. On the night before the reassembly of Parliament, Guy Fawkes was discovered in the cellars making his final preparations. He and his fellow plotters were seized and put to death.

The Gunpowder Plot struck deep into the popular imagination. Coupled with Foxe's account of the Marian persecutions in the *Book of Martyrs*, it created in the minds of

Englishmen a distrust and hatred of 'Popery' that lasted for well over two centuries.

James's First Parliament (1604–1611)

James soon found himself involved in quarrels with his first Parliament. A certain Sir Francis Goodwin, who was an outlaw, was elected member for Buckinghamshire. The election of outlaws had been prohibited by royal proclamation, and James demanded that the House of Commons should exclude Goodwin from membership. The Commons asserted that it was their own privilege to decide disputed elections, and James replied that they held all privileges from him. Finally, a new election was held, and the King quietly let the matter drop.

Soon more serious disputes arose over questions of taxation. James regarded England as a rich country after Scotland; he lived a life of extravagance and bestowed many presents upon his courtiers. He soon found himself in debt, and to raise money he imposed extra taxes on certain goods coming into the country. These impositions had not been sanctioned by Parliament and were unpopular; they could be defended, however, on the ground that they fell within the royal control over matters of foreign and commercial policy. In 1606 a London merchant named Bate, who traded with Turkey, refused to pay the imposition on currants. He was brought to trial, and the judges decided that the extra taxes were legal. Thus encouraged, James issued in 1608 a new Book of Rates imposing fresh duties upon many other articles. Parliament realized that with these powers the King would be able, in view of the growing commerce of the country, to make himself independent of Parliament. In 1610 Bate's case was hotly debated, and Parliament declared impositions without its own consent to be illegal.

In the same year Cecil made an attempt to place the royal revenues on a more satisfactory footing. He drew up what was called the Great Contract, whereby the King was to give up certain feudal dues and the claim to levy impositions in return for an annual income of £200,000. Owing to distrust on both sides this excellent scheme was never adopted.

Rule by Favourites

In 1612 James lost his chief minister by the death of Robert Cecil, Earl of Salisbury. Thereafter the King ruled by means of favourites of little ability, and as far as possible he did without Parliament. From 1611 to 1621 there was only one Parliament (1614). Within a few weeks it was angrily dismissed by the King before it had passed a single measure, and is known to history as the Addled Parliament.

James's first favourite was Robert Carr, who had been one of the King's pages in Scotland. Carr was vain, empty-headed, and worthless, but his good looks and flattery charmed the King, who created him Earl of Somerset. For several years Somerset was supreme and carried on the government by bestowing and receiving lavish bribes and presents. In 1616 Somerset and his wife were implicated in a murder; they were found guilty and were permanently banished from court.

Somerset was succeeded by George Villiers, a far abler person. Villiers was a handsome and attractive young man and a brave soldier. He quickly won James's favour, and in 1617 he was made Earl (later Duke) of Buckingham. James affectionately called him his 'Steenie.' Till his assassination in 1628 Buckingham was supreme, first as adviser to James I, and after 1625 to James's son, Charles I. Although he had ability, he was too impulsive to become either a wise statesman or a good general. His arrogance angered the peers and the traditional councillors of the Crown, and his flippancy gave great offence to the Puritans.

James's policy continued to offend a large part of the nation. In 1616 he dismissed from his judgeship Sir Edward Coke, who was the foremost champion of the common law against the claims of the royal prerogative. His foreign policy, as we shall soon see, was too pro-Spanish for a Protestant nation that still remembered the exploits of the Elizabethan sea-dogs. As time went on, James's financial difficulties became more acute. He revived Elizabeth's practice of selling monopolies, which gave their holders the sole right of dealing in certain commodities. This led to a rise in prices and was really a form of indirect taxation. James also raised money by selling baronetcies on the instalment system—the price being £1080, payable in three instalments. Much of the money raised by this means was used for settling Scottish Presbyterians in confiscated lands in northern Ireland. From this 'plantation' originated the un-Irish character of Ulster and the problems it entails.

The Parliament of 1621

James's financial difficulties eventually forced him to summon another Parliament. When it met, it was in no mood to grant supplies without first seeking redress of its grievances.

Parliament first declared the granting of monopolies illegal, and James was obliged to cancel his grants. Some of the holders of monopolies were punished. Eventually a law of 1624 forbade the granting of patents of monopoly to individuals except actual inventors.

Parliament next attacked Sir Francis Bacon, who since 1618 had been Lord Chancellor and Viscount St Albans. Bacon was one of the most remarkable men of his age— scientist and author as well as a great lawyer (see pp. 303, 313). Parliament disliked his support of the royal despotism, and it now accused him of allowing bribes and presents from suitors to influence his legal decisions. In accepting presents Bacon was only following a common custom of his time, but he was none the less impeached—the House of Commons prosecuting him and the House of Lords sitting as judges. He was found guilty and deprived of his offices.

Thirdly, Parliament turned to foreign affairs and urged

the King to adopt a more vigorous Protestant policy and to abandon the pro-Spanish measures he had set his heart upon. James regarded foreign policy as peculiarly his own prerogative and ordered the debates in Parliament to cease. At this the House of Commons drew up a memorable Protestation asserting its right to discuss all questions, "concerning the King, state and defence of the realm, and of the Church of England, and the making and maintenance of laws, and redress of mischiefs and grievances." In his anger the King himself tore out the Protestation from the Journal of the House and straightway dissolved Parliament (January, 1622).

A Peaceful Foreign Policy

From the very beginning of his reign, when James had made peace with Spain, foreign affairs had produced friction between king and nation. James set out with the praiseworthy object of establishing a general European peace, and, priding himself on his knowledge of foreign affairs, began his task with great confidence. He hoped to create better feeling between England and Spain, and to settle the discord between Catholic and Protestant on the Continent. Unfortunately national and religious animosities were too strong for him, but he deserves credit for his ideals, which were far in advance of those of his age.

James's policy involved two marriage schemes: the first between his daughter, Elizabeth, and the Calvinist Frederick, Elector Palatine; the second between his son, Henry (the Prince of Wales), and a Spanish Infanta, or Princess. The first of these marriage schemes was popular, and in 1613 the marriage was celebrated with extravagant luxury. It is interesting to note that from this union sprang the later Hanoverian dynasty (see table on p. 148). The second of the proposed marriages was, however, extremely unpopular, as most Englishmen viewed with dislike a union which would result in the future King of England being brought up by a

Catholic mother. It was even disliked by Cecil and by Prince Henry himself, but after the death of both in 1612, James was able to proceed more boldly with the scheme, as the new Prince of Wales, Charles, was much more amenable. James fell more and more under the influence of the Spanish ambassador, Count Gondomar, who was able to obtain relaxations of the laws against the Catholics. Gondomar soon became as unpopular as James's favourites.

The Tragedy of Sir Walter Raleigh

Sir Walter Raleigh was still in the Tower under sentence of death for his alleged participation in the Main Plot of 1603. He had spent his time in writing a *History of the World*. In 1617 James and Buckingham were badly in need of money, and Raleigh was

SIR WALTER RALEIGH
From an engraving in Raleigh's *History of the World*.

released to go in search of a gold-mine, of whose existence he claimed knowledge, up the river Orinoco in South America. He was given strict orders not to fight the Spaniards or interfere with their possessions. This was an almost impossible condition, especially as James gossiped to Gondomar about the expedition, and the Spaniards were forewarned. The inevitable conflict took place, in which Raleigh's own son was killed. The expedition was also unsuccessful in its search for gold, and on Raleigh's return the death-sentence, which was by now fourteen years old, was carried out (1618). The execution of the last of the Elizabethan sea-dogs, to please Gondomar and the Spanish court, disgusted the nation. The subservience of James to Catholic Spain was inevitably contrasted with the staunch opposition of Elizabeth thirty years before.

The Thirty Years' War and the Spanish Marriage Question

In 1618 James's son-in-law, Frederick, the Elector Palatine, became involved in the Thirty Years' War (see Chapter X). It was against James's advice that Frederick had accepted the crown of Bohemia, and when Frederick was driven out of Bohemia, James felt under no obligation to help him. Soon afterwards a Catholic army, which included Spanish as well as imperial troops, drove Frederick and his wife out of their hereditary possessions in the Palatinate as well. Opinion in England, especially among the extreme Protestants and Puritans, was strongly in favour of help being sent to the exiled Elector and his wife, and the Parliament of 1621 urged James to adopt this course before it drew up its famous Protestation.

But James merely pushed on with the marriage negotiations between Prince Charles and the Spanish Infanta, fondly hoping that if the proposed union took place Spanish troops would help to regain the Palatinate for Frederick. Spain in return demanded toleration for the Catholics in England, and, in any case, had no intention of meeting James's desires. In 1623 Prince Charles and Buckingham (who had gained complete ascendancy over the Prince of Wales) journeyed in person to Spain, but the Infanta loathed Charles, and the Spanish courtiers hated the haughty Buckingham. A contemporary letter informs us that on one occasion

> the Infanta was in the orchard, and there being a high partition wall between, and the door doubly bolted, the prince got on the top of the wall and sprang down a great height, and so made towards her: but she, spying him first of all the rest, gave a shriek and ran back.

When James's 'twa boys' returned home empty-handed there was universal relief and rejoicing in England. Buckingham, who enjoyed his newly found popularity, was now as anti-Spanish as the extremest Puritan and persuaded the aged King to declare war upon Spain. A Parliament met in 1624 and welcomed the change of policy, but the war brought no victories, and in March, 1625, the King died. He had earned twenty years' unpopularity for a foreign policy which in the last year of his reign he had been compelled to reverse.

The Beginning of the British Empire

Raleigh's attempts in Elizabeth's reign to colonize Virginia had failed, but in 1606 James granted a charter to a new Virginia Company. In 1607 a band of emigrants landed in America and founded

THE "MAYFLOWER"
From a model at Washington.

Jamestown. It was mainly due to the energy and heroic leadership of Captain John Smith that the colony succeeded. He forced the settlers to cultivate the soil and brave the dangers from Indian tribes. It was soon discovered that the soil and climate of Virginia were suitable for the growth of tobacco. Thereafter the success of the colony was assured, as, despite the opposition of the Puritans and of James I himself, the habit of tobacco-smoking was steadily growing. In 1624 the original company came to an end, and Virginia became a crown colony with a governor appointed by the king and a legislative assembly elected by the colonists.

Meanwhile religious persecution was responsible for another colony farther north. Both Elizabeth and James I had driven many Brownists, or Congregationalists, into exile. Many had fled to Holland, but, dissatisfied with their lives there, a band of them decided to seek a new home across the Atlantic. In 1620 these Pilgrim Fathers, numbering about one hundred, sailed from Holland to Plymouth to make their final preparations. They then crossed the Atlantic in the *Mayflower* and landed near Cape Cod at a place they called New Plymouth. They had to face many hardships: the icy winters, the poor soil, and the attacks of Indian tribes. But their staunch determination overcame all obstacles, and in the next two decades they were reinforced by thousands of other Puritans who fled to escape the religious persecution of the Stuarts. In this 'New England,' however, the Puritans proved quite as intolerant as the persecutors from whom they had fled.

In 1623 the first of the West Indian Islands, St Kitts, was colonized. In the next reign the number grew, and negro slaves were imported to work on the valuable sugar-plantations.

In the East also the foundations of empire were being laid by the East India Company, which, in pursuit of trade, was extending its influence and acquiring possessions (see pp. 291–292).

QUESTIONS AND EXERCISES

1. Illustrate the truth of the description of James I as "the wisest fool in Christendom."

2. Describe carefully the financial disputes between James I and his Parliaments.

3. Give an account of the activities of the Puritans under James I.

4. Describe the main points in James's pro-Spanish policy. Why was it unpopular?

5. Write notes on the following remarks: "Redress precedes supply"; "No Bishop, no King"; "Lions under the throne."

CHAPTER XII

CHARLES I: TO THE OUTBREAK OF WAR

The New King

IN many ways Charles I was a direct contrast to his father. He looked every inch a king, was handsome, dignified, and athletic, and without his father's love of theorizing and arguing. But he believed as firmly as James in the Divine Right of Kings and looked upon any opposition to his will as mere faction or knavery, which it was justifiable to outwit by any kind of trickery. This often led him to make mental reservations in his dealings with Parliament and to treat his promises lightly, so that he soon appeared to his critics as one whose word was worthless. Although conscientious in the work of government, he lacked real ability and was unable to discern it in others. Hence his advisers were generally unsuitable for their position.

CHARLES I
From the painting by Daniel Mytens in the National Portrait Gallery, London.

From the outset Parliament regarded him with distrust. He was completely under the influence of the fickle Duke of Buckingham. Moreover, his religious policy soon offended the Puritans. Charles supported the High Church party, or, as it was then called, the Arminian party—so named from Arminius, a Dutch theologian, who had attacked the Calvinist doctrine of predestination and the Calvinist opposition to Catholic ceremonial. In the eyes of the Puritans Arminianism was concealed Popery. To make matters worse, Charles married a French Catholic princess, Henrietta Maria, soon after his accession, and the new Queen used her influence to obtain greater freedom for the Catholics.

Charles's First Parliament (1625)

In the first year of his reign Charles summoned a Parliament, which he hoped would grant supplies for the war with Spain. To the King's surprise it showed little enthusiasm. It would have supported a naval war with Spain, but it distrusted the leadership of Buckingham and was in no mood to let him squander the nation's money on continental expeditions. It made a grant of £140,000, which was quite inadequate for carrying on the war.

Parliament then showed its disapproval of Charles's marriage and obliged the King to withdraw the promised relaxation of the laws against Catholicism. The custom—by now centuries old—of granting the king tunnage and poundage for life was broken by Parliament's making the grant for one year only. Charles regarded this as a personal insult and continued to levy the taxes without Parliamentary sanction. When it was intimated that a more generous grant might be made if Buckingham were dismissed, the King felt so angry that he dissolved Parliament in disgust.

Charles's Second Parliament (1626)

Before summoning another Parliament, Charles and Buckingham hoped to silence their critics with the *fait accompli* of a successful attack upon Spain. Accordingly they scraped together every penny they could find and, by means of press-gangs, raised a motley force for an attack on Cadiz. The result was a dismal failure. The fleet had been neglected since the days of Elizabeth, and the army, on arriving in Spain, found itself short of rations but with plenty of wine.

Despite the check to his plans, Charles was so short of money that he summoned his second Parliament (1626).

A new Parliamentary leader now appeared in Sir John Eliot, a Devonshire squire of noble character and forceful eloquence. Eliot attacked the King for levying tunnage and poundage without Parliamentary consent, and the House of Commons then authorized Eliot to draw up articles of impeachment against Buckingham. In a powerful speech Eliot compared Buckingham with the evil minister of one of the old tyrannical Roman Emperors. To save himself from further insults and his minister from further attacks, Charles dissolved Parliament without its having granted him a penny.

A New War and a Forced Loan (1627)

Soon afterwards the country found itself involved in a war against France. Buckingham had at first hoped for a French alliance as a result of Charles's marriage with Henrietta Maria, but events turned out otherwise. Cardinal Richelieu refused to fall in with Buckingham's plans for an attack on the Emperor; while Charles, faced with reluctance on the part of the English crews, was unable to send help to Richelieu for his attack on the Huguenots at La Rochelle. The failure of Charles to carry out his promises concerning the position of the Catholics in England further offended the French court.

With two wars on his hands Charles was in desperate financial straits, although he was still levying tunnage and poundage without Parliament's consent. He decided to levy a forced loan—a form of taxation that English kings had used in the past. Soon about eighty men were in prison for refusing to pay. At the same time press-gangs were busy raising men for the army, and soldiers were being billeted in private houses without payment to the householders, so as to save the government expense. Disputes between these soldiers, who were often unruly in their behaviour, and their civilian hosts were tried by martial law. Five knights who were in prison for refusing to contribute towards the forced loan decided to test the legality of their imprisonment. They obtained from the judges writs of *habeas corpus*, which were orders to the gaoler to produce his prisoners in court and state why they were imprisoned. When the five knights were thus produced, the judges decided that imprisonment by the King's special command was sufficient reason in law; but this involved no decision concerning the legality of the forced loan (1627).

Once more Charles and Buckingham tried to confront their critics with a military victory. In 1627 Buckingham himself led an expedition to relieve La Rochelle. Buckingham was personally brave and enthusiastic and managed to occupy the Isle of Rhé (off La Rochelle) to serve as a base. But the expedition was ill organized, and after losing over half his men, the Duke admitted failure and returned home. The King was then obliged to summon a third Parliament.

Charles's Third Parliament (1628–1629)

The leaders of the new Parliament included the orator Eliot, the lawyer Coke, and Pym and Hampden. Among the new members was one who sat silent throughout its sessions, the Huntingdon squire, Oliver Cromwell.

True to tradition, Parliament insisted on 'redress before supply,' and mindful of the forced loan and the case of the five knights, drew up the Petition of Right (1628) with its four famous clauses:

(1) "No gift, loan, benevolence, tax, or such like charge" was to be levied in future without the consent of Parliament.

(2) No one was to be imprisoned "by the king's special command" without a proper trial according to the law of the land.

(3) Soldiers and sailors were not to be billeted in private houses.

(4) Civilians were not to be subject to martial law.

After a week's hesitation the King was obliged by his

financial necessities to give his assent to the Petition, which thus became the law of the land. Popular rejoicing followed this decision; but Parliament was determined to press home its advantage. It once more raised the question of tunnage and poundage and requested the dismissal of Buckingham. Charles replied by proroguing—*i.e.*, adjourning—Parliament (1628).

In August of the same year Buckingham was murdered at Portsmouth. He was planning a second expedition to La Rochelle when a discontented officer, named Felton, who had been on the first expedition, stabbed him to death. Cheering crowds hailed Buckingham's funeral procession on its way to Westminster Abbey—an untimely display of rejoicing for which Charles never forgave his people. The second expedition to La Rochelle went forward, but it failed as miserably as the first. Charles was now in further financial difficulties. He wisely made peace with Spain and France, and summoned his third Parliament for another session (1629).

Two questions occupied the attention of Parliament. One was the continued levying of tunnage and poundage without Parliamentary consent. This, Parliament contended, was contrary to the Petition of Right which the King had signed. The other question concerned religion. Parliament was largely Puritan and protested strongly against the Arminian policy that Charles was pursuing by placing High Church-men in important positions in the Church of England. Charles decided to dissolve Parliament, but when the members received word that the royal messengers were on their way to the House, they took drastic action. The Speaker, a royal nominee, tried to leave the chair and thus bring the sitting to an end. He was firmly held in the chair, the doors were locked, and under the leadership of Eliot three resolutions were hurriedly passed. They condemned as enemies of the kingdom anyone who introduced Arminian-ism or Popery into England, anyone who advised the King to levy tunnage and poundage without Parliament's consent, and anyone who voluntarily paid such a tax. The doors were then flung open, and the excited members poured forth. Charles straightway dissolved Parliament (1629), and for the next eleven years he refused to summon another. Nine Parliamentary leaders were imprisoned by royal authority in the Tower—despite the Petition of Right. Sir John Eliot was among them; he refused to apologize for his conduct and died in the Tower in 1632.

The Eleven Years' Tyranny

From 1629 to 1640 Charles ruled without Parliament. During this period he was influenced by three persons: his wife, Henrietta Maria, who wanted a relaxation of the laws against Roman Catholics; his Archbishop of Canterbury, William Laud, who strove to make the Church of England more Arminian, or High Church, in its character; and Thomas Wentworth (later Earl of Strafford) who worked ruthlessly to make his master an absolute despot. Charles probably had no intention of doing without Parliament altogether, but as the years passed Englishmen could not help wondering whether their country was going to suffer the fate of France, where the States-General had not met since 1614.

Thomas Wentworth, Earl of Strafford

Wentworth, a Yorkshire gentleman, had been one of the Parliamentary leaders during the attacks upon Buckingham and the momentous debates leading up to the Petition of Right. But just about the time of Buckingham's death (1628) he changed sides and was henceforth regarded by Parliament as a traitor. Wentworth had no sympathy with the Puritans. Nor did he believe, after his experiences in Parliament, that an assembly of five hundred squires and merchants could carry on the king's government efficiently. He had attacked Buckingham because of the Duke's failures. With the Duke out of the way, he saw no reason why he should not take Buckingham's place and carry on the government more efficiently. This he did with his ruthlessness, his vigour, his masterful personality, and his undoubted loyalty to his new master. But he never replaced Buckingham in the King's affections, and Charles failed to appreciate to the full the value of his new minister till it was too late. For six critical years during the tyranny Wentworth was kept in Ireland.

Wentworth's first task was to overhaul the government of the north of England. In 1628 Charles made him President of the Council of the North, one of the King's prerogative courts. The semi-civilized state of the northern counties gave Wentworth ample scope for his ruthless policy—a policy that he himself described as 'thorough.' Abuses were checked, slackness was rebuked, and magistrates were called to strict account.

In 1633 Wentworth was sent to Ireland as Lord Deputy, and for the next six years he enforced his 'thorough' policy. Wentworth governed Ireland with a strong hand, hoping to make it prosperous and loyal so that it could furnish his master with men and money. He completely ignored local sentiment, though he gave Ireland peace for the time being and improved its industries. He suppressed the pirates that interfered with Irish commerce, established fisheries, and improved the breed of native cattle. Above all, he started the great Irish linen industry. But all this was done to make Ireland useful and subservient to the English Crown. He offended the native Catholics by attempting a plantation of Connaught with English settlers, and offended the Presbyterians of Ulster (descendants of James I's plantation) by his attempts to introduce the Church of England. Although Wentworth left Ireland peaceful on the surface, he is largely to blame for the Irish rebellion of 1641, when the Catholics rose in fury and massacred thousands of Protestants.

William Laud, Archbishop of Canterbury

The religious policy of Charles I is associated with the name of William Laud, an Oxford don who had proved eminently successful as the head of his college. In 1628 Charles made him Bishop of London, and in 1633 Archbishop of Canterbury.

Archbishop Laud was a convinced and conscientious Arminian, eager to reform the Church of England and to

stamp out all traces of Puritanism. In his own sphere he believed as strongly as Wentworth in the value of discipline and authority. Hence he was a firm upholder of the royal authority in Church and state, of the rule of bishops inside the Church, and of the sacred character of the clergy. Possessed of immense energy and zeal, he organized a visitation throughout the whole province of Canterbury. Commissioners inquired into the characters and views of the clergy, and offenders were brought before the Court of High Commission, of which Laud was president. He ordered elaborate vestments to be worn; he impressed upon the clergy the sacred nature of the Communion service and ordered all Communion tables to be moved to the east end of the churches and railed off. He punished unauthorized preachers and put down 'conventicles,' or private meetings for worship, that the Puritans had started. The censorship was tightened up to prevent any criticism by means of the printed word.

The Puritans naturally hated Laud and his system, much of which they misunderstood. They accused him of undermining the Protestant character of the Church of England and introducing Popery. In reality Laud was opposed to the Roman Catholics and worked hard against the influence of Henrietta Maria. But he was not altogether successful. A papal agent attended the Queen's court, and she was allowed to celebrate Mass publicly; the fines against recusancy were also suspended.

In the short space of just over ten years about 20,000 Puritans left England for America to escape the Laudian persecution. Charles placed no obstacle in their emigration, perhaps being glad to get rid of such troublesome people. In their new homes the Puritans were as intolerant as Archbishop Laud, and in 1633 Lord Baltimore founded the tobacco-growing colony of Maryland (named after Henrietta Maria), as a refuge for Catholics.

Government and Taxation

The Eleven Years' Tyranny was a period of prosperity, as far as the ordinary life of the country was concerned. England was at peace, and there were no Parliamentary disputes to distract the government's attention. Consequently the Privy Council had ample leisure to carry on the work of government and to see that the local magistrates or Justices of the Peace performed their duties efficiently. Elizabeth's Act of Apprentices and Poor Law were enforced; wages were regulated, apprenticeships insisted upon, and the poor looked after. In many ways it was a golden age for the mass of the people.

But those who took their religion or their politics seriously found many grounds on which to attack the government. First, there was Charles's apparent intention to rule without Parliament. Secondly, there was the Puritan hatred of Arminianism. Thirdly, there were the prerogative courts— the Court of High Commission, the Court of Star Chamber, and the Councils of Wales and of the North. These courts were not bound by the ordinary laws and rules of procedure, but were closely controlled by the King and his council. The Court of High Commission enforced Laud's religious policy and was hated by the Puritans. The Court of Star Chamber had in Tudor times done much good work and was still doing so. It was often quicker and cheaper than the ordinary courts, and much of its business was of quite an ordinary nature. But it was becoming increasingly the instrument for enforcing the royal policy. A climax was reached in 1637 when a lawyer, Prynne, was imprisoned, and Bastwick, a physician, and Burton, a clergyman, had their ears cut off in the pillory, were fined £5000 each, and were placed in solitary confinement for life—all for writing Puritanical pamphlets attacking the bishops. The crowd that witnessed the mutilation in the pillory clearly expressed its disapproval of the sentence.

A fourth objection to Charles's personal rule was his continued raising of money without Parliamentary consent. The Lord Treasurer, Weston, practised strict economy, but still found the royal revenues insufficient. To raise more money Charles revived old and almost-forgotten laws and practices that had never been repealed. How far this was legally justified is open to the gravest doubt, especially after the Petition of Right. Tunnage and poundage and impositions were levied. Then it was discovered that a law of Edward I compelled all men with land worth £40 a year to be knighted; many had unwittingly omitted to observe this and were heavily fined for this 'distraint of knighthood.' Heavy fines were also imposed on all who had built within the long-forgotten boundaries of the royal forests. The granting of monopolies to individuals had been declared illegal in 1624; Charles got round this by selling them to companies instead.

The device that attracted most attention was the levying of ship-money. It was an ancient right of the Crown to call upon the sea-ports to provide ships for the country's defence; Elizabeth had used this right at the time of the Armada. The Stuarts had neglected our fleet, and Algerian pirates were preying upon English commerce in the Channel. To

build a fleet Charles, in 1634, ordered the sea-ports to provide money. In 1635 and 1636 he extended the levy to inland counties—an unexampled procedure that could be
justified, however, on the grounds that the safety of the
country concerned everyone alike. Opposition to this new
tax soon appeared. Much of the money so far had been
spent upon ship-building, but if the tax became permanent
(as it seemed to be doing) there was no guarantee that it
would continue to be so spent. Above all, it was being levied
without Parliamentary consent. John Hampden, a Buckinghamshire gentleman, refused on principle to pay the twenty
shillings at which he was assessed. His case was tried before
the judges, seven of whom voted against him, and five in his
favour (1637). Although he had lost his case, it was only by
the narrowest possible margin of votes. Charles's position
was not really strengthened, and the remark of one of the
judges, that "No Acts of Parliament make any difference,"
was regarded as an insult to the nation.

The End of the Eleven Years' Tyranny

The tyranny was eventually brought to an end by events
in Scotland. In 1637 Laud introduced a new Prayer Book
on the English model into the Scottish Kirk. At once there
was fierce opposition—symbolized for ever by the scene in
St Giles's Church, Edinburgh, when a market-woman named
Jenny Geddes threw a stool at the Dean who was using the
new Prayer Book for the first time. Soon thousands of Scots
signed the National Covenant, pledging themselves to defend
their Presbyterian religion, as established by John Knox, to
the bitter end. In 1638 the General Assembly of the Scottish
Kirk abolished all traces of episcopacy in Scotland and
showed its determination to hold fast to the Presbyterian
system.

Charles was thus faced by a first-class crisis. He resolved
to try force, but, having no standing army, was obliged to
rely on a feudal levy of nobles and tenants from the northern

counties. These were no match for the Scottish soldiers, many of whom, including their leader, Alexander Leslie, had served in the Thirty Years' War under the Swedish warrior King, Gustavus Adolphus. Charles realized the hopelessness of the situation and brought the 'First Bishops' War' to an end by the Treaty of Berwick (1639).

Charles then summoned Wentworth from Ireland, made him Earl of Strafford, and sought his advice (1639). Strafford advised Charles to summon a Parliament and obtain supplies; he thought the old English hatred of Scotland would flare up, and in any case he was confident that he could bully Parliament by the methods he had used in Ireland. His mistake was shown when Parliament met (April, 1640). The grievances of eleven years were uppermost in men's minds, and in John Pym Parliament found a leader who was a match for Strafford and his 'thorough.' Parliament refused to grant supplies until it had obtained redress of its grievances, and within three weeks the so-called Short Parliament was angrily dissolved by the King.

The result was the 'Second Bishops' War' (1640). Charles raised a motley army by means of the press-gang and sent it north. The Scottish army easily swept it aside and invaded England. Charles had to agree to the Scottish demands, and by the Treaty of Ripon (1640) he promised to pay the Scots £850 a day so long as they remained in England, and to leave them in possession of Northumberland and Durham as security. There was now no other course for Charles but to summon another Parliament. On November 3, 1640, the Long Parliament began its fateful history.

The Long Parliament (1640–1660)

This Parliament lasted, in various forms and with one long interval of seven years, from 1640 to 1660. Its history can be summarized as follows:

(1) 1640–1642, the period of reforms.

(2) 1642–1649, the period of the civil war, during which

about two-thirds of the House of Lords and one-third of the Commons went over to the King's side.

(3) 1649–1653, the period of the 'Rump,' which was the name applied to the fifty or so members left after the army had expelled about one hundred and fifty members. In 1653 Cromwell dissolved the Rump.

(4) 1660, the surviving members of the Long Parliament were recalled to arrange for the restoration of the monarchy.

During its first two years the Long Parliament was in a strong position. Distrust of the King and indignation against his personal rule were strong, and the Commons had worthy leaders in 'King Pym,' John Hampden, and Oliver Cromwell. Moreover, the Scottish army still held the north, and the King needed money to pay them. Charles was, therefore, for the time being, completely at Parliament's mercy.

The Execution of Strafford (1641)

Several of Charles's ministers fled abroad, but the two most hated, Strafford and Laud, bravely stuck to their posts. Their safety was guaranteed by the King, but Parliament immediately ordered their arrest and proceeded forthwith to procure the execution of Strafford. He more than any other minister typified the personal rule of the King. He was scorned as a traitor to Parliament, while his outstanding abilities and masterful personality made him the most feared enemy of Parliament. He was also known to be intriguing to obtain men and money from Ireland to help the King's cause.

In March, 1641, the House of Commons impeached Strafford for high treason. Pym led the attack, but his case was not very strong from the legal point of view. Treason was an offence against the King; but Strafford's 'crime' had lain in strengthening the royal power, not in plotting against it! In vain Pym argued that Strafford had been guilty of treason against the nation, especially in advising Charles to bring over an army from Ireland. The Commons therefore brought in a Bill of Attainder, condemning Strafford to death; in voting for this members could ignore strictly legal questions. Both Houses passed the Bill; but the royal assent was still required, and the King had promised Strafford that not a hair of his head should be touched. A howling mob in front of Whitehall Palace demanded the death of 'Black Tom the Tyrant,' and even threatened the Queen's life. Strafford nobly advised Charles to give way. The royal assent was

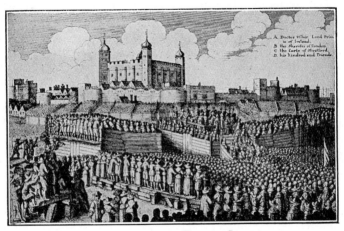

THE EXECUTION OF THE EARL OF STRAFFORD
After a contemporary print. The Tower of London can be seen in the background.

given, and the Bill became law. "Put not your trust in princes," was the only reproach that escaped Strafford's lips when he heard the news. In May, 1641, he was executed. He had fallen because his belief in absolute monarchy was repugnant to the England of his time.

Four years later (January, 1645) Archbishop Laud, the other prop of Charles's despotism, was taken from the Tower and executed.

Constitutional Reforms (1641)

Parliament now proceeded to carry through a number of reforms intended to prevent any repetition of the Eleven

Years' Tyranny. Already, in February, 1641, a Triennial Act had been passed, which stated that not more than three years were to pass without the summoning of Parliament. A few months later another Act forbade the King to dissolve the existing Parliament without its own consent. Further Acts declared ship-money, distraint of knighthood, and all similar devices illegal; and Parliament was empowered to withhold tunnage and poundage and impositions if it desired. To ensure the supremacy of the common law the Court of High Commission, the Star Chamber, and the Councils of Wales and the North were all abolished.

Parliament was practically unanimous over these measures, and Charles was obliged to give his consent. This part of the Long Parliament's work was quite constitutional, and was retained at the Restoration in 1660.

The Root and Branch Bill (1641)

In the second half of 1641 Charles's position grew somewhat stronger. The Scots were paid off and sent home, and in August the King journeyed to Scotland and pacified the northern kingdom by promising not to interfere again with the Presbyterian organization of its Church. Moreover, the Long Parliament itself was becoming divided over the question of religion, and for the first time a 'royalist' party appeared.

The point at issue concerned the organization of the Church of England. In December, 1640, a petition, signed by 15,000 Londoners, had been presented to Parliament asking for the abolition of episcopacy (or the rule of bishops) "with all its roots and branches." The result was the Root and Branch Bill, introduced to make the petition law. Broadly speaking, four religious parties now made their appearance. First, there were the Anglicans. Although some of these felt that Laud and his followers had gone too far in introducing Arminian practices, they were none the less convinced supporters of episcopacy, the royal supremacy over the Church, and the English Prayer Book. This party, ably led by Edward Hyde (later Earl of Clarendon) and Lord Falkland, henceforth supported the King and formed the nucleus of the future Royalist party. The other three parties were all Puritan in their outlook. There was the party of Pym, the strongest in numbers, which desired to abolish episcopacy, to bring the Church under the control of Parliament, and to introduce Puritan ideas. Then there were the Presbyterians, who wished to substitute the rule of presbyters for the rule of bishops, as in Scotland. Finally, there were the Independents (descendants of the Elizabethan Brownists), who opposed all forms of national Church government and wished each congregation to be free to decide its own form of worship; this party was to emerge, in the next few years, as the distinctive party of Oliver Cromwell and the army.

Religious divisions were so deep that when the Long Parliament adjourned in September, 1641, no decision had been reached concerning the Root and Branch Bill.

The Grand Remonstrance (1641)

When the Long Parliament reassembled in October, 1641, it was faced with a new problem. A Catholic revolt had broken out in Ireland, and thousands of English and Scottish Protestants were massacred. Puritan feeling in England ran high and exaggerated the atrocities, bad as they actually were. All parties agreed that an army should be sent over to quell the revolt. By law the army was under the King; and those members who felt that the King's powers had already been sufficiently curtailed wished for no alteration. The Puritans, however, refused to place a weapon in the King's hands which he might use to dissolve Parliament and crush Puritanism once more.

At this juncture Pym and his followers, feeling that their position was gradually weakening, drew up the Grand Remonstrance. This document of over 200 clauses was an attempt to justify all that the Long Parliament had done and all that the extremists still hoped to do. It catalogued and condemned all the misdeeds of Charles, defended the reforms that Parliament had enacted, demanded a reformation of the Church along Puritan lines, and required that in future the King's ministers should have the approval of Parliament. After a long and bitter debate that lasted well into the night, the Commons approved this manifesto by a majority of only eleven votes (November, 1641). If it had been rejected, Oliver Cromwell had decided to go to America, and the course of English history would have been different.

The Outbreak of Hostilities (1642)

The position of Charles had been steadily improving during the last few months, and if he had acted wisely the Civil War might have been averted and the monarchy retained. Unfortunately he now committed a disastrous blunder by appealing to force and attempting to override the privileges of Parliament. In January, 1642, prompted by his wife, who felt herself threatened with impeachment, Charles announced his intention of impeaching five members of the Commons (including Pym and Hampden) and one member of the Lords for carrying on treasonable negotiations with the Scots. When the House of Lords refused to arrest the members, Charles himself came down to the House with a swaggering band of soldiers to perform the deed in person. The members had already fled to take refuge in the City of London, and Charles, finding, as he put it, that 'the birds had flown,' returned baffled to Whitehall.

The King's appeal to force was really an act of war. During the next few months both sides began to prepare for the coming struggle. Charles left London, where feeling was strongly against him, for the north. He was soon joined by about two-thirds of the House of Lords and one-third of the Commons, including Edward Hyde, who remained at his side during the coming years. In March Parliament, finding it could not obtain legal control of the militia, began to raise a militia on its own authority. In April the Governor of Hull, acting on Parliament's instructions, refused the King admission to the city. On August 22, 1642, Charles raised his standard at Nottingham, and the Civil War had begun.

QUESTIONS AND EXERCISES

1. Give an account of the career of the Duke of Buckingham.

2. Write an essay on the Petition of Right. Did Charles break his word after signing it?

3. Write notes on: Sir John Eliot, John Pym, John Hampden, Henrietta Maria, Edward Hyde.

4. Write an essay on Charles's ways of raising money during the Eleven Years' Tyranny.

5. Describe the life and work of either Thomas Wentworth or William Laud.

6. Summarize the chief measures passed by the Long Parliament (1640–1642).

7. Discuss in class which side was the more to blame for the outbreak of the Civil War.

CHAPTER XIII

CHARLES I: THE CIVIL WAR

The Two Sides

ONLY a small proportion of the nation took an active part in the Civil War. Most of the labouring classes kept apart from the struggle, and the armies that fought the battles were relatively small. In general the north and west supported the King, the south and east, Parliament. The division, however, was by no means definite, and there were considerable minorities in most districts. Similarly it is impossible to say that the two sides were divided on any definite class-basis. Generally speaking, the nobility and the gentry were Royalists, and the business men and yeomen farmers were Parliamentarians. But there were plenty of exceptions. Many of the Parliamentary generals were drawn from the nobility. On the other hand, some of the less extreme Puritans were Royalists out of traditional loyalty to the Crown. Even families were divided among themselves. The only unanimous party was the Catholics, who supported Charles in the knowledge that a Parliamentary victory would mean the triumph of Puritanism. This lack of any clear-cut class-division explains largely why the war was carried on in a relatively humane manner, for men were sometimes fighting against their own friends and for reasons that were not always very apparent.

A CAVALIER

At first the Royalists were in the stronger position. Their cause was more easily understood and appealed to the deeply rooted tradition of loyalty to the Crown. They were also superior in cavalry, as many of their supporters were

Districts held by Parliament and
the Scots at the end of 1643.

Glencoe 1692
Killiecrankie ✕1689
Loch Leven
Dunbar ✕1650
Kilsyth ✕1645
Langside ✕1568
Edinburgh
Bothwell Bridge ✕1679
Carberry Hill ✕1567
Berwick
Philiphaugh ✕1645
Flodden ✕1513
Solway Moss ✕1542
Carlisle
Durham
Marston Moor ✕1644
York
Adwalton Moor ✕1643
Hull
Preston ✕1648
Lathom House
Wigan
Manchester
Winceby ✕1643
Newark
Nottingham
Stoke ✕1487
Bosworth ✕1485
Leicester
Fotheringay
Norwich
Naseby ✕1645
Holmby House
Lowestoft ✕1665
Southwold ✕1672
Worcester ✕1651
Edge Hill ✕1642
Northampton
Newmarket
Cambridge
Ipswich
Gloucester
Oxford
Rye House
Chalgrove Field ✕1643
Hounslow Heath
London
Tilbury
Newbury ✕1643, 1644
Blackheath
Bristol
Lansdown ✕1643
Hampton Court
Basing House
Chatham
The Downs ✕1666
Dunk
Roundway Down ✕1643
Sedgemoor ✕1685
Bridgwater
Langport ✕1645
Salisbury
Winchester
Dover
Calais
Beachy Head ✕1690
Dungeness ✕1652
Boulogne
Exeter
Lyme Regis
Portland ✕1653
Carisbrooke Castle
Lostwithiel ✕1644
Plymouth
Torbay
Brixham

ENGLAND AND SOUTHERN SCOTLAND UNDER THE TUDORS AND
STUARTS: POLITICAL MAP

nobles or country gentlemen accustomed to spending their time in the saddle, and they often brought with them their grooms, gamekeepers, and menservants. Cavalrymen armed with pistol and sword were more than a match for foot-soldiers, whose pikes were long and clumsy and whose muskets could only be reloaded at the muzzle after an interval of several minutes. At the outset the King found himself with a ready supply of wealth, for his supporters were quick to melt their plate on his behalf.

But Parliament possessed several advantages of its own which were likely to become increasingly important if the war dragged on. It had the support of London and the south-east, the wealthiest and most populous parts of the country. London was by far the richest town and the busiest port in the kingdom. In addition, most of the other ports were in Parliament's hands. Parliament was thus able to collect more taxes than the King, while the fact that the

A ROUNDHEAD

navy declared in its favour enabled it to control the country's commerce and prevent Charles from obtaining help from the Continent. After the first year Parliament gained two other advantages: the support of the Scots, and the organization of a strong body of cavalry of its own under Oliver Cromwell. The Scottish alliance, however, held good only in the First Civil War of 1642 to 1646. In the so-called Second Civil War of 1648 the Scots supported the King.

Edgehill and Turnham Green (1642)

The Parliamentary armies were placed under the command of the Earl of Essex, an experienced but slow soldier, whose actions were hampered by his instinctive loyalty to the throne. On the King's side a body of cavalry was collected by Prince Rupert, the King's nephew. Rupert was the very opposite of Essex; he was dashing and quick, but he failed to teach his men the value of discipline.

Charles's aim was to capture London, and at Edgehill, on the borders of Warwickshire, the first important battle of the war took place. Rupert's cavalry easily routed the 'decayed serving-men' who constituted the Parliamentary horse—and then chased them several miles across country. When they returned they found the Parliamentary infantry firm and the Royalist infantry broken. The result was a drawn battle. The King continued his march towards London and occupied Oxford, which remained his headquarters for the rest of the war. It was an excellent base for launching further attacks upon London, and the Oxford colleges showed their loyalty by melting their plate on the King's behalf. After reorganizing his forces Charles pushed on towards the capital. At Turnham Green he was faced by Essex and a hastily gathered force of about 20,000 Londoners. Charles hesitated to attack so numerous a force and retired to Oxford for the winter. Never again was he so near to London.

The Triple Advance on London (1643)

The Royalist plan in the following year was to encircle London by a triple advance. The King himself was to advance from Oxford, Sir Ralph Hopton from Devon and Cornwall, and Lord Newcastle from Yorkshire. At first the plan went well. Hopton was victorious at Lansdown and Roundway Down, and Newcastle defeated Lord Fairfax and his son, Sir Thomas Fairfax, at Adwalton Moor. Prince Rupert was able to capture Bristol, the second seaport in the kingdom. But the Royalist advance was delayed by two facts: the reluctance of Cornishmen and Yorkshiremen to move far from their own homes, even in support of their King; and the Parliamentary control of an important city in each of the three royalist districts—Plymouth in the south-west, Hull in the north, and Gloucester in the west. Deeming it unwise to leave these enemy strongholds behind them, Hopton attacked Plymouth, and Newcastle attacked Hull. Neither met with success; Plymouth and Hull, and the Parliamentary fleets that helped them, saved the cause of Parliament.

Nor did Charles fare any better in the west. Parliament had failed to dislodge him from Oxford, and in a skirmish at Chalgrove Field, John Hampden had been killed. With his death Parliament lost one of its ablest and noblest leaders. But the plan for the triple advance had to be abandoned, and Charles decided to lay siege to Gloucester. The city held out bravely under Colonel Massey till Pym sent a relief expedition under the Earl of Essex from London. Charles tried to stop London's citizen army on its way back from Gloucester, and at Newbury a hard-fought battle took place. The result was a draw, but Essex was able to bring his army safely home after an absence of five weeks.

Cromwell's Eastern Association

Oliver Cromwell (1599–1658) was a Huntingdonshire squire whose ancestors had for long been settled in the eastern counties. His great-grandfather was the nephew of Thomas Cromwell, Henry VIII's vicar-general. The young Oliver was educated at the Grammar School of Huntingdon and at Sidney Sussex College, Cambridge. Thereafter he settled down as a gentleman farmer, and in 1628 he was chosen to represent Huntingdon in Parliament. Cromwell's language and thoughts, like those of many other Puritans of his time, were deeply influenced by the Bible, and he resolutely opposed the Arminianism of Charles I and Laud. But he did not take a very prominent part in the Parliamentary proceedings of 1628 or in those of 1640–1642. His chance came with the outbreak of war.

The Battle of Edgehill (1642), at which Cromwell commanded a troop of horse of about sixty men, convinced him that Parliament could win only if it reorganized its armies.

Your troops [Cromwell had told Hampden before the battle] are most of them old decayed serving-men, and tapsters, and such kind of fellows; and their troops [meaning the Royalists] are gentlemen's sons, younger sons, and persons of quality; do you think that the spirits of such base mean fellows will ever be able to encounter gentlemen, that have honour and courage and resolution in them?

Consequently Cromwell says:

I raised such men as had the fear of God before them, as made some conscience of what they did.

Cromwell spent the year 1643 organizing from Cambridge a new army called the 'Eastern Association.' This was the first regular army on either side and soon formed the backbone of the Parliamentary forces. The men were well drilled and disciplined, received regular pay, and were willing to serve in any part of the country. They were exceptionally strong in the cavalry arm, many of them being yeomen farmers and their sons riding their own horses. Above all, Cromwell insisted upon the religious nature of their task, and in this way he gave them enthusiasm together with self-discipline.

A news-letter of May, 1643, describes the Eastern Association as

2000 men, well disciplined; no man swears but he pays his twelve-pence; if he be drunk, he is set in the stocks, or worse; if one calls the other Roundhead he is cashiered; insomuch that the countries where they come leap for joy of them, and come in and join with them. How happy were it if all the forces were thus disciplined!

But Cromwell's Puritanism was not confined to any one sect. He welcomed all God-fearing men and allowed them to worship as they liked. His army became the resort of the Independents (later Congregationalists), who believed in toleration and the independence of each congregation. It was this that eventually drove a wedge between the army and Parliament, for the latter had in the very same year (1643) concluded an alliance with Presbyterian Scotland.

In the autumn of 1643 the Eastern Association gained its first victories, and the Earl of Manchester compelled Newcastle to raise the siege of Hull; Cromwell and Fairfax then defeated a strong force of cavalry at Winceby in Lincolnshire.

The Search for Allies

Meanwhile Charles had been seeking assistance from France, Denmark, and other foreign powers, but without success. By making a truce with the Irish Catholic rebels he managed to bring over some of his Irish army, but his new soldiers were too wild and undisciplined to be of much use.

Parliament was more fortunate, though at a price. By the middle of 1643 the Parliamentary cause had been in such grave danger that both Parliament and Scotland had been alarmed—the latter realizing that a Royalist victory would be followed by attacks on the Scottish Presbyterian Church. Parliament and Scotland therefore signed an alliance called the Solemn League and Covenant (September, 1643). The Scots promised to send an army to help Parliament, and in return Parliament promised to reform the religion of England and Ireland "according to the word of God and the example of the best reformed Churches"—vague phrases that were intepreted by the Scots and by many English as a promise to introduce Presbyterianism.

The Scottish alliance was the last work of Pym, who died in December, 1643. By his courage and eloquence he had served the Parliamentary cause well, and his death removed the one person who might have kept Parliament and the army together.

Marston Moor (1644)

The results of the Scottish alliance and of Cromwell's military genius were shown in the following year in the biggest battle of the Civil War, Marston Moor.

The campaigns leading up to the battle centred round York and were really for the control of the north of England. In January, 1644, a Scottish army under Lord Leven invaded England, joined forces with Fairfax, and compelled Newcastle to take refuge in York. In the summer the army of the Eastern Association, under Manchester and Cromwell, marched northward from East Anglia. Newcastle's plight was desperate, and he appealed to the King for help. Prince Rupert was in Lancashire putting down the Puritan manufacturing-towns, and after relieving Lathom House, where the Royalist Countess of Derby was being besieged, he crossed the Pennines to York. He released Newcastle, and the Parliamentary armies withdrew to Marston Moor, about eight miles west of York. On the evening of July 2, 1644, the battle took place. On the left wing of the Parliamentary army Cromwell faced Rupert for the first time. Cromwell's cavalry scattered Rupert's forces, and the Royalist leader only saved himself by running away. As a tribute to his victor he nicknamed Cromwell "old Ironside," a name that was later transferred to Cromwell's men. After his victory, Cromwell, with admirable discipline, wheeled his horsemen round to aid the Parliamentary centre and right, under Manchester, Fairfax, and Leven, whose position was becoming precarious. Cromwell saved the situation, and the Royalists were routed. The battle gave Parliament control of the north of England and established direct contact between Scotland and the Parliamentary territory. Cromwell's military supremacy was now undisputed, as, although not commander-in-chief, he had been the real victor.

In the south the fortune of war favoured the King. Essex, instead of attacking the King's army at Oxford, marched into the Royalist stronghold of Cornwall. His communications were soon cut off, he himself had to escape by sea to London, and although his cavalry cut through the Royalist lines, his starving infantry had to surrender at Lostwithiel.

Encouraged by this success, Charles moved his army eastward, and Parliament, fearing an attack upon London, summoned the Earl of Manchester from the north. At the second Battle of Newbury, Manchester, out of loyalty to the King, failed to press home his advantage, and the result was a drawn battle. Charles retreated safely to Oxford.

The Self-denying Ordinance and the New Model Army (1645)

In the winter of 1644–1645 plain words were spoken on the Parliamentary side. Cromwell complained that the King would never be defeated so long as the Parliamentary forces were commanded by half-hearted men like Essex and Manchester. He also demanded the reform of the whole Parliamentary army along the lines of his Eastern Association. Parliament was not altogether anxious to comply with his demands, as the numerous body of Presbyterian members viewed with distrust the growing power of the army, which, under Cromwell's influence, was becoming more and more Independent. Although both were Puritan in their outlook, Presbyterianism, with its rigid organization and its intolerance, was far removed from the broader-minded outlook of the Independents. In January, 1645, the intolerance of Parliament had been shown by the execution of Archbishop Laud. But Parliament had to face the fact that it was dependent upon the army, and the army was dependent upon Cromwell. Hence Cromwell eventually got his way. In April, 1645, Parliament passed a Self-denying Ordinance, by which members of both Houses resigned their military commands. This got rid of Manchester and Essex—and Cromwell as well, for the time being. But there was nothing to prevent members from being reappointed, and Cromwell was soon made second-in-command of Parliament's new army, which had been placed under the supreme command of Sir Thomas Fairfax. Parliament's New Model Army was based upon the principles that had been so successful in the

Eastern Association, namely, regular pay, strict discipline, and liability for service in any part of the country. Cromwell commanded the cavalry, and his Eastern Association formed the nucleus of this new army.

Naseby (1645) and the End of the First War (1646)

While the organization of the New Model Army was still proceeding, the King, with his main force, invaded the Midlands. Fairfax and Cromwell hastily gathered their men and marched to intercept Charles. On June 14, 1645, the rival armies met at Naseby, in Northamptonshire. Rupert's cavalry chased their foes from the field, but failed to return. Cromwell, on his wing, was equally successful, but *did* return to help the Roundhead infantry. The result was an overwhelming victory for Parliament. The King lost most of his infantry and his ammunition; his private papers, which revealed his intrigues with foreign powers, fell into his enemy's hands, and he himself fled to the Welsh border. In the following month the last Royalist army in the south-west was beaten at Langport, in Somerset.

Only in Scotland were the Royalists victorious. There the Earl of Montrose had quarrelled with the extreme Presbyterians under Argyll and had rallied the Highland clans in support of the King. In the same year as Naseby and Langport, Montrose invaded the Lowlands and defeated the Covenanters at Kilsyth. Many of his Highlanders then returned home to carry their plunder with them, leaving their leader with a depleted army to face a Scottish detachment sent north from England. In September, 1645, the Scottish Royalists were annihilated at Philiphaugh, and Montrose fled abroad.

Throughout the winter and spring of 1645–1646 the New Model Army was busy reducing isolated cities, castles, and strongholds still held by the Cavaliers. In April, 1646, Charles fled from Oxford disguised as a servant and surrendered to the Scottish army at Newark. In June came the fall of Oxford, the Royalist headquarters. The First Civil War was ended.

Rival Policies (1646–1648)

The events of the next two years are best understood if two important facts are borne in mind:

First, Charles had learnt nothing from the war; he was still contemptuous of his enemies, and ready to make and break promises and stoop to any sort of intrigue to gain his own ends—these being the political supremacy of the Crown and the continuance of the Church of England under king and bishops.

Secondly, the King's three enemies were by no means united, and their divisions gave the King plenty of scope for intrigue. The English Parliament was strongly Presbyterian; but it lacked capable leaders and indulged in a revengeful policy towards the Cavaliers, many of whose lands it confiscated. It both feared and hated the New Model Army and tried to disband it without giving it its legitimate arrears of pay. The army was strongly Independent in religion and included also many Baptists. The army was prepared to grant toleration to all Puritan sects and even, in certain circumstances, to members of the Church of England. It opposed the rigid Presbyterianism of Parliament, which had not only abolished the English Prayer Book and expelled thousands of Anglican clergy from their livings, but also threatened Independents and Baptists with heavy punishments, including death. Cromwell, who was a member of both Parliament and the army, tried to bridge the gap between them, but finding it impossible, threw in his lot with the army. Finally, the Scots desired the continuance of Presbyterianism in Scotland and its establishment, in an even stronger form than Parliament wished, in England and Ireland. This was the situation that eventually led to the Second Civil War, when the Scots found themselves fighting on the side of their former enemy, Charles.

Charles's Intrigues (1646–1648)

Charles aimed at weakening his enemies by playing them off against one another. In April, 1646, he had surrendered to the Scots, hoping to obtain the best terms from them. In July, 1646, the Scots presented their terms in the Newcastle Propositions, which provided for the establishment of Presbyterianism in England and Ireland. Charles pretended to consider these proposals for the rest of the year, until finally the Scots wearied of the business. The English Parliament had already set up a Presbyterian Church, and when Parliament suggested that it would pay the Scots their arrears of pay if they would hand the King over, the Scots accepted. Consequently in January, 1647, Charles was taken to Holmby House, in Northamptonshire, under Parliamentary guard.

Parliament's terms closely resembled those of the Scots, namely, the establishment of Presbyterianism and the diminution of the royal power. The King, however, was holding his hand, for during the summer of 1647 the quarrel between Parliament and the army came to a head. Parliament had established an intolerant Presbyterian Church which threatened to persecute all other Puritan sects, including Independents and Baptists. In May, 1647, Parliament issued an order disbanding the army without its arrears of pay. When the army refused to obey, Parliament schemed with the Scots and even with some of the Royalists to enforce their demand. This was too much for Cromwell and the army. Recognizing that whoever held the person of the King held the trump card, the army decided to seize Charles. Accordingly in June, 1647, Cornet Joyce, at the head of a troop of cavalry, raided Holmby House and carried the King off to the army headquarters at Newmarket. Still finding it impossible to come to terms with Parliament, the army occupied London, expelled eleven of the most prominent Presbyterian members from Parliament, and moved its headquarters to Hampton Court, whence Charles was also removed (August, 1647). From now till the Restoration in 1660 the country was under a military dictatorship, however disguised.

In the same month the army's terms were presented to Charles in the famous Heads of the Proposals. The King henceforth was to be advised by a Council of State under the authority of Parliament. Control of the army was to remain in Parliament's hands for ten years and then to be restored to the King. An indemnity was to be granted to all Royalists. As for religion, the Church of England, together with the Prayer Book and rule by bishops, was to be restored, provided all other Protestants (but not Catholics) were granted freedom of worship. These generous and statesmanlike terms were the work mainly of Cromwell and his son-in-law, Ireton. They were much more moderate than many members of the army desired, for among the rank and file extreme views were beginning to find favour. 'Honest John' Lilburne and his followers, known as Levellers, were preaching that as all men were equal, there was no need for a king at all, and everyone should have the vote; some even preached that all wealth should be divided equally between rich and poor. These views did not commend themselves to Cromwell, who believed in rich and poor, in upper, middle, and lower classes.

Charles rejected the Heads of the Proposals. He was still playing for time and hoping for assistance from the Scots. In order to carry on his intrigues more freely, he escaped from Hampton Court in November, 1647, and fled to the Isle of Wight. There the governor lodged him in Carisbrooke Castle, half-guest and half-prisoner.

The Second Civil War (1648)

From his new abode Charles completed his negotiations with the Scots, who hated the anti-Presbyterian rule of the army. The Scots undertook to send an army to restore the

King's authority, and Charles, in return, promised to establish Presbyterianism in England for three years. The scattered Royalists throughout England planned to rise at the same time. By May, 1648, the Second Civil War had broken out, with revolts in Wales, Kent, and Essex, and a Scottish army beginning its march through the Lake District into Lancashire.

THE TRIAL OF CHARLES I

The King's intrigues united, for the time being, the army and the English Parliament. Republican sentiment, especially in the army, increased, and the Council of Officers declared its intention "to call Charles Stuart, that man of blood, to an account for the blood he had shed." While Fairfax swept the eastern counties, Cromwell put down the rising in South Wales and then marched north into Yorkshire. He crossed the Pennines and threw his forces on the straggling line of Scots who were marching through Lancashire. At the Battle of Preston (August, 1648) the main Scottish force was defeated, and in the next few days the rest were rounded up. With the defeat of the Scots the remaining Royalists surrendered, and the Second Civil War was over.

The Execution of Charles I (January, 1649)

The Second Civil War, short though it had been, produced embittered feelings. Parliament was still inclined to negotiate with the King, but the army resolved otherwise. In December, 1648, one of the army leaders, Colonel Pride, went to the House with a regiment of soldiers, and excluded about one hundred and fifty Presbyterians from any further

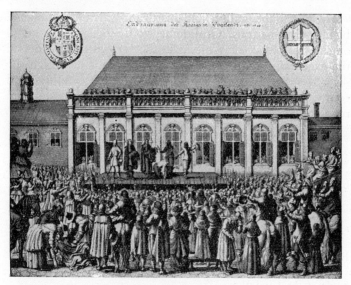

THE EXECUTION OF CHARLES I

Charles insisted on wearing two shirts lest any shivering on his part through cold should be mistaken for trembling.

sittings. 'Pride's Purge' transformed the Commons into a mere 'Rump' of fifty or sixty Independents.

The army, working through the Rump, now appointed a High Court of Justice to try the King for treason against the people. When the few remaining members of the House of Lords refused to participate, the Rump abolished the Upper House altogether. Of the 135 persons appointed to the High Court, less than half attended the trial, which took place in Westminster Hall. Throughout the proceedings Charles, with perfect dignity, refused to defend himself, rightly maintaining that the Court was an illegal creation and lacked power to try him.

G

The King smiled at the reading of his charge, and after reading of it, demanded of the lord president, by what lawful authority he was brought thither. Being answered, in the name of the commons of England: he replied, he saw no lords there, which should make a Parliament, including the King.

He was found guilty, and his death-warrant was signed by fifty-eight persons. On January 30, 1649, he was executed outside his palace of Whitehall. The crowd that witnessed the execution groaned when the executioner held high the severed head. Charles met his death with calmness and courage—unshaken to the end in those ideas of kingship and religion which he had held throughout his reign.

QUESTIONS AND EXERCISES

1. Describe and illustrate the respective advantages enjoyed by the two sides during the Civil War.

2. Give an account of the activities of the Scots (1642–1649).

3. In what ways did Oliver Cromwell help to win the war against the King?

4. Explain clearly and describe the rivalry between the English Parliament and the army.

5. On an outline-map of England put in the chief battle-fields of the Civil War.

6. Do you think the execution of Charles I was justified? Give your reasons.

CHAPTER XIV

OLIVER CROMWELL AND THE COMMONWEALTH

A New Form of Government

SOON after the King's execution the Rump Parliament passed laws establishing a Commonwealth, or Republic, throughout the British Isles and its overseas possessions. The monarchy and the House of Lords were abolished. The government was vested in Parliament (represented by the Rump—a mere fifty members out of the original Commons of 1640) and a Council of State of forty-one members, mostly members of Parliament or army officers. This government was far from democratic. A general election would have returned a different sort of Parliament, while a vote of the whole people would certainly have favoured a restoration of the monarchy in the person of Prince Charles, the elder son of Charles I. A book called *Eikon Basilike*, describing the meditations of Charles I before his execution and supposed to have been written by the King himself (though really by a Royalist who later became Bishop of Worcester), proved so popular that the Council of State employed its Latin secretary, the poet John Milton, to answer it in his *Eikonoklastes*.

OLIVER CROMWELL
From the National Portrait Gallery, London.

Despite the new constitution, real power lay with Cromwell's army, a well-disciplined force of 50,000 men attracted by generous rates of pay. The army alone stood between the newly established Commonwealth and its many foes. Royalist sentiment was widespread but dared not raise its head. Even parts of the army were disaffected, arguing that the Commonwealth did not go far enough in establishing equality. Cromwell quickly put down these Levellers and then turned to Ireland, which was in rebellion. The Irish and Scots occupied his attention till the end of 1651.

Ireland under the Commonwealth

In Ireland all classes united under the Royalist Lord Lieutenant, the Duke of Ormonde, to oppose the newly established Commonwealth. The Catholic peasantry hated the Puritanical rule of the New Model and its execution of a king with High Church views; the Anglican landlords believed in Divine Right and the established Church of England; the Presbyterian Scots in Ulster hated the Independent views of the new English government. Soon most of Ireland was in Royalist hands, and Dublin itself was besieged.

In August, 1649, Cromwell landed in Ireland with over 10,000 Ironsides. He was grimly determined to quell the rebellion and avenge the massacre of Protestants in the Catholic revolt of 1641. In September he stormed Drogheda and massacred soldiers and priests in cold blood. Probably over 2000 men were thus slaughtered. Cromwell tried to justify his action on the twofold plea that he was avenging '1641' and that his cruelty was the quickest way of ending the rebellion. He wrote to the Speaker of the Commons:

> I am persuaded that this is a righteous judgment of God upon these barbarous wretches, who have imbrued their hands in so much innocent blood; and that it will tend to prevent the effusion of blood for the future. Which are the satisfactory grounds to such actions, which otherwise cannot but work remorse and regret.

Despite his "satisfactory grounds," the massacre at Drogheda remains one of the blackest stains on Cromwell's character. A similar, though less deliberate, massacre followed the capture of Wexford in October, 1649. Soon the coalition of forces against the Commonwealth began to break up, and in May, 1650, Cromwell was recalled to deal with the situation in Scotland. He left his son-in-law, Ireton, behind him, and the subjection of Ireland was completed by 1652. In Leinster and Munster nearly one-third of the population had perished.

For the rest of the period Ireland was quiet. Cromwell united the Parliaments of England and Ireland and introduced free trade between the two countries. He tried to stamp out Catholicism and confiscated Irish lands for his soldiers and other Protestant settlers. Like many before and after him, he failed to solve the Irish problem. The peasantry remained Catholic, and the Protestant planters were regarded as heretics and robbers.

Cromwell and the Scots

In Scotland opposition to the Commonwealth was based upon two facts: the execution of a Stuart king and the Presbyterian hatred of an Independent army.

Several attempts were made to restore Prince Charles to the throne. The first was by the old Cavalier leader, the Earl of Montrose, who returned from exile to raise the Highland clans. The Covenanters, or Scottish Presbyterians, would have none of Montrose and his Cavaliers. They hunted him down and hanged him in Edinburgh (May, 1650). Charles, who was negotiating with the Covenanters, did nothing to save his devoted follower.

Soon afterwards Charles landed in Scotland and took the Covenant, promising to continue Presbyterianism in Scotland and to establish it in England. His promises were probably as worthless as his father's; his aim was to regain his throne, no matter how, and then to pursue his own policy. The Scots proclaimed Charles King and prepared an army for the invasion of England. Cromwell was quickly dispatched to nip the movement in the bud; he marched north by the east-coast route, keeping in touch with his fleet as he went. He found the Scottish forces, under David Leslie, firmly entrenched in front of Edinburgh, and he fell back to Dunbar. His army was in a most dangerous situation. Food-supplies were running short, and the Scots occupied the

BOSCOBEL HOUSE

Here Charles found a brief hiding-place after the Battle of Worcester, and here, according to legend, hid in the oak tree while Puritans searched beneath.

Frith & Co. Ltd.

Lammermuir Hills, which penned the English army close to the sea-coast. Leslie's policy was to wait for the weakening of Cromwell's forces, but the Presbyterian ministers who filled his camp urged him to descend at once to the plains for battle. "The Lord hath delivered them into our hands!" exclaimed Cromwell, as the Scottish forces descended. The Battle of Dunbar (September 3, 1650) was a complete victory for Cromwell, who proceeded to occupy Edinburgh and to attempt the conversion of the Scots from their Presbyterian 'errors.' Failing in this, he moved towards Perth to subdue the Highlands.

Prince Charles now seized his opportunity. He collected another army and invaded England by the western route through Lancashire. Few English Royalists joined him, as the Scots were still 'foreigners.' Cromwell hurried back through Yorkshire and the Midlands and overtook Charles at Worcester. On the anniversary of Dunbar (September 3, 1651) Cromwell again defeated the Scots. The Battle of Worcester (referred to by Cromwell as his "crowning mercy") finished the Scottish resistance. Charles himself escaped, despite the notices offering a reward for the capture of "a tall, dark young man above two yards high." After many adventures, including his famous concealment in the oak-tree, he took boat from Brighton to France.

An army of occupation under General Monk kept Scotland quiet for the remainder of Cromwell's life. Like Ireland, its Parliament was united with the English Parliament and its separate trade-system abolished. Like Ireland, too, it was never reconciled to the English Commonwealth and only waited its time to throw off the yoke.

Command of the Sea

Naval problems also faced the Commonwealth. Prince Rupert had collected a fleet and soon showed himself as dashing a sailor as he had been a soldier. For two years he preyed upon the merchant-ships of the Commonwealth before he met his match in Robert Blake. Blake was formerly a Bridgwater merchant who had distinguished himself at the siege of Taunton in the Civil War. Till the age of fifty he had never been to sea; but he showed himself even more adaptable than Rupert and became one of the greatest of English admirals. The Commonwealth had reorganized and improved the navy, and Blake drove Rupert's ships into the Mediterranean, whither he followed and destroyed them. This was the first appearance of English warships in these waters.

The First Dutch War (1652–1654)

The revival of English naval power soon brought us into conflict with the Dutch, who, during the quarrels between the first two Stuarts and their Parliaments, had become the leading carriers of the world's trade (see Chapter X). In 1651 the Rump Parliament passed an important Navigation Act, which stated that all goods brought to England or her colonies should be carried in English or colonial ships or the ships of the country where the goods were actually produced. This Act was clearly directed against the Dutch, for Dutch ships could now bring to England only Dutch goods, and the thriving Dutch trade in English colonial goods was consequently destroyed (see pp. 292–293).

The Dutch refused to take the new law lying down, and when England demanded also that foreign ships should salute the English flag in English waters, the Dutch refused, and war broke out. For two years (1652–1654) the English fleet under Robert Blake fought the Dutch under Van Tromp. The latter defeated Blake off Dungeness in 1652, but Blake soon regained command of the Channel by defeating his great adversary in a three days' battle off Portland (1653). So long as Blake controlled the Channel, through which the Dutch ships passed to and from home, the issue was never in doubt. In 1654 the Dutch were compelled to accept our terms, namely, acquiescence in the Navigation Act and the English right of salute in home waters. The decline of Holland as a commercial power had begun, although two further Dutch Wars had to be fought in the following reign before English supremacy was assured. The resources of Holland were proving too small against her new competitors.

The Dutch War had not been altogether popular. Cromwell and the army opposed a war against the leading Protestant power on the Continent, and the nation as a whole grumbled about the heavy taxation that resulted. In the middle of the war the rule of the Rump had been brought to an end in dramatic circumstances.

Cromwell's Dismissal of the Rump (1653)

After the battle of Worcester Cromwell and the army felt free to turn to matters of government. The Rump was very unpopular. A mere fifty or so members out of the original Commons of the Long Parliament of 1640, it could no longer claim to represent the wishes of the country. It attracted the hatred of all the enemies of the Commonwealth and even of

CROMWELL DISSOLVING THE LONG PARLIAMENT

some of its friends. The cost of Cromwell's army and the reorganization of Blake's navy necessitated high taxation, which was still further increased by the Dutch War. The army desired a more 'Protestant' foreign policy than the Dutch War signified, and demanded a wider measure of religious toleration than the Rump had provided. The last straw was a scheme, brought forward by the self-important members of the Rump, of perpetuating their own existence and allowing them to fill any vacancies that occurred at their own discretion. With a company of soldiers Cromwell went down to the House, upbraided the members, and expelled them by force.

"You are no Parliament!" he exclaimed. "I say you are no Parliament. Come, come, we have had enough of this; I will put an end to your prating." Catching sight of the Speaker's Mace, the emblem of Parliament's authority, he continued, "What shall we do with this bauble? Here, take it away!"

With the expulsion of the Rump (April, 1653) the last survivors of the Long Parliament disappeared, and the military dictatorship of Cromwell's army was undisguised.

Constitutional Experiments

For the remainder of his lifetime Cromwell was the real ruler of England. He ardently desired to win the confidence of the people and rule by their consent, but he realized that a freely elected Parliament would contain a majority of his enemies, probably of enemies of the Commonwealth itself. The Royalists would wish to restore Church and king, the Presbyterians to establish Presbyterianism and persecute the sects, the Levellers and other extremists (who numerically were a small minority, but had considerable influence in the army) to introduce much more democratic forms of government. In the resulting confusion the Scots and Irish would strike for independence once more. In truth Cromwell alone at this period stood between settled government and anarchy. Herein lies the justification of his military dictatorship, which was more despotic than the very monarchy which had recently been overthrown.

In July, 1653, Cromwell's first Parliament met. The Independent and Baptist congregations throughout the country had sent in lists of 'godly men,' and from these and other sources the Council of State selected 140 'saints' to constitute a Parliament. From the name of the first member on its list, 'Praise-God' Barebone, a London leather-merchant, it has passed into history under the name of Barebone's Parliament. The 'saints' set about their task with enthusiasm and many good ideas, but they lacked practical experience and quarrelled with one another and with Cromwell. Early one morning a moderate group met and, with Cromwell's approval, brought the 'rule of the saints' to an end (December, 1653).

In the same month the army officers drew up a regular constitution called the 'Instrument of Government.' The Commonwealth was to be governed by a Lord Protector with the help of a Council of State composed mainly of officers. A Parliament of one House was to meet for at least five months every three years with the power of passing laws and granting taxes. It was to consist of 400 English, 30 Scottish, and 30 Irish members, but Royalists and Roman Catholics were debarred either from voting or from being elected.

In January, 1654, Cromwell (dressed in black to indicate the civilian nature of the new Government) was solemnly inducted as Lord Protector. His first Protectorate Parliament was not due to meet till September 3, and for nine months the new Protector and his Council applied themselves vigorously to the work of clearing up the confusion left by the Civil Wars. When Parliament met fresh quarrels immediately broke out. Despite the exclusion of a hundred Republicans who refused to promise allegiance to the Protectorate, the remainder soon began to discuss Cromwell's powers, to press for a reduction of the army, to oppose religious toleration, and to criticize the Instrument of Government. In January, 1655, Cromwell angrily dismissed his first Protectorate Parliament.

Cromwell's difficulties encouraged his enemies, and in March, 1655, a Royalist rising under Penruddock took place at Salisbury. It was easily suppressed, but Cromwell decided on stern measures to prevent further outbreaks. He divided the country into ten districts, each under a major-general supported by a special military force. The expenses were to be met out of a special tax of ten per cent. levied on Royalist incomes. All this was quite illegal, even under the constitution as it stood. The rule of the major-generals was efficient but extremely unpopular. They suppressed all kinds of popular amusements and pastimes, and twelve months of their government confirmed most Englishmen in their hatred of military rule and Puritanical interference.

In September, 1656, Cromwell summoned his second Protectorate Parliament. Again the Protector excluded a hundred of the more discontented members. The rest criticized Cromwell's illegal actions of the previous year; but recognizing the need for a settled form of government, they drew up a new constitution called the 'Humble Petition and Advice' (March, 1657). In many ways it was a return to the past. Cromwell was offered the title of king, but this he refused, foreseeing strong opposition from the army if he accepted. He continued therefore as Protector, but with more pomp and splendour, and with the important additional powers of naming his own successor and of nominating an Upper House of Parliament.

In January, 1658, the second Protectorate Parliament met for its second session. Cromwell's strongest supporters in the previous House of Commons had been raised to the new Upper House, and the hundred members that had previously been excluded were allowed to return to the Commons. The reconstituted Commons soon began to attack the powers of the Upper House, and in February, 1658, Cromwell once more dissolved his Parliament in anger. "The Lord judge between you and me," he told the members.

This was Cromwell's last Parliament. By September, 1658, the Lord Protector was dead. The problem of reconciling his own authority with government by consent remained unsolved to the end.

Cromwell's Domestic Policy

From the dismissal of the Rump in 1653 till his death in 1658 Cromwell was the real ruler of England. After the confusion of the Civil Wars there was much to be done, and

Cromwell applied himself to his task with all the seriousness of purpose and high ideals, as well as with the shortcomings, of his Puritan character.

True to the Independent views he had long held, he allowed a large measure of religious toleration. All "God's people," by which he meant Puritans, were allowed to worship as they chose. Hence the ministry was filled with Independents, Baptists, and moderate Presbyterians—most of them earnest and sober men, who performed their parochial duties conscientiously. The Jews, who had been excluded from England since the reign of Edward I (1290), were allowed to return. A new religious sect, the Quakers, or Society of Friends, grew up during these years. It had been founded by George Fox at the end of the Civil Wars, and its members aimed at a return to the primitive purity of the Christian religion. They believed in non-resistance to evil and refused to take part in any wars whatsoever. They avoided outward ceremonies, teaching that true religion sprang, not from the forms of worship, but from the spirit that dwelt in every man. Although never large in numbers, the Quakers from their earliest days have exercised an important influence upon the life of the nation.

Cromwell's toleration did not extend to every religion. The Book of Common Prayer was abolished, and Anglicans and Roman Catholics were forbidden to worship in public. The Protector's motives were partly religious and partly political, and so long as Anglicans and Catholics were loyal to the Commonwealth they were sometimes allowed to continue their meetings in private.

In some respects the Protector's rule was the reverse of tolerant. Puritanical interference in the everyday life of the nation reached under him its highest point. The major-generals of 1655 were closely associated with this policy. They abolished most of the pastimes of 'merrie England,' and men and women were forced to forgo the theatre, cock-fighting, bear-baiting, horse-racing, and even country dancing. Ale-houses were closely regulated, and drunkenness was severely punished. The Sabbath, the only free day for the bulk of the population, was strictly enforced as a day of rest and worship. It is small wonder that this grandmotherly interference provoked strong resentment, and led, when the rule of the Puritans was over, to an even more foolish outburst of gaiety and frivolity under Charles II.

Cromwell and his advisers held progressive views on education and law, though much of what they did was undone at the Restoration. Education was encouraged, and a beginning was made in the establishment of a new university at Durham for the north of England. Legal procedure was simplified and cheapened, and the number of capital offences reduced.

The Protector was as despotic as any Tudor or Stuart king, and on one occasion he imprisoned judges and lawyers who questioned his right to levy customs duties without Parliamentary consent. But he worked earnestly and with much enlightenment for the welfare of his country, regarding himself as God's agent in carrying out the Divine Will. His theory of toleration excluded large masses of his countrymen, but it was the widest measure of toleration so far granted in our history and provided a valuable opportunity for the growth of those Nonconformist sects which have exerted a steadying influence upon our national life.

Cromwell's Foreign Policy

"Cromwell's greatness at home was a mere shadow of his greatness abroad," wrote the Royalist historian, Lord Clarendon, in his *History of the Great Rebellion*. If greatness is measured by military and naval exploits, then the judgment must be accepted.

Cromwell's foreign aims were three: to prevent Prince Charles from obtaining help, to promote the expansion of English commerce, and to champion the cause of Protestantism. In pursuit of these aims a vigorous foreign policy was pursued, reminding us of the days of Queen Elizabeth and contrasting sharply with the ineffectiveness of English policy under James I and Charles I.

In 1654 Cromwell brought the Dutch War to an end on terms favourable to England. He was anxious to make peace with the leading Protestant country on the Continent so as to form an alliance among the chief Protestant powers of Europe. He tried to unite England, Holland, Denmark, Sweden, and the north German princes into a Protestant League; but his efforts were not successful. In truth, much of Cromwell's foreign policy was based on assumptions that no longer held good. With the end of the Thirty Years' War at the Peace of Westphalia (1648) the era of religious warfare had passed away, and a new era of territorial and commercial warfare was beginning. Thus two Protestant states (England and Holland) were vying with each other for commercial supremacy, and two Catholic states (Spain and France) for the leadership of Europe. Cromwell lived in a period of transition and cannot altogether be blamed for sometimes looking backward instead of forward.

In 1655, in pursuance of his plan for extending English commerce (a plan, be it noted, that definitely looked to the future), two naval expeditions set sail from England. Admiral Blake sailed to Tunis, burnt the Barbary corsair fleet that had preyed upon English commerce, and laid the foundations of English naval supremacy in the Mediterranean. The other expedition, under the elder William Penn, was in the Elizabethan tradition—to attack the Spanish possessions in the West Indies. Cromwell had demanded of the Spanish ambassador that Englishmen should be allowed to trade freely with Spanish America and to exercise their Protestant religion in those parts, and the astonished ambassador had replied, "It is to ask for my master's two eyes!" Hence Spain became, in Cromwell's words, our "natural enemy," and Penn's expedition was dispatched. An attack upon the large island of San Domingo failed miserably, the soldiers fleeing from a mere handful of half-blacks that rushed at them from the forests. The expedition then sailed to Jamaica, which was only lightly held by the Spaniards, and succeeded in capturing it (1655). Jamaica is still the largest of our West Indian possessions.

Such actions naturally provoked Spain into declaring war. On the Continent Spain and France were still fighting each other in what was really the aftermath of the Thirty Years' War. Cromwell's obvious ally therefore was Catholic France, but he exacted a price that fitted in well with his Protestant policy. The Duke of Savoy, on the south-eastern border of France, had commenced a savage massacre of his Vaudois subjects, whose Protestantism went back to long before the Reformation. Cromwell obliged France to exert pressure to bring these massacres to an end, while Milton, who acted at times as Cromwell's secretary, gave vent to popular feeling in one of his noblest sonnets beginning:

> Avenge, O Lord, thy slaughtered saints whose bones
> Lie scattered on the Alpine mountains cold.

This was in 1655, and by the following year the stage was set for the Spanish War, with France and England in alliance.

Blake, as usual, was the English naval hero. In 1656 he captured a Spanish treasure-fleet in the Atlantic, and in 1657 he chased another Spanish fleet into the harbour of Santa Cruz in the Canaries and, despite the gunfire of the Spanish shore-batteries, succeeded in destroying it. The intrepid 'soldier-turned-sailor' died on the return journey as his ship entered Plymouth Sound (August, 1657). In the following year it was the turn of the soldiers. Six thousand red-coated Ironsides helped the French to defeat a Spanish force at the Battle of the Dunes, among the sandy flats near Dunkirk. As a result Dunkirk, part of the Spanish Netherlands fell into allied hands. Before the end of the year Cromwell died (September 3, 1658), but when peace was made in 1659

Dunkirk remained in English hands as a visible token of the prowess of English arms under the Protector.

Cromwell's foreign policy has been much criticized. He engaged in war when perhaps the truest interests of the country demanded peace. His idea of a Protestant alliance was out of date, and by helping France against Spain he was aiding a future enemy fast-growing in power against an old one that was declining. His wars also entailed high taxation that did much to turn the merchant and middle classes against him. All this is true. But few, if any, in his time could foresee the depths to which Spain would sink or the heights to which France would rise. And no one can deny that his vigorous naval and commercial policy promoted the true interests of England, which lay in overseas trade and colonization.

The End of the Commonwealth

Cromwell's death on September 3, 1658—the anniversary of Dunbar and Worcester—ushered in a period of confusion. Oliver had named his son, Richard, as his successor, but the new Lord Protector was an unambitious country gentleman, more interested in sport than in affairs of state. Moreover, he soon found that he lacked his father's prestige in his dealings with the powerful army officers. In January, 1659, he summoned a Parliament, and immediately a quarrel began between its members and the officers over the important question of the control of the army. In April, 1659, the officers compelled Richard to dissolve his Parliament. They then recalled the Rump of the Long Parliament, which declared for a republic without a Protector or an Upper House. Richard Cromwell resigned his office in May, 1659, and at the Restoration he went into exile; he later returned to England, settled down in the country with his dogs and horses, and died in 1712. Meanwhile the army and Rump had begun to quarrel, and the army once more dissolved the Rump (October, 1659).

By this time the inability or unwillingness of the army to provide a settled form of government was apparent to all. The Royalists were in revolt, the Presbyterians and Scots hated the arrogance of the army chiefs, while moderate opinion everywhere realized that the restoration of the monarchy offered the best hope of putting an end to a state of uncertainty that was fast degenerating into anarchy. Strangely enough, a leader appeared in the army itself to focus the prevailing discontent. This was General Monk, a moderate-minded soldier who commanded the army of occupation in Scotland. With the moral and financial support of the Scots, Monk crossed the border in January, 1660, and as he marched south he realized that a restoration of the monarchy was the ardent desire of the majority of Englishmen.

Monk's first step on reaching London was to restore the full Long Parliament, so far as its members still survived. After arranging for a general election, the Long Parliament dissolved itself in March, 1660—thus fulfilling, after twenty years, its own demand not to be dissolved without its own consent. The new Parliament (called a Convention Parliament, because it was summoned without royal authority) met later in the same month. Monk was already in communication with Charles in Holland, and on Monk's advice Charles issued the Declaration of Breda (April, 1660). It contained four promises: a general pardon, subject to any exceptions that Parliament itself might make; "liberty to tender consciences," by which was meant freedom of worship so long as the peace of the country were not disturbed; a settlement by Parliament of questions of land-purchase arising out of the war; and arrears of pay for the army. The Convention Parliament accepted these terms and proclaimed Charles King. On May 29, 1660, on his thirtieth birthday, Charles II entered London amid tremendous enthusiasm, "the ways strewed with flowers, the bells ringing, the streets hung with tapestry, and the fountains running with wine," as John Evelyn's *Diary* informs us.

QUESTIONS AND EXERCISES

1. Describe the various attempts under the Commonwealth to establish a constitutional form of government. Why were they unsuccessful?

2. Describe Cromwell's foreign policy. Do you agree that it was already out of date?

3. Give an account of the career of Robert Blake.

4. To what did Cromwell refer by the following remarks:

   (a) "The Lord hath delivered them into our hands."

   (b) "A crowning mercy."

   (c) "What shall we do with this bauble? Here, take it away!"

   (d) "The Lord judge between you and me."

5. Write notes on: Levellers, Quakers, Navigation Act, Declaration of Breda.

6. What were (a) the general causes, (b) the immediate events, that produced the Restoration?

7. Summarize the main facts in the relations between England and Scotland (1640–1660).

CHAPTER XV

EUROPEAN SURVEY (IV): THE AGE OF
LOUIS XIV

Chief Rulers

Louis XIV	(France)	1643–1715
Charles II	(England)	1660–1685
James II	(England)	1685–1688
William III	(England)	1689–1702
Anne	(England)	1702–1714
Charles II	(Spain)	1665–1700
Philip V	(Spain)	1700–1746
Frederick William, The Great Elector	(Prussia)	1640–1688
Frederick I	(Prussia)	1688–1713
Charles XII	(Sweden)	1697–1718
Peter the Great	(Russia)	1689–1724

General Survey

The period 1660–1715 is aptly called 'the Age of Louis XIV.' Louis ascended the French throne in 1643 at the age of four, but until 1660 France was governed by Cardinal Mazarin, who continued Richelieu's policy of centralizing the government under royal control and of extending the power and influence of France abroad. From 1660 till his death in 1715 Louis was the dominant personality in European politics, and France occupied the foremost place in the affairs of Europe.

The growing power of France coincided with the decline of the Empire and of Spain. Germany was exhausted as a result of the Thirty Years' War, and Spain had failed to adapt herself to changing conditions. Her kings were mediocre, and when, in 1700, the Spanish royal house came to an end, the rulers of Europe gathered round like vultures to divide and devour the prey. The only Continental power that could withstand France was Holland, but she had not the resources to oppose for long both the military might of

France and the commercial power of England, and by the end of the period the star of Holland had obviously set. The position of England in the European rivalries was at first not clear. Both Charles II and James II were Catholics and also cousins of the French King. They therefore desired the friendship of their powerful relative—a desire which led to the same end as England's commercial rivalry with Holland. But although religious antagonisms had declined, they had by no means disappeared, and Louis XIV of France appeared to most Englishmen as another Philip II of Spain, to be opposed as naturally as their forefathers under Elizabeth had opposed the Spanish menace. After James II had been turned off the English throne in 1688, England and Holland joined forces under William of Orange to oppose France.

The Leadership of France

For more than a century after the accession of Louis XIV France was the pattern of European civilization. European manners, dress, art, literature, science, furniture—in fact all the varied elements of modern civilization—were based upon those of France. French civilization in this period was often too artificial for modern tastes, but its perfection in its own sphere cannot be doubted.

Inside France the position of the King was unchallenged. Richelieu and Mazarin had destroyed the power of the French nobility, and the French Parliament, or States-General, had fallen into disuse. Louis XIV is supposed to have made the famous remark, "L'état c'est moi" ("I am the state"). Whether he actually used those words or no, they sum up accurately his position in the state. At enormous cost to the French tax-payer, Louis built for himself the Palace of Versailles, near Paris. There he held his court with every splendour imaginable. The arts and sciences were patronized, the French nobility left their country estates to bathe in the genial rays of 'Le Roi Soleil,' and statesmen and ambassadors decided peace or war and redrew the boundaries of Europe. Louis was vanity personified; but he took his 'trade of a king' seriously and worked many hours daily on affairs of state.

France under Louis XIV

From 1661 to 1683 Louis' chief minister for domestic affairs was Colbert, who applied himself particularly to improving the French financial and economic system. French finances were in a very bad state. The nobility and the higher clergy were exempt from taxation, officials were corrupt and pocketed much of the public money, and the tax-payer paid far more than went into the government's coffers owing to the system of contracting and sub-contracting out the collection of taxes. Colbert succeeded in remedying many of these evils for the time being, but was unable to subject the upper classes to taxation.

Colbert took the prevailing mercantile view that commerce, agriculture, and industry should be organized to increase the strength of the country (see Chapters IX and XX). Hence native industries were protected by the placing of taxes upon foreign imports, and bounties were given to encourage native exports. Roads and canals were built, numerous local barriers to trade were swept away, industries were encouraged, and overseas trade was increased. Colbert was particularly keen upon French colorization, which, in the seventeenth century, had proceeded apace. In 1608 Champlain had founded Quebec, and French Canada can be said to have begun. In Louis XIV's reign the great French explorer, La Salle, explored the Mississippi valley, which he named Louisiana in honour of his King. Colbert founded trading-companies and increased the French navy, but after his death in 1683 Louis XIV undid much of the good work of his great finance minister. By the end of Louis' reign the French financial system was once more rotten, and the French King's neglect of commerce and colonization in favour of more spectacular military campaigns had weakened France for the colonial struggle with England in the eighteenth century.

Few things illustrate Louis' attitude to domestic affairs better than his policy towards the Huguenots, who, under the Edict of Nantes, still enjoyed freedom of worship. While Colbert lived the Huguenots had been safe, as they included some of the most industrious and skilful of French artisans. But Louis was a bigoted Catholic, and in 1685 he revoked the Edict of Nantes. The Huguenots were now forbidden to practise their religion, and about 300,000 of them emigrated to England, Holland, and Prussia, where they strengthened anti-Catholic feeling and introduced their industries and trades. In England they commenced the silk-industry of Spitalfields, just outside London (see p. 289).

Louis XIV's Foreign Policy

Louis XIV aimed at extending the boundaries of France and making himself master of Europe. His numerous attempts to reach the River Rhine brought him into conflict with the countries along his eastern frontier—with Spain (which possessed the Spanish Netherlands and Franche Comté), with the Empire, and with Holland. Both Spain and the Empire were declining, and the task of opposing Louis fell mainly upon the Dutch, who were ably led by William of Orange, the great-grandson of William the Silent. Time after time the Dutch stood between Louis and victory, and the proud French King regarded his Protestant and Republican foe with implacable hatred.

Louis' ambitions led France into four great wars. The French King was served by some of the ablest men of his day, by Louvois, his war minister, by Vauban, his military engineer, and by Condé and Turenne, his generals. From 1667 to 1668 Louis engaged in the War of Devolution, when by a legal fiction he claimed the whole of the Spanish Netherlands for his Spanish wife. He was thwarted by the Dutch and by the formation of the Triple Alliance between

England, Holland, and Sweden. Thereafter Louis aimed at detaching England from Holland, which he did by the secret Treaty of Dover in 1670 (see pp. 233–235).

This led to the second of Louis' wars, the Dutch War from 1672 to 1678, when France faced a large coalition of European powers. For two years (the Third Dutch War, 1672–1674, p. 235) England aided France by attacking Holland, until the English Parliament forced Charles II to abandon his French ally. By the Treaty of Nymwegen (1678) the Dutch did not lose a foot of territory, but Spain had to give to France the important province of Franche Comté.

The next war, the War of the League of Augsburg or the English Succession (1689–1697), coincided with the accession of William of Orange to the English throne. During this war England wrested the control of the sea from France, and when peace was made at Ryswick in 1697, France gained nothing in territory and had to recognize William as King of England (see pp. 259–261).

The last of Louis' wars, the War of the Spanish Succession (1702–1713), was fought to decide the fate of the Spanish Empire, whose royal line had come to an end in 1700. It was concluded in 1713 by the Treaty of Utrecht (see Chapter XIX).

Louis XIV died in 1715 after a reign of seventy-two years. He had added to French territory along the eastern frontier; but his dream of reaching the Rhine and dominating Europe remained unfulfilled. Moreover, he had neglected French interests overseas, and his military adventures and courtly extravagance bequeathed to his country a legacy of bankruptcy.

Prussia and Russia

Prussia—originally the electorate of Brandenburg—was ruled by the family of Hohenzollern. Frederick William, the Great Elector (1640–1688), was able, patriotic, and unscrupulous. He added to his dominions by the Treaty of

Westphalia (1648), extended his own personal authority by overriding the rights of his towns and nobles, and improved the economic resources of his possessions. He used the skill of about 20,000 Huguenots, who had fled from the persecutions of Louis XIV, to develop his country. His successor, Frederick (1688–1713), in return for his support of the imperial cause during the War of the Spanish Succession, extorted from the Emperor the title of King of Prussia.

At the same time the Czar Peter the Great (1689–1725) was laying the foundations of a new Russian Empire. He forced his backward subjects to adopt western habits of dress, dancing, social intercourse, and even personal appearance. Russians who refused to shave off their heavy beards were either taxed or forcibly deprived of them. But these reforms did little more than touch the surface of Russian life. For twenty years Peter waged war against Charles XII, the last of the warrior kings of Sweden, and when peace was made in 1721 he forced Sweden to yield valuable Baltic provinces along the Gulf of Finland. Thus Russia acquired her 'window on to the Baltic,' and the new town of St Petersburg arose to remind later generations of the Czar whose vigorous policy had found Russia her outlet to the sea.

England was little affected at the time by these changes in eastern Europe, but they were fraught with far-reaching consequences for the future. In the nineteenth century Prussia created the new German Empire, and the growing power of Russia was a nightmare to English statesmen.

QUESTIONS AND EXERCISES

1. Mention briefly the chief ways in which the reign of Louis XIV affected England.

2. Explain why English policy towards Louis XIV was more clearly defined after 1689 than before.

3. Write notes on: Colbert, the Great Elector, Peter the Great.

4. In what ways do you think the reign of Louis XIV illustrates the dangers of personal dictatorship?

CHAPTER XVI

CHARLES II AND THE RESTORATION

The Restoration (1660)

On his thirtieth birthday, May 29, 1660, Charles II entered London amid scenes of tremendous enthusiasm. Charles dated his reign from the year of his father's execution (1649), thus stigmatizing the period of the Commonwealth as an illegal usurpation. This was a pleasant enough fiction, but no one could pretend that the 'clock of history' could be so easily put back.

CHARLES II
Samuel Cooper

Much of the old order was naturally restored. The Crown once more directed English policy at home and abroad through ministers of its own appointment. The Church of England was also restored to its previous position of power and privilege, and in many a parish republicans and Puritans had to retire into obscurity in favour of squires and parsons of undoubted orthodoxy and loyalty. But the Long Parliament, the Civil War, and the Commonwealth had not been in vain. If King and Church were restored in 1660, so also to a great extent was Parliament, which had been scurvily treated by Cromwell and his army. Most of the laws passed by the Long Parliament in 1641 were not repealed, so that it was still illegal for the king to levy prerogative taxation or establish prerogative courts. The Triennial Act of 1641 (which had ensured the meeting of Parliament at least once every three years) was indeed repealed, but in 1664 it was again passed, without any machinery to make it effective. Moreover, although the restored Church of England indulged in bitter persecution of the Nonconformist sects for the next thirty years, it was found impossible to enforce religious uniformity upon the country. The sects had grown too strong, and the only solution eventually was to grant them toleration.

' The Merry Monarch '

The new King resembled his French mother rather than his martyred father. He was witty, gay, and charming, but

COSTUMES OF THE NOBILITY: TIME OF CHARLES II

lacked that devotion to a cause which had led his father to choose death rather than renounce his principles. Charles II had spent nearly half of his thirty years in exile, and if he returned devoted to any cause at all, it was to the cause of self. He was determined never to go on his travels again, and succeeded, not only in keeping his throne for twenty-five years, but in finishing his reign in a stronger position than he had begun it. In matters of business he was lazy and easy-going, but where his own personal position was concerned he was astute and adaptable. He trod cautiously and was ever ready to draw back if he overstepped the mark.

Thus his religious sympathies were Roman Catholic, and he desired toleration for the Catholic faith; but he kept his religious views a secret and pursued his Catholic aims with great caution.

After the 'rule of the saints' England swung to the other extreme, and amusements of every sort flourished. The moral tone of the nation sank very low, and sober-minded Nonconformists and others were aghast. The King himself led the country in its reaction against Puritanism. His life abroad had demoralized him, and he returned to England devoid of high principles or even of ordinary morality. The Court was corrupt, and women like Lady Castlemaine and the Duchess of Portsmouth exercised an evil influence. Charles II has passed into history as 'the merry monarch,' and the Restoration period has become a byword for frivolity and licence.

The Restoration Settlement

The Convention Parliament had recalled Charles on the basis of the four promises contained in the Declaration of Breda (see p. 214). Charles himself was easy-going and chose as his chief adviser a man of moderate, though naturally of Royalist and Anglican, views. This was Edward Hyde, who, twenty years before, had supported Hampden over ship-money and the Long Parliament over its impeachment of Strafford and its attack on the prerogative powers of the Crown. But Hyde had quarrelled with Parliament over the Root and Branch Bill and the Grand Remonstrance, and thereafter he had acted as the trusted adviser of Charles I during the Civil War and of Charles II during his exile. Charles II now made him Lord Chancellor with the title of the Earl of Clarendon, and the ties between King and minister were soon strengthened by the marriage of Anne Hyde, Clarendon's daughter, to James, Duke of York, the King's brother.

In 1660 the Convention Parliament passed an Act of

Indemnity and Oblivion granting a general pardon to all except actual regicides, *i.e.*, those who had signed the death-warrant of Charles I. Thirteen of these, together with one other person, were put to death, while the bodies of Cromwell, Ireton, and Bradshaw were dug up from Westminster Abbey, hanged at Tyburn, and buried beneath the gallows. The regicides thus became the scapegoats for all other rebels, and their execution closed the account.

Mindful, perhaps, of the fatal refusal of the Long Parliament to pay the New Model their wages, the Convention Parliament took care to honour the promise to pay the army its arrears. Most of the soldiers thereupon returned to civil life and quickly settled down. Charles was allowed to retain about five thousand soldiers, of whom Monk's regiment, the Coldstream Guards, was the most important. Monk himself was created Duke of Albemarle and continued in command. This was the beginning of the English standing army—a small force compared with the armies kept by despotic monarchs on the Continent. Fortunately for English liberties, the Royalists distrusted armed forces so much after their experience of Oliver Cromwell that they resisted all attempts on the part of Charles and his successors to enlarge the standing army.

The settlement of the land question raised wide and complicated questions of vested interests, as much land had changed hands during the Commonwealth. It was decided eventually that all Crown and Church lands should be restored, without compensation to the existing owners; likewise with respect to Royalist lands which had been definitely confiscated by the Puritans. But where Royalists had sold their acres to help the King or to pay the heavy fines inflicted upon them after the Civil War, the new owners were to retain possession, even though the land had often changed hands at ridiculously low prices. Many Royalists felt aggrieved at this and, remembering the generous pardon extended to ex-rebels, complained bitterly that the Act of

Indemnity and Oblivion was one of indemnity for the King's enemies and oblivion for his friends.

The final promise of the Declaration of Breda, namely, a generous settlement of the religious question, was left for the next Parliament to settle—with, as we shall see, distinctly unfortunate results. Before it dispersed, however, the Convention re-enacted the Navigation Act of 1651, with the important addition that the colonies should first send certain enumerated goods (including sugar and tobacco) to England before being passed on to the Continent. A settlement of the royal income was also arrived at and was confirmed by later Parliaments. The King agreed to give up certain traditional feudal dues and was granted taxes to make his income up to £1,200,000 a year. This sum was not always realized in actual fact, and as it had to cover the cost of government as well as the King's own personal expenses, it was not really sufficient even in time of peace. Consequently the King was still financially dependent upon Parliament, unless he could find (as Charles II often succeeded in doing) alternative sources of income.

The Religious 'Settlement'

In 1661 the first lawful General Election since 1640 returned the Cavalier Parliament (1661–1679), whose members it has been said were "more zealous for royalty than the King, more zealous for episcopacy than the bishops." Parliament restored the control of the militia to the King (though opposing any increase in the small standing army) and declared passive obedience to the King's wishes to be the subject's duty in all circumstances. It then applied itself to the religious problem.

The Cavalier Parliament was fanatically Anglican and proceeded to exact vengeance upon the Puritans for their treatment of the Anglican Church during the Commonwealth. It did so by means of the four Acts known collectively as the Clarendon Code, though it is fair to say that neither the moderate Chancellor nor the easy-going King altogether approved of the severity of these measures.

In 1661 the Corporation Act stated that all members of the municipal corporations which governed the towns and which, in many cases, controlled the election of members of Parliament, must take the oath of passive obedience to the King and receive the Communion according to the rites of the Church of England. Thus the Puritans, especially the Presbyterians, were deprived of their hold over the towns and the House of Commons. In 1662 the Act of Uniformity stated that every clergyman must declare his "unfeigned consent and assent" to everything contained in the English Prayer Book, to which a number of alterations of an anti-Puritan nature had recently been made. About two thousand clergymen refused to conform and were deprived of their livings; their expulsion marked the beginning of Nonconformity in the strict sense of the word. To prevent these Nonconformists and others from continuing to hold their own religious meetings, or conventicles, the Conventicle Act of 1664 laid down severe penalties where more than five persons met together for any other service than that according to the Church of England. Finally in 1665 Parliament, which had removed to Oxford during the Plague, passed the Five Mile Act, occasioned largely by the jealousy felt towards the Nonconformist clergy who returned to London to minister to their flocks. Henceforth Nonconformist clergymen and schoolmasters were forbidden to come within five miles of any corporate town or of the place of their previous employment.

The vindictiveness of the Clarendon Code was a flagrant betrayal of Charles's promise of "liberty to tender consciences," though the King himself cannot be blamed for its harshness. Nonconformists of every kind—Baptists, Independents, and Quakers, as well as the Presbyterians who had helped Charles to regain his throne—were bitterly persecuted. The country gentlemen, in their capacity as Justices of the Peace, together with the Anglican parsons, exacted a stern revenge for the Puritan rule of the Commonwealth, and many offenders against the Code languished and even died in prison. John Bunyan, the tinker-preacher, spent twelve years in prison and wrote his immortal book, *Pilgrim's Progress*, in Bedford gaol; its account of the temptations and sufferings met with by Christian in his journey through life is a record, not only of the normal difficulties of the Christian life, but also of those specially applicable to Bunyan's own lifetime.

But the Nonconformists were too strong to be stamped out by persecution. Some of the wealthier Puritans, anxious to retain their wealth and political power, joined the Church of England; but they remained anxious to help their former co-religionists and became the basis of the later Whig party. Most Nonconformists, however, held fast to their faith. After 1689 they were granted religious freedom, but their continued exclusion from political power and from the numerous educational and social advantages enjoyed by members of the Church of England made them for the next two centuries a race apart. Unable to enter the professions, they devoted themselves to trade and industry and became one of the most prosperous sections of the community.

The Restoration in Scotland and Ireland

At the Restoration separate Parliaments for Scotland and Ireland were once more created, and free trade between those two countries and England was abolished.

Presbyterian Scotland now entered upon one of the most distressing periods in Scottish history. The Marquis of Argyll, the leader of the Presbyterians, was executed; the Covenant was burned by the hangman, and the rule of the bishops was restored. Over three hundred Scottish ministers refused to recognize episcopacy and were expelled from their livings. They and their Presbyterian followers were subjected to even worse persecution than the Nonconformists in England, even torture by 'the Boot' being used against them.

In the south-west of Scotland the Covenanters, known as Whigamores or Whigs, were strong in numbers and continued their meetings, or conventicles, despite fierce persecution. For a time the Earl of Lauderdale, who governed Scotland, attempted reconciliation, but without success. In 1679 the Covenanters murdered Archbishop Sharp of St Andrews (a turncoat Presbyterian minister) and rose in revolt. The Duke of Monmouth, an illegitimate son of Charles II, defeated the Covenanters at Bothwell Bridge, near Glasgow (1679), but his leniency towards his defeated toes led to his recall. Under the King's brother, James, Duke of York, and John Graham of Claverhouse (Viscount Dundee) the persecution of the Covenanters was so fierce that the period following Bothwell Bridge is known in Scottish history as the 'killing-time.' Scotland remained discontented for the rest of the reign.

The story of Ireland is quite different. Here Ormonde, who became Lord-Lieutenant again, allowed the Catholics toleration, and Ireland enjoyed a period of religious peace. But the land-question continued as a source of trouble. Much of the land that Cromwell had confiscated was restored to its original owners, but much, too, was left in the hands of Cromwell's Protestant settlers. The result of this, added to the plantations under Elizabeth and James I, was that about two-thirds of the land of Ireland was held by Protestant usurpers.

Foreign Affairs under Clarendon (1660–1667)

Clarendon continued the Elizabethan and Cromwellian tradition of friendship with France and hostility to Spain. In 1661 he arranged a marriage between Charles II and Catherine of Braganza, the sister of the King of Portugal. Catherine's dowry to her husband consisted of the welcome sum of £800,000, together with Tangier and Bombay. The former proved too costly to garrison and was abandoned to the Moors in 1684. As for Bombay, Charles personally had

H

little use for it and presented it to the East India Company
for £10 a year. In 1662 Clarendon sold Cromwell's conquest
of Dunkirk to the French. It was a wise move, as it got rid
of what would have proved a troublesome possession; but
Clarendon incurred much unpopularity at the time and was
accused of pocketing some of the proceeds. As well as
obtaining a large sum in ready cash, Charles was also saved
the yearly garrison charge of £100,000.

Very soon commercial and colonial rivalry between England and Holland led to the Second Dutch War (1665–1667).
Already in 1664 the English had seized the Dutch colony of
the New Netherlands, in North America. By 1665 war was
officially declared and soon spread to European waters.
James, Duke of York, the King's brother, won a great victory
off Lowestoft in 1665, but in the following year the Dutch
de Ruyter defeated Prince Rupert and the Duke of Albemarle in the 'Four Days' Battle' in the Downs, off the North
Foreland. The war proved very costly for Charles. Parliament gave only niggardly supplies, and, to prevent the King
from mis-spending the money, appointed auditors to see that
the money was spent on the objects for which it had been
granted. This marked the beginning of the important check
on government expenditure known as appropriation of supplies. The government, being short of money and antici-
pating peace, laid up the fleet at Chatham. In June, 1667,
de Ruyter sailed unmolested up the Thames and burnt
many of the ships lying in the Medway. This was regarded
as a national disgrace, and many people compared Charles's
government unfavourably with the brave rule of Oliver
Cromwell. But the Dutch, who were involved in a war with
Louis XIV as well as with Charles II, were ready for peace.
By the Treaty of Breda (1667) England returned the Dutch
colony of Surinam on the South American coast, but retained the New Netherlands, whose capital, New Amsterdam, was renamed New York in honour of the King's
brother. The New Netherlands proved a useful addition to

our overseas possessions. They linked up the New England States in the north with Virginia in the south, and, by means

THE EARLIEST PICTURE OF NEW AMSTERDAM
Sketched by a Dutch officer in 1635.
From "A Graphic History of the United States" (Harrap)

of the Hudson valley, gave access to Canada and the interior.

Domestic Calamities

In 1665 London was visited by the bubonic plague, which killed about one-fifth of the city's population. It was produced by insanitary living-conditions, the narrow streets with their overhanging houses, and an abnormally dry winter and spring. The people, however, regarded it as a divine punishment for the wickedness of the times. The *Diary* of Samuel Pepys reveals the terrible nature of the visitation:

FLEEING FROM THE PLAGUE
After an old print

August 31 This month ends with great sadness upon the public, through the greatness of the plague everywhere through the kingdom almost. Every day sadder and sadder news of its increase. In the City died this week 7496, and of them 6102 of the plague. But it is feared that the true number of the dead this week is near 10,000; partly from the poor that cannot be taken notice of, through the greatness of the number, and partly from the Quakers and others that will not have any bell rung for them.

In the following year (1666) London suffered again, this time from the Great Fire, which raged for four days. Most of the City between the Tower and Temple Bar was laid in ashes, and the fire was only checked by the blowing up of houses in its path. In their bitterness the people blamed the government, the Roman Catholics, and even the French. The fire, however, did much good in cleansing the city and enabling a new start to be made. Sir Christopher Wren's plans for rebuilding London in an orderly manner were turned down; but St Paul's Cathedral and over fifty churches were rebuilt by him in the graceful and dignified Renaissance style (see Chapter XXI).

The Fall of Clarendon (1667)

By 1667 the dismissal of Clarendon was demanded. He was, quite absurdly, held responsible for the plague and the fire. The King had grown tired of his minister's sermons on the wickedness of the court, and wished to pursue a more Roman Catholic policy than Clarendon would sanction. The nobles regarded him as self-seeking in arranging the marriage between his daughter, Anne Hyde, and James, Duke of York. The Cavaliers held him responsible for the Act of Indemnity and Oblivion, the Dissenters for the Clarendon Code. The sale of Dunkirk was remembered against him, and he was blamed for the episode of the Dutch in the Medway. Charles dismissed his old friend, who was then impeached by Parliament. Many of the charges were untrue, but Clarendon did not wait to hear his fate. He fled to France, where he spent the remaining seven years of his life writing his *History of the Great Rebellion*, the most complete first-hand account of the troubled period of the Civil Wars.

The Cabal (1667–1673)

For the next six years Charles ruled through five ministers known as the Cabal. The word 'cabal' had previously been used to denote a small group of ministers, and by a curious coincidence the initials of Charles's new ministers now spelt the word 'cabal' itself. The new ministers were Clifford and Arlington (both Roman Catholics), Buckingham (the son of Charles I's favourite, who posed as a champion of the Independents), Ashley (later Lord Shaftesbury, a former Roundhead who believed in religious toleration), and Lauderdale (the Scottish peer who governed Scotland and who had some sympathy with Presbyterianism).

This ill-assorted collection of ministers was quite unlike a modern Cabinet. It had no leader and no collective responsibility, but its members had one thing in common: they were all opposed to the Anglican Church and its continued supremacy. Charles was tired of the Cavalier Parliament, with its niggardly finance and its persecuting Anglicanism, and was determined through his new ministers to pursue a less Anglican policy and, if possible, to make himself financially independent of Parliamentary grants.

Charles II and Louis XIV

Henceforth Charles's policy was closely linked with those ambitions of his cousin, Louis XIV, that have been outlined in Chapter XV. Louis' desire to extend French rule and influence throughout Europe gave Charles just the chance he needed of selling the support, or at any rate the neutrality, of England to his cousin.

In 1665 the King of Spain, Philip IV, died, and left his crown to a sickly child, Charles II. Few people expected Charles II of Spain to live long, and as there were no other near heirs to the Spanish throne, the kings and statesmen of

Europe soon began to weave plots for the dismemberment of the Spanish Empire. As it happened, Charles II of Spain lived till the year 1700. Louis, however, was determined to seize the bird in the hand at the very outset of the new King's reign. On the ground that his wife was the daughter of the late Spanish King and his first wife, he laid claim to the whole of the Spanish Netherlands under a local law known as the Law of Devolution. His claim was sheer arrogance, but his real argument was shown when Marshal Turenne invaded the Spanish Netherlands and defeated the weak Spanish garrison (1667). England and Holland were immediately alarmed by this War of Devolution. Both countries feared French naval and commercial rivalry if France obtained the Spanish Netherlands. The prosperity of London and Amsterdam would be threatened by the competition of Antwerp, while the very existence of Holland would be endangered if France reached the Dutch frontier.

England and Holland had just ended the Second Dutch War by the Treaty of Breda (1667), and the English ambassador at the Hague, Sir William Temple, was able to form a Triple Alliance (1668) between England, Holland, and Sweden. The three countries threatened to make war upon France if the invasion of the Netherlands were not stopped. Louis was obliged to make peace in 1668 with only a small part of his ambitions realized. He was infuriated against the allies, but more particularly against Holland. Henceforth he aimed at isolating and subduing the rich Dutch Republic.

This was just the situation that Charles II desired. The King of France, having felt the power of England, was now anxious for its friendship and willing to pay a price. In 1670 Charles and Louis concluded the Treaty of Dover. This contained many secret clauses, known only to the King himself and to Clifford and Arlington, the Catholic members of the Cabal. At a favourable moment Charles was to declare himself a Catholic and attempt the restoration of the Catholic Church in England; Louis was to support Charles by men and money to put down any revolts that might occur. In the following year all the members of the Cabal signed the second and open Treaty of Dover, whereby England and France were to renew the war upon Holland, and Louis was to pay Charles subsidies in return for England's help.

The two Treaties of Dover indicate clearly the real aims of Charles II's policy, namely, alliance with France, war against Holland, the restoration of Catholicism, and independence of Parliamentary control as a result of French subsidies. Within a year or two this policy was patent to everyone.

The Declaration of Indulgence (1672) and the Third Dutch War (1672–1674)

In 1672 Charles II, without Parliamentary authority, issued a Declaration of Indulgence, freeing both Roman Catholics and Dissenters from the penal laws against them, though the former, for the time being, were to enjoy liberty of worship only in their own homes. By coupling the Puritan Dissenters with the Roman Catholics the King vainly hoped to win the support of the former.

Meanwhile Charles had been making preparations for his war against Holland. First he obtained supplies from Parliament on the understanding that they were to be used in favour of the Triple Alliance against France. Parliament was then prorogued. To obtain more money Charles then informed the London goldsmiths, who had lent the Government large sums of money, that he was unable to continue repayment of these loans. This Stop of the Exchequer (1672) ruined many commercial houses, caused great discontent, and lowered the government's credit.

The Third Dutch War (1672–1674) between England and Holland was only part of a bigger struggle between Louis XIV and the Dutch Republic from 1672 to 1678. The Dutch took desperate measures to preserve their independence. They elected as Stadtholder, or head of the state, the 21-year-old William of Orange (later our William III and great-grandson of William the Silent), and ordered the cutting of the dykes to impede the French advance. Within a year William had organized a European alliance against France. At sea the Dutch admiral, de Ruyter, held his own against a combined English and French fleet off Southwold (1672), and, in the following year, drove off an allied attack upon the Texel.

The End of the 'Dover' Policy

With no victories to commend his cause and with in-sufficient money to carry on the war, Charles was soon obliged to recall the Cavalier Parliament. Opposition to his recent policy flared up. The Declaration of Indulgence had raised the cry of "No Popery," and the Dissenters, who had benefited under its terms, were as loud in their opposition as the Anglicans. It was now attacked as illegal, since it had been issued without Parliamentary consent. The Lord Chancellor, Ashley (now the Earl of Shaftesbury), feeling that Charles had tricked him over the secret Treaty of Dover, joined the opposition, and the Cabal began to break up. The Declaration of Indulgence was withdrawn, and Parliament passed the Test Act (1673), which restricted all offices under the Crown to members of the Church of England. The Test Act was fatal to the Cabal, as the Roman Catholic Clifford immediately resigned his office. The King's brother, James, Duke of York, likewise resigned his position at the Admiralty. This open avowal of Catholicism by the heir to the throne, as well as his recent marriage to the Catholic Mary of Modena after the death of his first wife, Anne Hyde, caused many people to view the future with misgiving.

In 1674 Charles was obliged, through lack of money, to bring the Dutch War to an end. The treaty made no important changes, but the commercial power of Holland was gradually declining before English rivalry and the con-tinued attacks of Louis XIV.

The Ministry of Danby (1673-1678)

Charles's next minister was an orthodox Anglican after the style of Lord Clarendon. This was Sir Thomas Osborne, created the Earl of Danby. Danby was a firm believer in Church and King, and under him the persecution of Catholics and Dissenters once more commenced. The foreign policy of the country reverted to that of the old Triple Alliance—alliance with Holland and hostility to France. In 1677 Danby scored his greatest triumph in obtaining the King's consent to the marriage of the Duke of York's elder daughter, Mary, to the Dutch leader, William of Orange. The Duke of York's accession to the throne on his brother's death was looked forward to with much misgiving by many Protestants, but, as he had as yet no sons, his Protestant daughter, Mary, was the next in succession after him. Hence the importance of her marriage to the Protestant leader of Holland.

Although Charles was chastened, he was unrepentant and still lived in the shadow of his 'Dover' policy. He continued to receive secret subsidies from Louis XIV in return for his promises not to ally with the Dutch in an attack upon France. Danby disapproved of this, but at times he was obliged to give his official, though secret, sanction.

The Court and Country Parties

During Danby's ministry the English two-party system began to emerge, though as yet it was only in its infancy. The Cavalier Parliament still existed; but it was less Royalist than at its beginning, and Puritans were sometimes returned at by-elections. Danby therefore began to organize a definite party to support the government, and he obtained members by bestowing offices and bribes. It was called the Court party, and its leading principles were the support of Church and King.

The Earl of Shaftesbury, who felt resentment against Charles over the secret Treaty of Dover, then organized the

Country party, which stood for greater recognition of the rights of Parliament, opposed the ascendancy of the Church of England, and advocated toleration for Dissenters. It also attacked the Catholic leanings of Charles and the Duke of York. Although it opposed Charles's pro-French policy, Louis XIV encouraged the Country party in its attacks upon Danby.

Shaftesbury's first aim was to force the dissolution of the Cavalier Parliament; an unexpected event gave him his chance.

The Popish Plot (1678)

In the late summer of 1678 the details of a Catholic plot were revealed to the country by one Titus Oates, an un-principled scoundrel who had been in turn Puritan minister, Anglican clergyman, and Jesuit. Oates had been living in a Jesuit seminary on the Continent, and had learnt something of the plans for the conversion of England. He now related this plot, plus numerous details supplied by his own imagination, to the authorities. The Catholics, he said, were to murder the King, massacre numerous Protestants, and place the Duke of York on the throne with the aid of a French army. Oates was proved a clumsy liar; but his story was widely believed. The memory of 'Bloody Mary' and the Gunpowder Plot made Englishmen ready to attribute any catastrophe or wickedness to the Catholics, who had already been blamed for the Fire of London and the Third Dutch War. Oates had accused the Duke of York's secretary of complicity in the plot, and among his papers were found letters from Louis XIV's Jesuit confessor dealing with the despatch of French troops to England. Soon afterwards, Sir Edmund Berry Godfrey, the magistrate before whom Oates had made his declaration of the plot, was found murdered in a ditch near London. His death is still a mystery, but at the time it was regarded as the beginning of the Protestant massacre foretold by Oates.

The country was now in a state of panic. London was barricaded as if for a siege, and citizens walked about with 'Protestant flails' to brain Catholic assassins. The word of Oates sent scores of Catholics to prison and even some to the block—while the unscrupulous ex-Puritan-Anglican-Jesuit waxed rich on the rewards of his information.

The Fall of Danby (1678) and the End of the Cavalier Parliament (1679)

Shaftesbury probably believed little of Oates's story, but he used it to inflame Parliament and the country against the Catholics, against the Duke of York, and against Danby. The exclusion of the Duke of York from the throne began to be urged. Louis XIV, who had never liked Danby, now supplied Danby's enemies with the evidence necessary for his overthrow. This was a document in Danby's handwriting promising that England would not take action against France if Louis would continue his subsidies. In vain Danby pleaded that he had acted under the King's orders; he was held personally responsible for his actions—an important principle in our constitutional law. Articles of impeachment were drawn up against him (1678); but Charles prevented the matter from going any further (and more of the truth from being divulged !) by dissolving the Cavalier Parliament in January, 1679. Danby remained in the Tower for the next five years.

The Exclusion Policy (1679–1681)

The critical events of the next two years were conditioned by two facts. First, the country was in a state of mental panic as a result of Titus Oates's story. Secondly, Charles II had no legitimate descendant, and the next heir to the throne was a Catholic—the King's brother, James, Duke of York.

In these circumstances Shaftesbury and the Country party

worked out a policy of excluding James from the throne in favour of the Duke of Monmouth, a weak and vain person, who was the illegitimate son of Charles II. This exclusion policy ensured the Protestant succession and was popular in the anti-Catholic state of the country. But it ignored the principle of hereditary succession and the doctrine of Divine Right. Charles naturally opposed it, but realized the need for caution. Fortunately for him, Shaftesbury found a strong opponent in Lord Halifax, a former member of the Country party. Halifax, nicknamed 'the Trimmer,' felt that Shaftesbury was going too far and realized that personal ambition underlay Shaftesbury's actions. He proposed instead that James's accession should be allowed, provided his powers were strictly limited by Parliament.

The First Exclusion Parliament (1679)

The elections following the dissolution of the Cavalier Parliament gave Shaftesbury a large majority. The Country party, from its headquarters at the Green Ribbon Club in Chancery Lane, knew how to turn the anti-Catholic feeling of the nation to its own account after the fashion of the most up-to-date electioneering-methods.

The new Parliament passed one Act of considerable constitutional importance, namely, the Habeas Corpus Amendment Act of 1679. Persons imprisoned without trial had for long possessed the right of demanding a writ of *habeas corpus*, which ordered the gaoler to bring them up for trial. This ancient constitutional right had been overridden in various ways. The new Act tried to stop these evasions by allowing judges to issue writs during a vacation, setting a time-limit to the period of imprisonment without trial, and forbidding the imprisonment of people in remote places.

In Parliament's eyes its main business was the Exclusion Bill to prevent the accession of the Duke of York. Before the Bill had even passed the Commons the King killed it by dissolving Parliament (1679).

The Second Exclusion Parliament (1680-1681)

Fresh elections were held in the autumn of 1679, and again the Country party obtained a majority. This time the King resorted to the trick of delaying the meeting of Parliament after its first preliminary sitting. For a whole twelvemonth, from October, 1679, to October, 1680, the newly elected members were unable to meet. The Exclusionists organized demonstrations which petitioned the King to summon Parliament, while their opponents replied with counter-petitions in which they abhorred the idea of interfering with the King's constitutional rights. In consequence Shaftesbury's party were called Petitioners and their opponents were called Abhorrers, but these new names were soon replaced by others savouring more of the political arena. The Abhorrers were nicknamed Tories—a name applied to the Catholic cut-throats and bandits who attacked unwary Protestants in Ireland. The Abhorrers replied by calling their opponents Whigs, which was the name given to the Scottish Covenanters, who at this time were engaged in one of their outbursts against the King's government. These party-labels, applied in the political dog-fights over the exclusion policy, lasted for the next two centuries.

In October, 1680, financial difficulties obliged Charles to summon Parliament. The Commons soon passed a new Exclusion Bill, but in the Lords it met with the fierce opposition of Lord Halifax, whose commanding eloquence, coupled with his moderate views, secured its rejection. The Commons were furious, and Charles dissolved Parliament in January, 1681.

The Third Exclusion Parliament (1681)

New elections once more gave Shaftesbury and the Whigs a majority, so the King decided that the new Parliament should meet at Oxford, which was much more Royalist in its atmosphere than London. The Whigs were flushed with triumph and confident of success when they rode into Oxford with bands of armed supporters and banners proclaiming "No Popery, no slavery." They did not know that Louis XIV, afraid of the anti-French policy that a Whig government and its puppet King would pursue, had just promised Charles a three years' subsidy to make him independent of Parliament. On March 28, 1681, just seven days after its first meeting, Charles suddenly dissolved Parliament. The surprised Whigs were completely cowed and quickly dispersed.

The Personal Rule of Charles II (1681-1685)

For the remaining years of his reign Charles ruled without Parliament, despite the Triennial Act of 1664. His financial position was assured by Louis XIV's grants and by the growth in the royal revenue from customs duties consequent upon expanding trade. The French King, sure now of English neutrality, used these years to undermine the freedom of the Huguenots, preparatory to the final revocation of the Edict of Nantes in 1685.

The positions of the English parties were now completely reversed; the Tories were supreme, the Whigs discomfited. The Clarendon Code was strictly enforced against the Dissenters, who were the bulwark of the Whig party. The doctrines of Divine Right and of Passive Obedience—even, it was said, if the King were as wicked as Nero—were proclaimed from the pulpit. The Whig leader, Shaftesbury, was brought to trial for treason (1681), and the poet Dryden, in his famous satire, *Absalom and Achitophel*, attacked him as being

> In friendship false, implacable in hate;
> Resolved to ruin or to rule the state.

Shaftesbury was acquitted by the London jury (London being a Whig stronghold), but in the following year (November, 1682) he fled to Holland, where he died at the beginning of 1683.

At this stage some of the more violent of Charles's enemies hatched a plot to assassinate the King and the Duke of York as they passed Rye House on their return from the Newmarket Races (1683). This Rye House Plot and other plans for a general rebellion were betrayed to the government. Many Whig leaders were imprisoned and in some cases put to death, notwithstanding the obvious innocence of some of them. The Duke of Monmouth was banished from the country.

Thereafter Charles's power was greater than ever. He attacked the corporations which had for long been Whig strongholds. London and sixty-five other towns were brought under royal control; their charters were remodelled to allow them less independence, and their officials henceforth were royal nominees. Since the corporation officials often appointed the borough members of Parliament, Charles was also ensuring that Parliament, when it should next meet, would possess a Tory majority. In contravention of the Test Act the Duke of York, who had recently been busy persecuting Scottish Covenanters, was recalled from Scotland and reinstalled as Lord High Admiral.

Lord Halifax, 'the Trimmer,' protested as strongly against the Tory excesses of these years as he had previously protested against Shaftesbury's excesses, but his protests were unavailing. Charles's power continued supreme to the end, which came in February, 1685. On his death-bed Charles confessed himself a Catholic and was received into the arms of Mother Church by the old priest who had saved his life after the Battle of Worcester over thirty years before. Characteristically, also, the dying monarch apologized to those round him for being "such an unconscionable time dying."

The Growth of the Empire under Charles II

Most of the leading statesmen of Charles II's reign—the Duke of York, Prince Rupert, Clarendon, and Lord Shaftesbury—were interested in maritime and colonial affairs.

The Duke of York at the Admiralty, and Samuel Pepys, the diarist, who was for long secretary to the navy, worked hard to make the fleet efficient.

We have already seen how Charles's marriage with Catherine of Braganza brought us Bombay and Tangier. The latter was abandoned in 1684, but Bombay was handed over to the East India Company, whose affairs continued to prosper. In 1672 Charles II granted a charter to the Royal African Company, formed mainly to promote the slave-trade between Africa and America (see Chapter XX for the trading-companies).

It was on the American mainland, however, that the most important steps for the future were being taken. In 1663 the lands south of Virginia were colonized (mainly by colonists already in America) under the names of North and South Carolina. Their very name, together with that of Charleston, their chief port, reminds us of the reign in which they were founded. Prominent among their founders were Lord Shaftesbury and the philosopher, John Locke. The Second Dutch War (1665–1667) gave us the New Netherlands (see p. 230), which linked the English colonies together. These New Netherlands were afterwards formed into three separate colonies: New York, New Jersey, and Delaware. In 1670 the Hudson's Bay Company was formed, under the governorship of Prince Rupert. Its object was to trade in furs, and it provided an opportunity for English traders to gain a footing in Canada, which hitherto had been a French preserve (see Chapter XX). Finally, in 1681 was established the colony of Pennsylvania. This was the work of William Penn, the son of Admiral Penn who had captured Jamaica in 1655. Charles II owed the younger Penn the sum of £16,000, and in settlement of the debt he made over certain lands in North America. These Penn colonized as Pennsylvania, meaning 'Penn's wooded country.' William Penn was a Quaker, and his colony became a refuge for his co-religionists. Penn treated the Indian natives fairly, bought land from them instead of stealing it, and refused to allow his colonists to bear arms. The capital was named Philadelphia, which means 'brotherly love.' For a time Penn's ideals worked successfully, but later settlers departed from them.

By the end of Charles II's reign twelve of the thirteen American colonies had been established—the thirteenth being Georgia, founded in 1732. They varied considerably among themselves, the Puritan colonists of the northern New England states having little in common with the slave-owning aristocrats of the south. Each colony was allowed to elect its own Parliament, but the everyday work of government was performed by a Governor sent out from England. These colonies and all others were subject to the mercantile system, which regulated their trade for the benefit of the mother country and subjected them to the restrictions of the Navigation Laws (see Chapter XX).

QUESTIONS AND EXERCISES

1. Write a character-sketch of Charles II.

2. Illustrate the importance of the religious question in the reign of Charles II.

3. Describe the life and career of Edward Hyde, Earl of Clarendon.

4. Distinguish clearly the attitudes of (a) the nation, (b) the King towards (i) Holland, (ii) France.

5. Show how the 'Dover' policy illustrates the main aims of Charles II.

6. Write notes on: the Act of Indemnity and Oblivion, the Clarendon Code, the Test Act, the Habeas Corpus Amendment Act.

7. Summarize the growth of the Empire under Charles II.

8. Describe the growth of the party-system under Charles II, paying special attention to (a) the aims, (b) the membership of the two parties.

CHAPTER XVII

JAMES II AND THE GLORIOUS REVOLUTION

The New King

ON his brother's death, James, Duke of York, became King as James II. In many ways the two brothers were dissimilar, and the differences between them are reflected in their respective fates. While Charles II kept his throne for twenty-five years, James II lost his in less than four years. The new King was bigoted, stubborn, and obstinate, though his sincerity contrasts strongly with his brother's underhand methods. James lacked both his brother's charm of manner and his faculty of knowing just how far to go. He was an open and avowed Catholic, whose object was to use the royal power to re-establish the Catholic faith in England. His record against the Scottish Covenanters bespoke the strain of cruelty in his character.

Nevertheless, James was in a strong position in 1685. The Whigs and their exclusion policy were thoroughly discredited, and James chose his ministers from the Royalist Tories. The laws against Dissenters were rigidly enforced, and the mischief-maker, Titus Oates, was almost flogged to death through the streets of London. The Parliament elected in May, 1685, under the new town charters, voted the King £1,900,000 a year for life, while James's promise to regard his own religion as a personal matter and to respect the English Church promised well for the future.

The Rebellions of Argyll and Monmouth (1685)

Two rebellions marked the opening months of the new reign. In Scotland the Presbyterian Duke of Argyll tried to rouse the Covenanters against their new Catholic King. He met with little support even from his own clan, the Campbells, and was soon captured and executed. James, after all, was of another Scottish house, the Stuarts.

In England a rising was led by the Duke of Monmouth, the one-time darling of the Whigs. Monmouth returned from exile and landed at Lyme Regis in Dorset in June, 1685. The gentry of the south-west held aloof, but the peasantry rallied to the cause of the handsome Duke, who had been a popular figure among them several years before. The south-west woollen-manufacturing district was largely Nonconformist and was ready to support their new Protestant champion. Monmouth marched towards London, and at Taunton he was proclaimed King. Meanwhile a Royalist army, led by Lord Feversham and John Churchill (later Duke of Marlborough), was sent against him. On the night of July 5 Monmouth's rustic army tried to surprise the royal forces at Sedgemoor, near Bridgwater. The professionals were prepared, and although Monmouth's countrymen put up a stout resistance, they were eventually beaten. Many of the rebels were cruelly rounded up by Colonel Kirke's soldiers (nicknamed 'Lambs') just back from Tangier.

Sedgemoor had important consequences. Monmouth himself was captured and put to death, and with his disappearance the enemies of James, if they should desire to strike again, would now have to choose the more statesmanlike William of Orange as their champion. James made the rebellion an excuse for increasing the size of the standing army and for wreaking a cruel vengeance upon the rebels. The brutal and drunken Lord Chief Justice Jeffreys was sent down to punish Monmouth's misguided supporters. At the so-called 'Bloody Assize' he sentenced 300 rebels to be hanged and 800 more to transportation to the West Indies, where they lived in virtual slavery. Two of the women put to death (Alice Lisle and Elizabeth Gaunt) had only been guilty of aiding fugitives after the battle! On his return Jeffreys was rewarded by being made Lord Chancellor. The failure of the rebellion had demonstrated the strength of

James's throne; but his cruel vengeance was the first of those mistakes that caused him to lose it.

James's Catholic Policy: the Dispensing Power

James soon began the fatal policy of relieving Catholics from the laws against them. In this he was encouraged by Louis XIV; but the latter's despotism and recent revocation of the Edict of Nantes made Englishmen suspicious of the pro-French policy of the English King.

James began by asking Parliament to repeal the Test Act, but Parliament, for all its Tory loyalty, was strongly Anglican and refused to yield. In November, 1685, Parliament was dismissed and was never again summoned by James. The King also dismissed his Anglican advisers, including the moderate Halifax and the High Churchman Rochester; their places were filled by Catholics. An army of 13,000 men was stationed at Hounslow Heath, ominously near the capital in case trouble threatened.

James now made use of an old prerogative power known as the dispensing power, which enabled the king to dispense with (or do without) the laws in particular cases. In flat defiance of the Test Act, Roman Catholics were placed in important state positions. A Catholic Lord-Lieutenant was appointed in Ireland with the task of enrolling a Catholic army for the King's use. Similarly, a number of Catholics were given commissions in the English army. When the legality of this was questioned in the famous case of Godden v. Hales, the King dismissed the judges that were hostile to him and obtained from the remainder a decision that the dispensing power was quite legal (1686).

This spurred James on to greater activity. In 1686 he defied the law of 1641 which had prohibited the erection of prerogative courts by establishing the Court of Ecclesiastical Commission, similar to the old Court of High Commission. This court, with Jeffreys as its president, was given the task of enforcing the King's religious policy. James next attacked the Universities of Oxford and Cambridge, which were in those days the exclusive preserves of the Anglican Church. In 1686 he appointed a Roman Catholic as Dean of Christ Church, Oxford. In 1687 the fellows of Magdalen College, Oxford, refused to elect James's Catholic nominee as their president and were in consequence expelled. This was, in effect, to deprive them of valuable properties, and it alarmed the holders of Anglican property throughout the country. Many Tories began to wonder if after all the doctrine of 'Passive Obedience' was so valid as they had previously maintained. If so, then parsons might be asked to yield their livings to Roman Catholics, and squires their former monastic property to the Catholic Church!

James's Catholic Policy: the Suspending Power

James refused to see the dangers that lay ahead and now proceeded to use an even wider power—the power of suspending laws altogether, and not just dispensing with them in particular cases. In 1672 Charles II had used this power when he issued his Declaration of Indulgence; but he had wisely withdrawn the Declaration in the following year when Parliament objected. Would James profit by his brother's example if opposition flared up?

In 1687 James issued his first Declaration of Indulgence, which, like his brother's, freed Roman Catholics and Dissenters from the laws against them. Religious toleration is praiseworthy if honestly pursued; but James's idea was to use it as a stepping-stone to something quite different. The English Catholics were small in number, and James hoped that by granting Dissenters toleration he would win them to his side. Then, when he had consolidated his power, he would enforce Catholicism against Anglicans and Dissenters alike. The latter realized this and received their freedom with a coolness that must have surprised their shortsighted King.

In the following year (1688) the second Declaration of

Indulgence was issued, with orders that the Anglican clergy were to read it to their congregations—from those very pulpits that had recently proclaimed obedience even to a Nero! This was indeed to place the clergy in a dilemma; they were obliged to choose between loyalty to their King and loyalty to their Church. They chose the latter. Seven bishops, including Sancroft, the Archbishop of Canterbury, petitioned the King to excuse the clergy from reading out the Declaration on the grounds that it was contrary to the law as laid down by Parliament. James was furious. He imprisoned the seven bishops in the Tower and had them tried for seditious libel. London was in a state of great excitement, Dissenters and Anglicans, Whigs and Tories being whole-heartedly on the bishops' side. When, on June 30, 1688, the accused were found 'not guilty' there were scenes of tremendous enthusiasm, in which even James's soldiers on Hounslow Heath joined.

Exit James

During the trial a further event had occurred to bring the opposition to James to a head. This was the birth of a son to James's Catholic wife, Mary of Modena. Hitherto the next in succession after James had been the Protestant Mary, the daughter of James's first wife, Anne Hyde, and the wife of the Protestant champion, William of Orange. But now quite a different prospect appeared—the succession of another Catholic king. The story was put about that the baby (known to later history as the Old Pretender) was not really James's son, but had been smuggled into the bedroom in a warming-pan; but this unproven gossip would obviously not keep him off the throne.

On the very night, therefore, of the bishops' acquittal a decisive step was taken. Seven of the leading men of the country, both Whig and Tory, sent a letter to William of Orange inviting him to England to safeguard the nation's liberty. William cared little for English liberty; but he cared a great deal for Protestantism and the independence of Holland, which would be in great danger if James succeeded in his Catholic policy and allied England with Louis XIV. At this very moment Louis was contemplating a fresh invasion of Holland, which, if it had taken place, would probably have kept William too busy at home to interfere in English affairs. But Fate played into William's hands. When Louis offered to send help to James, the latter replied that he was quite capable of looking after himself. Louis in annoyance then sent the troops that were to have invaded Holland into the Rhineland instead. His intention probably was to teach James not to be too independent of French help; little did he realize that William's invasion would turn out quite differently from Monmouth's Rebellion three years before.

On November 5, 1688, William of Orange, helped by the 'Protestant wind' that blew his fleet safely down the Channel, landed at Brixham in South Devon. He had with him a mixed but capable army of 15,000 men, but his object was to proceed slowly and avoid every appearance of leading an armed invasion. His banners proclaimed his object—"A Free Parliament and the Protestant Religion"—and his hope was that the country would support him so wholeheartedly that an armed conflict would be unnecessary. His hopes were completely fulfilled. When James dismissed his Catholic advisers and promised a Parliament, the nation was not impressed. When James tried to meet force with force and advanced as far as Salisbury, his most capable general, Churchill (the Duke of Marlborough) went over to the enemy; on his return to London James learned that his younger daughter, Anne, had also deserted him. The game was up. In December, 1688, he tried to escape, but was brought back by some over-zealous fishermen. William had no desire to be burdened with his father-in-law and allowed him to make a second effort to escape. On Christmas Day, 1688, the fugitive King landed in France, where Louis maintained him in regal state for the rest of his life.

The Glorious Revolution

The flight of James marks the first stage in the Glorious Revolution—so-called because of its bloodless nature. James

LOUIS XIV WELCOMING HIS FUGITIVE COUSIN, JAMES II

had lost his throne because his attacks on the Anglican Church and his championship of Roman Catholicism had alienated the vast majority of the nation, including the Tories, who had hitherto been the staunchest supporters of the royal power. England was without a King, for as yet the constitutional position of William and Mary had not been determined. But whatever the outcome, the Glorious Revolution had so far killed such notions as the Divine Right of Kings, Passive Obedience, and Absolute Monarchy, and had made it abundantly clear that Catholic kings were unwanted in Protestant England.

QUESTIONS AND EXERCISES

1. Write a character-sketch of James II as illustrated by his reign, and compare him with his brother, Charles II.

2. Summarize the successive steps in James II's Catholic policy.

3. Explain carefully how James II united all classes of the nation against him.

4. Write notes on: the Duke of Monmouth, Judge Jeffreys, John Churchill.

5. Explain why it was essential for William of Orange to proceed cautiously in his invasion of England.

CHAPTER XVIII

WILLIAM III AND CONSTITUTIONAL MONARCHY

William III and Mary—Joint Sovereigns

In January, 1689, a Convention Parliament met. The most pressing business was to settle the question of the monarchy. Few Tories were extreme enough to desire the recall of James. What, then, was to be the position of William and Mary? Three main answers were advanced. The Whigs wished to give the throne outright to William; but this was too complete a break with the idea of divine hereditary succession for many Tories. These suggested either that James should continue as titular King with William acting as his Regent, or that Mary should be made Queen (thus ignoring James's new-born son) and that William should be ruler in effect with the title of King Consort. Both the Tory suggestions contained difficulties, for if James was still really King he might be able some day to regain his power, while if William were to rule merely in his wife's name, what would be his position if Mary died before him? In any case, William himself decided the issue by refusing to be his wife's lackey. Parliament thereupon took the sensible step of declaring the abdication of James and making William and Mary joint sovereigns (February 13, 1689).

Divine Right and hereditary succession were now gone for ever, for William's hereditary claim to the English throne was very weak. The English monarchy appeared henceforth as a monarchy of convenience. To emphasize the new bargain between King and people, William and Mary had to agree to certain limitations on their royal power (contained in the Declaration of Rights) before they were accepted as sovereigns.

The Bill of Rights (1689)

With the authority of the new sovereigns behind it the Convention Parliament now became an ordinary English Parliament and proceeded to legalize the new situation. The Declaration of Rights was first transformed into a regular Act of Parliament under the title of the Bill of Rights. Henceforth it was illegal for the king to use the suspending power or the dispensing power, to levy money without Parliament's consent, to establish courts for ecclesiastical cases, or to keep a standing army in time of peace. The subject's right of petitioning the Crown, and Parliament's right to be freely elected, to exercise freedom of debate, and to be summoned frequently were also affirmed.

An Act of Succession also declared that if William and Mary had no children the throne should pass to Mary's younger sister, Anne, and her children. Furthermore, no Roman Catholic or person married to a Roman Catholic could ever become sovereign.

The Mutiny Act and Financial Settlement (1689)

Parliament knew from experience that it was not enough to express the pious hope that Parliament should meet frequently; it was necessary to devise means of ensuring it. This was indirectly effected in two ways.

Firstly, the Bill of Rights had declared standing armies illegal; but an army was essential, as Louis XIV was on the point of attacking England for daring to choose his arch-enemy, William, as its King. Consequently a Mutiny Act was passed to legalize the army and the martial law by which it was controlled; but as the law was given effect for one year only, it was necessary to summon Parliament annually to re-pass it. The Mutiny Act has since become the Army Act and is still passed every year.

Secondly, the royal revenue was henceforth regulated

to make it impossible for the King to become financially independent of Parliament. A sum, estimated at £1,200,000, was voted to the King; but only £700,000 of this (later known as the Civil List) was for the expenses of king and court and was voted for life. The rest was for the expenses of government and was voted by Parliament from time to time as required, and very soon only for each year. A system of audit was established to prevent the King from spending government money on his own personal needs.

The Religious Settlement (1689)

Religion, as ever, proved a thorny problem. William's sympathies were with the Low Churchmen and Dissenters, and he tried to induce the Church to broaden its basis by admitting Dissenters within its ranks. This was stoutly opposed by the High Church Party, and the scheme had to be abandoned. Several hundred High Churchmen (including six of the seven bishops who had opposed James II over the Declaration of Indulgence) went so far as to refuse altogether to recognize William as their new King. They refused to take the oath of allegiance, were expelled from their benefices, and formed a separate Church of Non-jurors.

It was obvious, however, that in the circumstances the persecution of Dissenters under the Clarendon Code would have to cease. In 1689 Parliament passed a Toleration Act, which allowed freedom of worship to all Dissenters; Roman Catholics were not included in this grant of freedom, but even they henceforth were able to worship as they pleased provided they did so unobtrusively. The Tories succeeded in keeping the Corporation and Test Acts on the Statute Book, which meant that Dissenters and Roman Catholics were still ineligible for positions in the municipalities or the state. These laws were not repealed till the beginning of the nineteenth century, but they were rarely enforced during the eighteenth century against Protestant Dissenters.

Subsequent Acts of the Glorious Revolution

In 1694 the Triennial Act limited the length of Parliament to three years; this was intended to keep members more closely in touch with public opinion and to prevent such long-lived Parliaments as the Long Parliament and the Cavalier Parliament. In 1695 the Licensing Act was not renewed, and many restrictions upon the freedom of the Press were thus removed. In 1701 the Act of Settlement was passed to prevent a return of the Stuarts; the terms of this important Act are more fully discussed on p. 263.

The Glorious Revolution and Scotland

Presbyterian Scotland, which had suffered persecution at the hands of successive Stuart kings, welcomed the accession of William III. A Convention Parliament met at Edinburgh and offered the Scottish Crown to William and Mary in return for their allowing the Scottish Parliament a larger share in the government of the country. The Scots were also given the right to organize their own Presbyterian Kirk (1690), and the religious disputes between England and Scotland which had lasted from the time of Archbishop Laud were brought to an end.

The new King was not universally accepted, however. The Highlanders, as always, were eager for an opportunity to plunder the Lowlands and the lands of the Presbyterian Campbells. They found a leader in John Graham of Claverhouse, who had been created Viscount Dundee for his part in crushing the Covenanters in Charles II's reign. 'Bonny Dundee' led a wild charge of his Highlanders against the regulars of William at the Pass of Killiecrankie (1689) and succeeded in routing them, but he himself was killed in the battle, and the Highlanders dispersed with their plunder to their mountain-homes. They were offered a pardon provided they took the oath of allegiance by January 1, 1692. Unfortunately the head of the Macdonalds of Glencoe proudly left his submission to the very last moment and then turned up at the wrong place. This made his oath a day too late. A force of soldiers under one of the Campbells was sent to Glencoe, where the unsuspecting Macdonalds entertained them for a fortnight. The soldiers then treacherously rose against their hosts and massacred thirty-eight of them in cold blood (February 13, 1692). The massacre of Glencoe was in some ways an incident in the traditional Highland feuds; but William, who was in Holland, probably knew something about the scheme, and he certainly took no steps to punish those responsible.

The Glorious Revolution and Ireland

If Presbyterian Scotland in the main welcomed the Glorious Revolution, Catholic Ireland strongly opposed it. James II was a Catholic, and his Catholic Lord-Lieutenant, Tyrconnel, had raised a Catholic army and placed Catholics in important posts. The Protestants formed a small minority of the population (about one-tenth) and were regarded as foreigners and usurpers.

When James landed in Ireland in March, 1689, with an army of French soldiers, he met with strong support, and soon all Ireland, except Protestant Ulster, acknowledged him as King. For four anxious months the Protestants of Londonderry (called 'Orange-men,' after the new Protestant King) were besieged by the supporters of James (called 'Jacobites,' from the Latin *Jacobus* = James). At length on July 30, 1689, Londonderry was relieved by an English food-ship which burst the boom that had been placed by the besiegers across the River Foyle.

In the following year William himself landed in Ulster and marched south to capture Dublin. At the River Boyne his advance was checked by the Jacobites, but in the resulting battle (July 1, 1690) William won an easy victory. The Battle of the Boyne was a turning-point in British history. The scared James once more hurried off to France, and

William was able to leave the final subjugation of Ireland to his Dutch general, Ginkel, and to John Churchill. In 1691 the last Irish stronghold, Limerick, was surrendered by its gallant defender, Patrick Sarsfield, on terms contained in the Treaty of Limerick. Irish soldiers were to be allowed to emigrate to France to serve in French armies, and the Irish Catholics were to be given the same freedom as they had possessed under Charles II.

WILLIAM III AT THE BATTLE OF THE BOYNE
From a medal.

Unfortunately for the later relations between England and Ireland, the second part of the Treaty of Limerick was shamefully broken. In 1692 the English Parliament excluded Catholics altogether from the Irish Parliament, which thus became a mere instrument of the Protestant ascendancy. In the following years the two Parliaments seemed to vie with each other in suppressing Ireland. By a series of penal laws Catholics were excluded from all important offices and from the learned professions; their estates were broken up and their priests subjected to vexatious control or else banished. The Anglican Irish also excluded the Ulster Presbyterians from important offices, while the English Parliament penalized all classes and religions alike by prohibiting the export of Irish wool or cloth to any country except England—from which it was largely excluded by high tariffs! Small wonder that the Irish, especially the Catholics, grew discontented with their lot!

The War of the League of Augsburg (1689–1697)

The campaigns in Ireland were really part of a larger continental war, known as the War of the League of Augsburg (the League consisting of England, Holland, Spain, and the Empire), or the War of the English Succession (because of Louis' attempts to dethrone William in favour of the ex-King James).

In addition to Ireland, the main centres of operation that concerned England were the sea and the Low Countries. On June 30, 1690—the day before the Battle of the Boyne— a combined English and Dutch fleet was decisively beaten off Beachy Head. This gave France control of the sea for the time being, and two years later a large force was assembled at La Hogue, in Normandy, to invade England. James himself was there to see them off; but what he actually saw was the complete destruction of the French fleet (1692). The Battle of La Hogue gave England control of the sea for the rest of the war and marks the beginning of English naval supremacy, which was to prove the most important factor in the wars against France in the following century.

The Low Countries, commanding the opposite coast of the Channel, have always been of special importance to England, and it was also to William's interest, as ruler of Holland, to prevent France from conquering the Spanish Netherlands or Belgium. The actual warfare in the Low Countries was uninteresting, consisting mainly of sieges and campaigns that seemed to result in nothing. Twice William suffered defeat—at Steinkirk in 1692 and at Neerwinden in 1693. But the descendant of William the Silent refused to lose hope and was able to prevent his enemies from obtaining any real advantage from their victories. In 1695 his perseverance was rewarded by the capture of Namur.

By 1697 both sides were tired of the struggle, and peace was made by the Treaty of Ryswick. Louis had to give up all his recent gains except Strasburg, he had to acknowledge William as King of England and promise to give no further help to James, and he had to allow the Dutch to garrison certain barrier fortresses in the Spanish Netherlands as a guarantee against future French aggression. Louis' schemes had received their biggest check so far; but the Grand

Monarch was reserving his resources for the Spanish succession question, which was soon to torment the statesmen of Europe and set still larger armies in motion.

The National Debt and the Bank of England (1694)

It had been found impossible to pay for the heavy costs of the war out of ordinary taxation, and the government had been obliged to borrow money for the purpose. Hitherto the government had been in the habit of borrowing money from leading merchants for short periods only. For this war, however, the Whig Chancellor of the Exchequer, Montagu, devised a scheme for long-term borrowing from a group of merchants headed by a Scotsman, William Paterson. They lent the government £1,200,000 at the high rate of 8 per cent., as no time was specified for the repayment of the principal. This was the beginning of our National Debt (1693). It was the child of war, and subsequent wars have nourished their monstrous offspring till it now stands (1959) at about £27,000,000,000.

The merchants who lent William the money were allowed to form themselves into the first joint-stock bank to carry on all kinds of banking-business, including the issue of bank-notes. Thus was formed (1694) the Bank of England, which has developed into the most important bank in the country and has contributed greatly towards the country's economic development (see p. 294).

These financial transactions had important political effects at the time. The Whigs who lent William III's government the money became directly and personally interested in the stability of the Revolution settlement, knowing full well that if James II were restored he would refuse to pay his rival's debts.

William III and English Party Politics

William was never popular with his English subjects. His character was cold, aloof, and stern, and he was regarded

I

as a foreigner whose chief interest in his new kingdom was
to provide his Dutch friends with lucrative posts and use
English resources for his lifelong duel with Louis XIV.
Much of this was true, but Englishmen often forgot that
William had delivered them from James's tyranny, and that
William's continental struggles benefited England as well
as Holland. Many Englishmen, both Whigs and Tories,
kept up some sort of treasonable correspondence with James
so as to be on the safe side in case of a restoration. Among
these were the brilliant soldier, John Churchill, and the
victor of the Battle of La Hogue, Admiral Russell.

Fortunately, the English Queen, Mary, was extremely
popular, but after her death in 1694 William felt his
isolation from his subjects still more keenly.

He had tried at first to please the nation by choosing his
ministers from both Whigs and Tories; but the two parties
disliked each other so much that it was impossible to persuade them to work together, and Parliament, which was
Whig, showed clearly its desire that Whig ministers should
control the expenditure of the sums being voted for the war.
In 1696 William chose a ministry composed entirely of
Whigs. This was the so-called Whig 'Junto,' which marks
an important step in the direction of our modern system
of Cabinet Government. But it was still a long way off our
modern practice. The King still presided at Cabinet meetings, and so little was the connexion between ministers and
Parliament—the very essence of the Cabinet system—
realized that several attempts were made by Parliament to
exclude William's ministers from being elected members. Fortunately for our constitutional development, these attempts
failed. In 1693 William refused to give his consent to such a
Bill, although it had passed both Houses of Parliament.

The Act of Settlement (1701)

Towards the end of William's reign it became necessary for
Parliament to regulate the succession once more, as William

had no children to succeed him, and the Princess Anne (next in succession to the throne) lost the last of her nineteen children, the Duke of Gloucester, in 1700. Unless the Stuart descendants of James II were to be allowed to return, some new arrangement had to be made.

The Act of Settlement (1701) laid down that on Anne's death the Crown should pass to the Electress Sophia of Hanover and her descendants, provided they were Protestants. Sophia was the daughter of the Elector Palatine and Elizabeth, the daughter of James I (see the genealogical table on p. 148). In 1714 the Act of Settlement brought the Hanoverians to the throne in the person of Sophia's son, George I.

The Act of Settlement contained other causes designed to weaken the king's position and to prevent foreign kings from giving posts to foreigners and engaging England in wars on behalf of foreign powers. In addition the king had henceforth to be a definite communicant of the Church of England, and judges were to be freed from royal control by providing that they could be dismissed only by agreement between the Crown and both Houses of Parliament. Otherwise, their salaries were to be fixed and they were to remain in office so long as they carried out their duties efficiently and impartially (*quam diu se bene gesserint*). The resulting independence of judges from both royal and ministerial influence has been one of the most cherished safeguards of our constitutional liberties.

The Spanish Succession Question

The Spanish King, Charles II, who had been on the throne since 1665, was weak in mind and body, and his death had long been expected. He had managed so far to disappoint the vultures who were hovering round his possessions; but his end could not now be far off. With his death the Spanish Hapsburgs would come to an end.

Claimants to the vacant throne were not lacking. The

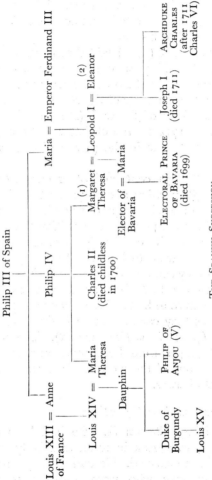

THE SPANISH SUCCESSION

The claimants, shown in capitals, were:

(1) The Bourbon, Philip of Anjou, who eventually succeeded.
(2) The Electoral Prince of Bavaria, who died before the King of Spain.
(3) The Hapsburg, Archduke Charles, who became Emperor in 1711.

French Bourbons based their claim on the marriage of Charles II's elder sister to Louis XIV. The Austrian Hapsburgs pointed out that this sister had renounced her claims to the Spanish throne on her marriage, whereas a younger sister had married the Emperor Leopold I. If it were objected that this younger sister had also renounced her claims, it could be replied that Leopold was also descended from an aunt of Charles II who had *not* renounced her claims. Finally, the royal house of Bavaria put forward a claim based on its descent from the same younger sister who had married the Emperor Leopold.

The question was even more complicated than would appear from this; but it soon became clear that the succession would be settled, not merely by an appeal to legal right, but by diplomatic bargaining and, if necessary, by force of arms. For the prize at stake was too valuable to be lightly surrendered. It included Spain itself, the Spanish Netherlands, possessions in Italy (Naples, Milan, Sicily, and Sardinia) which would give their ruler power over the central Mediterranean, and valuable trading-rights and colonies in Central and South America. Louis XIV, realizing that Austria would not allow a king of France to succeed to this vast empire, put forward his *second* grandson, Philip of Anjou, as the Bourbon claimant. Similarly the Emperor, fearing French opposition, put forward his *second* son, the Archduke Charles, as the Austrian Hapsburg candidate. England and Holland, who were not anxious to see Bourbon power extended either on the Continent or across the seas, favoured the Bavarian claimant, the five-year-old Elector Joseph, whose accession would not greatly upset the balance of power. Failing him, they favoured the Archduke Charles.

In 1698 the First Partition Treaty arranged for the Elector of Bavaria to succeed to the throne of Spain, while Austria and France were to receive compensation in Italy. Unfortunately in the following year the young Bavarian

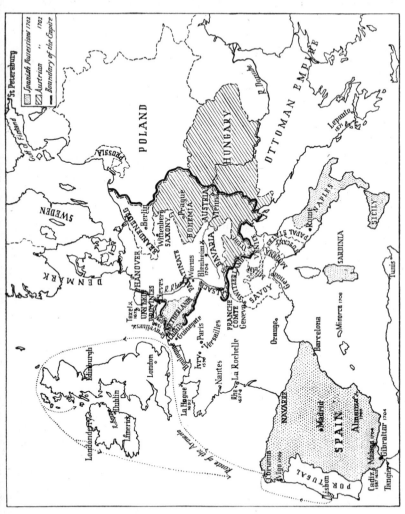

FUROPE IN THE 16TH AND 17TH CENTURIES

Elector died of smallpox, and the business had to be begun all over again. The Second Partition Treaty of 1699 arranged that the Austrian Archduke Charles should inherit Spain and most of its empire, but French compensation in Italy was to be increased.

This arrangement, which reflects credit on Louis' moderation, was suddenly upset in 1700 when the Spanish king died and left the *whole* of his empire to the Bourbon Philip of Anjou, and, failing his acceptance, directed that it should go to the Archduke Charles. Charles II's will reflected the quite natural reluctance on the part of Spain to seeing her empire cut up and parcelled out as if it were a huge cheese. After some deliberation Louis XIV decided to break his pledged word over the Second Partition Treaty and to accept the will. He dramatically appeared before the assembled French courtiers at Versailles, and leaning upon his grandson, Philip of Anjou, exclaimed, "Messieurs, voici le Roi d'Espagne !"

There was some excuse for Louis' action, as Austria had never consented to the Second Partition Treaty and persisted in claiming the whole of the Spanish Empire. But there was little excuse for Louis' subsequent actions. The Tories in England were not anxious to see England involved in another continental war on, as they thought, William's behalf. The independent burghers of Holland were also just now chafing under the strong rule of William. If Louis had acted with restraint, he might have won the Spanish inheritance for his grandson without a major European war. Instead, he announced that Philip of Anjou's claims to the French throne were not impaired by his succession to the Spanish throne. He began to exclude English and Dutch merchants from the Spanish American colonies, and expelled the Dutch from the barrier fortresses and imprisoned the garrisons. The last straw occurred when, on James II's death soon after the Act of Settlement (1701), Louis recognized James's son (the baby born in 1688 and known to history as the Old Pretender) as James III of England, although he had promised in the Treaty of Ryswick that he would no longer support the Stuarts.

The Death of William III (1702)

All this played into William III's hands, and Tories as well as Whigs reconciled themselves to the idea of another war. William had already been building up a Grand Alliance including Holland and the Empire to oppose French ambitions. But just before war broke out the English King died (March, 1702) as a result of a riding-accident in the grounds of Hampton Court Palace. His horse stumbled over a mole-hill, and Jacobites thereafter often toasted "the little gentleman in black velvet" whose burrowings had caused their enemy's death. William left the conduct of the war to the brilliant John Churchill, Earl of Marlborough, whom he had chosen as his envoy in building up the Grand Alliance and as the Captain-General of the allied forces.

QUESTIONS AND EXERCISES

1. Summarize briefly the chief results (a) at home, (b) abroad, of the Glorious Revolution.

2. Describe the difficulties of William III's position in England. How far was he himself to blame for not overcoming them?

3. What fresh checks were placed upon the royal power as a result of the Glorious Revolution?

4. Write out the terms of the following important Acts: Bill of Rights, Toleration Act, Mutiny Act, Triennial Act, Act of Settlement.

5. Write notes on: the Massacre of Glencoe, the Treaty of Limerick, the Whig Junto, the Partition Treaties.

6. Discuss the arguments for and against a government getting into debt (a) for war purposes, (b) for expenditure on peaceful projects.

7. Why did England go to war over the Spanish succession question?

CHAPTER XIX

ANNE AND THE WAR OF THE SPANISH SUCCESSION

Queen Anne

THE new Queen was a well-meaning and placid woman, influenced by two overpowering feelings—her devotion to the Church of England and her affection for the Tory party. She restored to the Church the income that had been seized by Henry VIII, which was formed into a fund called 'Queen Anne's Bounty' to increase the salaries of clergymen. She had for long been a close friend of Sarah, the Duchess of Marlborough, and we are told that "the Queen called herself Mrs Morley and addressed the Duchess as Mrs Freeman when they were together." Thus the Duke of Marlborough (as the Earl was soon made) had 'a friend at court,' while his own charming manner added to his influence over the Queen.

Although a Tory, Queen Anne chose her first ministry from both political parties. The two leading members of the Government were Marlborough and his friend, Lord Godolphin, both of whom were moderate Tories. From 1702 to 1710 Godolphin was really the first minister, and under him the ministry gradually became more and more Whig. Its main task was to prosecute the war.

John Churchill, Duke of Marlborough (1650–1722)

John Churchill was the son of Sir Winston Churchill, a Devonshire squire. He had been a page in the household of James, Duke of York; had seen service in our army at Tangier; and had gained valuable experience by fighting in the French army against the Dutch in the Third Dutch War. He had been responsible for the defeat of Monmouth at Sedgemoor in 1685, but had deserted James during the critical days at the end of 1688. William III had used Marlborough's brilliant gifts in the subjugation of Ireland after the Battle of the Boyne and in the Netherlands during the war against Louis XIV. But William soon discovered that Marlborough was in correspondence with the exiled

James II. For some time the King turned a blind eye to the slippery methods of his general, but eventually he stripped his servant of all his offices and even clapped him in the Tower. Marlborough was soon released and henceforth was content to await the accession of Anne, over whom he and his beloved wife, Sarah, had great influence.

JOHN CHURCHILL, DUKE OF MARLBOROUGH

William had chosen well in selecting Marlborough to command the allied forces, for it needed all Marlborough's brilliance and versatility to cope with the many difficulties of his task. The Grand Alliance of England, Holland, Austria, Denmark, Hanover, Brandenburg, and other smaller powers was often rent with jealousies and divisions. Each state was out for its own ends, and the only bond of unity was the fluctuating fear of Louis XIV's ambitions. The Dutch in particular, who constituted a large proportion of Marlborough's armies, often refused to move from their own frontiers, while the consent of their civilian 'field deputies' was necessary before they could be involved in battle. Louis XIV, moreover, was in many ways in a stronger position than at the outbreak of his previous wars. The inheritance of the Spanish Empire by his grandson, Philip, gave France control of Spain, north Italy, and the vital Spanish Netherlands without a blow; and the loyalty of most of Spain to their new Bourbon King made the expulsion of Philip from Spain almost an impossibility from the very outset. Finally, as the war proceeded, Marlborough had to cope with Tory opposition at home to what was regarded as a Whig war.

If the result of the war was to leave Philip of Anjou on the throne of Spain, Marlborough cannot certainly be blamed for this apparent failure of the allied cause. He achieved more than anyone else could have done in checking Louis XIV's ambitions, in depriving Philip of valuable parts of the Spanish inheritance, and in increasing the power and prestige of England. Marlborough's fame as a soldier has somewhat dimmed his ability as a statesman; but in truth he was one of the most successful diplomatists of his age, managing time after time by his charm of manner, his patience, and his ready wit to keep the allies from falling apart. As a military leader he was superb. The rank and file loved their 'Corporal John,' who always saw that they were well paid and well fed and who always led them to victory. The enemy feared the redoubtable 'Malbrouck,' who could conceive vast strategic plans, execute them with perfect precision, and, on the field of battle, manipulate his men with unsurpassed tactical skill to strike at the enemy's weakest point. Of Marlborough, whose achievements can be ranked with those of Julius Caesar and Napoleon, it has been written, "He never fought a battle which he did not win nor besieged a fortress which he did not take." But his military genius and his extraordinary achievements must not blind us to the bribery and other dishonest means (common faults of his age) by which he often obtained his own ends or enriched himself.

The Opening Years of the War (1702-1703)

The war was fought in many spheres—in the Netherlands, in Spain, in central Europe, in north Italy, at sea, and in the colonies. In 1702 an English fleet destroyed a Spanish treasure-fleet off Vigo, in north Spain. This induced

Portugal to conclude the Methuen Treaty with England
(1703), by which the ancient alliance between the two
countries was resumed. Portuguese wines were allowed
into England (to produce much gout during the eighteenth
century!), and English woollen goods into Portugal on
favourable terms. In the Netherlands Marlborough drove

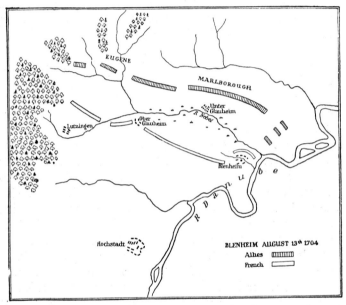

the French out of southern Holland; but they took up a
strong defensive position in the Spanish Netherlands, from
which he was as yet unable to dislodge them, especially as the
Dutch were reluctant to fight away from their own frontier.

1704: **Blenheim and Gibraltar**

Louis XIV now planned an attack upon Vienna by
joining forces with the Bavarian troops (Bavaria being his
only ally) and marching down the valley of the Danube.
The Emperor just now was occupied with a rebellion on

the part of his Hungarian subjects, and the situation for the allies was extremely critical. It was at this juncture that Marlborough conceived the most daring and brilliant campaign of his career, the Blenheim campaign. Despite the opposition of both the English and the Dutch Governments to having their troops moved far from the Netherlands, Marlborough planned to march into central Europe to intercept the Franco-Bavarian attack upon Vienna. He staked his whole reputation upon the success of his venture.

He deceived the Dutch by pretending that the object of his attack was the Moselle valley, but when he reached that river he pushed on with his mixed English, Dutch, and German army up the valley of the Rhine as far as Mainz, and then turned east across Germany. He stormed the key position of Donauwerth, joined forces with Prince Eugene (the ablest of the imperial generals), and placed his army between the Franco-Bavarian forces and Vienna. At Blenheim, just where the little River Nebel joins the Danube, the battle took place (August 13, 1704). An attack on the enemy's right wing distracted their attention from the centre, which they thought well protected by the marshy ground near the river. But Marlborough unexpectedly crossed the marsh, stormed the enemy's centre, and routed the French and Bavarian troops. Eleven thousand men, including the French marshal, Tallard, were taken prisoner. Vienna was saved, Bavaria was crippled, and the French army had suffered its first serious defeat for fifty years.

Characteristically Marlborough scrawled the first brief news of his victory to his wife, who received it ten days later and immediately showed it to the Queen at Windsor Castle:

August 13, 1704. I have not time to say more but beg you will give my duty to the Queen and let her know her army has had a glorious victory. Monsr Tallard and two other generals are in my coach, and I am following the rest. The bearer, my aide-de-camp, Colonel Parke, will give her an account of

THE NETHERLANDS

MILES
0 10 20 30 40 50

NORTH SEA

NORTH

SEA

Texel

FRIESLAND

Apingadam
GRONINGEN
Groningen   Emmingen
Heiliger-Lee

DRENTHE

Enkhuizen
Alkmaar   Hoorn

ZUIDER ZEE

Haarlem

Amsterdam   Naarden

OVERYSSEL
Deventer

Leyden   HOLLAND

The Hague   UTRECHT
Ryswick   Utrecht   Zutphen   GUELDERLAND
Delft   Gouda
Maaslandsluis   Rotterdam   Tiel
Briel   Gorinchem
Dordrecht   Nimeguen
Brouwershaven   Lot Bommel   Mookerhyde
Zierickzee   Breda
Walcheren   ZEALAND   NORTH BRABANT
Middelburg   Goes   Bergen
Flushing   Beveland   op Zoom

LIMBURG

Ostend   Sluys
Nieuport   Bruges   ANTWERP
Dunkirk   Ghent   R. Scheld   Antwerp   Roermonde
Mechlin   Da'lem
FLANDERS   Alóst   Brussels   Elslod   Cologne
Yprès   Courtrai   Oudenarde   BRABANT   Landen   Maestricht   Aix-la-Chapelle   Bonn
Tournay   Steinkirk   Ramillies   Liège
Fontenoy   Waterloo
HAINAULT   Namur   LIÈGE
Valenciennes   Mons   R. Meuse   Cohlenz
Malplaquet   NAMUR

LUXEMBOURG
Treves
Luxembourg

R. Ems   R. Ryssel   R. Yssel   R. Maas   R. Rhine   R. Meuse what has passed. I shall doe it in a day or two by another more at large.

In the same year the English fleet, under Sir George Rooke, appeared off Gibraltar. The Spanish garrison was at Mass, and the fortress was almost unguarded. The English sailors captured the famous rock and, by defeating a French fleet off Malaga in the same year, managed to retain it. The command of the Straits of Gibraltar, which has remained in British hands ever since, gave Britain control of the narrow entry into the Mediterranean. In 1708 Minorca was captured; it remained British till 1783, when it was restored to Spain.

The War continued

Inspired by the successes of 1704, the allies attempted to drive Philip V from the Spanish throne. This was an almost impossible task, as most of Spain, except Catalonia (which has always cherished separatist ambitions), was devoted to the new Bourbon King. In 1705 the Earl of Peterborough, accompanied by the Archduke Charles of Austria, captured Barcelona, the capital of Catalonia, and the Catalans acknowledged the Archduke as Charles III. Another English force, aided by the Portuguese, moved eastward from Lisbon, and in 1706 the allies occupied Madrid. But in the following year the English suffered a serious defeat at Almanza. Although Madrid was reoccupied for a short time in 1710, the Battle of Almanza and the hostility of the Spaniards had really settled the issue, and the allies were steadily driven back to Barcelona.

Elsewhere the war proceeded in favour of the allies. In 1706 Prince Eugene won a victory at Turin and drove the French out of north Italy. In the same year Marlborough won his second great victory of the war at Ramillies, when he once more deceived the enemy by a feigned attack and brought his main body of troops round to the other wing under cover of a hill. In 1708 his third victory at Oudenarde drove the French altogether out of the Spanish Netherlands, and soon Lille, the important fortress-town in north-east France, was in allied hands. Louis was now on the defensive and definitely shaken. He offered quite generous terms of peace, but the allies insisted that the Grand Monarch should join with them to expel his own grandson from the throne of Spain! This was too much to expect, and so the war dragged on. French resistance stiffened now that the war threatened to cross their own frontier, and Marlborough's fourth victory at Malplaquet was dearly bought; in this 'Pyrrhic' victory the allies lost more than the French, although the way into France was now open.

The end of the war, however, was determined as much by events at home as by battles abroad, and to these we must now turn.

The Whig Ascendancy (1702–1710)

Queen Anne's first ministry was chosen from both parties, with the moderate Tory, Godolphin, in charge. Divisions between the two parties soon appeared. The Tories were High Church and wished to revive the laws against the Nonconformists. As the land-owning party they also objected to the increasing Land Tax which was used to pay for the war—a war which they regarded as a Whig war to enrich Whig financiers and merchants who lent money to the Government at high rates of interest and supplied the army with goods at extortionate prices. As the war proceeded, the elections returned more Whigs to the House of Commons, and this, with the Whig ascendancy in the Lords, made them the predominant party in the state. From 1704 the Tory members of the Government began to resign, and by 1708, when the two leading Tories, Robert Harley and Henry St John, went out of office, the ministry had become completely Whig, though it still retained its two original leaders, Godolphin and Marlborough.

The Union of England and Scotland (1707)

Since the Glorious Revolution Scotland had enjoyed a new lease of freedom in Church and State. Her Parliament was strong, her Presbyterian Church was secure, and she had begun to lay the foundations of the educational system for which she has become famous. But her relations with England had not been happy. England excluded Scotland from her trading-ventures and taxed Scottish products imported into England. The ill-feeling between the two countries increased under William III, who would have liked to see the two Parliaments united. From 1696 to 1698 the Scots tried to develop a trading-company at Darien, on the isthmus of Panama. Many hard-earned savings were invested in the scheme, and in 1698, 3000 Scottish colonists went out to try their fortunes. The Darien Scheme was a complete failure, and the colony soon perished before the combined attacks of mosquitoes and Spaniards. The Scots blamed William III for not taking up their quarrel with Spain, but the King was at this moment occupied with the negotiations over the Spanish succession and probably feared also to incur the opposition of English merchants, who resented Scottish trading-schemes quite as much as the Spaniards.

Relations between the two countries grew worse in the next few years. In 1704 the Scottish Parliament, resenting the English Act of Settlement, passed an Act of Security rejecting the Hanoverian succession and claiming the right to choose its own sovereign on Queen Anne's death. This opened up disturbing possibilities of separate sovereigns once more, and perhaps of a Stuart king in Scotland during the English war against France. Despite opposition from extreme nationalists, commissioners from both countries, with the Queen's encouragement, arranged the terms of the Act of Union, which was passed by both Parliaments at Westminster and Edinburgh.

I²

By this Act Scotland brought her separate Parliament to an end and was henceforth represented in the British Parliament by forty-five members of the House of Commons (*i.e.*, about one-eleventh of the total membership) and sixteen members of the House of Lords chosen by the Scottish peers at the beginning of each Parliament. Scotland

PARLIAMENT HOUSE, EDINBURGH
In the seventeenth century. Used by the Scottish Parliament between 1639 and 1707.

was allowed to keep her own laws and law-courts, and the Presbyterian Church was recognized as the established Church. Free trade was established between the two countries, and Scots were allowed to settle in, and trade with, the Empire, as well as to engage in other trading-ventures on the same terms as Englishmen. A new flag, combining the red cross of St George and the white cross of St Andrew, symbolized the union.

Despite continued prejudices the union was eminently successful. Half a million Scots, in return for trading-concessions, had merged their separate Parliament with that of five million English. The threatened disruption of the two nations was averted, and Scotsmen have played a valuable part in the political and economic life of Great Britain and her Empire.

The Fall of the Whigs (1710)

Godolphin's ministry, which, since the dismissal of Harley and St John in 1708, had become purely Whig, was fast losing its popularity. The nation was becoming tired of the war, which the Tories alleged was being continued for the enrichment of Whig merchants and money-lenders and the enhancement of Marlborough's military reputation. The Whig refusal to conclude peace without the expulsion of Philip V from Spain appeared pig-headed in view of the obvious attachment of Spain to its monarch. The Tory Queen Anne, with her principles of Divine Right and her attachment to the Church, disliked her Whig ministers, with their doctrines of limited monarchy and religious toleration. She was also tiring of the imperious and sharp-tongued Duchess of Marlborough, and the Tories, sensing the estrangement, encouraged Harley's cousin, Mrs Masham, to undermine the influence of 'Mrs Freeman' over the Queen.

In 1710 events were brought to a head by a violent sermon preached by Dr Sacheverell before the Lord Mayor and aldermen at St Paul's Cathedral. Sacheverell, the High Church rector of a South London church, bitterly attacked the Whigs and their views; and the Government, in a fit of exasperation, decided to impeach the Tory parson before the House of Lords. This was to make Sacheverell into a martyr and invest the affair with undue importance. The cry of 'the Church in danger' was raised, and the Whigs were accused of violating the right of free speech. The House of Lords merely forbade Sacheverell to preach for three years—a sentence so light that everyone regarded it as an acquittal.

The Queen now felt it safe to dismiss Godolphin, and form a Tory government under Harley and St John (1710). The Tories obtained a majority at the General Election and continued in power for the rest of the reign.

The End of the War

Robert Harley, created Earl of Oxford, was a cautious and moderate ex-Whig, who was soon overshadowed by his more brilliant colleague, Henry St John. St John (1678–1751) was daring and ambitious as a politician and is best known by his title of Lord Bolingbroke. The two ministers immediately set about bringing the war to an end.

Party feeling ran very high towards the end of Anne's reign, and both sides availed themselves of the talents of distinguished writers. Addison and Steele, contributors to the famous *Tatler* and *Spectator* papers, were the two ablest Whig writers. In political satire and party venom they were easily surpassed by the Irish Tory Swift (the author of *Gulliver's Travels*), who published in 1711 a bitter attack on the war under the title of *The Conduct of the Allies*. Swift was a powerful influence among the leaders of the Tory party, and in 1713 he was made Dean of St Patrick's, Dublin. His pamphlet on the war made the demand for peace irresistible. Daniel Defoe, the author of *Robinson Crusoe*, was the first journalist in our history, writing with equal facility for whichever party paid him most. Party pamphlets and news-letters were eagerly discussed in tavern and coffee-house.

In the same year as Swift's pamphlet the Emperor died without heirs and was succeeded by his brother, the Archduke Charles, who now became Charles VI. This made the continuance of the war all the more futile, as to place the Emperor Charles VI on the Spanish throne would upset the balance of power more than allowing Philip V to remain there. At the same time the Marlboroughs fell from power. The Duchess was dismissed from her court appointments and replaced by the more amiable Mrs Masham. The Duke was recalled to England and charged with embezzling public money; the victor of Blenheim was met with cries of "Stop thief!" as his carriage drove through the streets of London.

He retired in anger to the Continent, whence he was recalled in the next reign; but his political and military career was ended by 1711. The Tories appointed the Duke of Ormonde as Marlborough's successor with instructions to avoid giving battle! Meanwhile Bolingbroke opened negotiations with France without informing our allies or safeguarding the liberties of our Catalan friends in Spain—practices which earned for England the title of 'perfidious Albion.' The Queen created twelve new Tory peers to pass the proposed terms through the House of Lords, and in 1713 peace was made by the Treaty of Utrecht.

The Treaty of Utrecht (1713)

Philip V was recognized as King of Spain and Spanish America on condition that he renounced his rights of succession to the French throne. But the Spanish Netherlands, Milan, Naples, and Sardinia were given to the Emperor, and Sicily was given to the Duke of Savoy. Louis XIV recognized the Hanoverian succession in Britain and agreed to give no further support to James II's son, the Old Pretender. Britain received valuable colonies and trading-rights: Gibraltar and Minorca in Europe, and Nova Scotia (or Acadia), Newfoundland, and Hudson's Bay Territory in America. She also received from Spain the right of sending one ship a year to trade with Porto Bello, on the Spanish main, and the right to supply the Spanish colonies with negro slaves. This was the famous Asiento Treaty, from the Spanish word *asiento*, meaning an agreement.

The main results of the war were, therefore, that despite allied victories, the Bourbons obtained the throne of Spain (which they retained till 1931), but that Austria obtained most of the Spanish possessions in Europe. France was exhausted, and Britain had embarked upon her career as the chief naval, colonial, and commercial power of the world.

Tory Policy at Home: the Problem of the Succession

Meanwhile the Tories were reviving the persecution of the Dissenters as a means of demonstrating their High Church principles and undermining the strength of the Whig party. The Occasional Conformity Act of 1711 punished those Dissenters who only occasionally attended the Anglican communion service so as to qualify for office under the Test and Corporation Acts. In 1714 the more vindictive Schism Act attempted to destroy all Nonconformist education by compelling everyone who taught anything except the rudiments of reading and writing to obtain a licence from the bishop of the diocese. Fortunately for English liberties, both these Acts were repealed early in the next reign.

The most thorny problem facing the Tories, however, was that of the succession. Who was to succeed Anne—the Hanoverian provided for by the Act of Settlement, or the son of James II? The Whigs were quite clearly in favour of the Hanoverians; they curried favour at Hanover and pointed out how the Tories had deserted Hanover, along with Britain's other allies, at Utrecht. The Tory leaders, Oxford and Bolingbroke, had, it is true, inserted the clause safeguarding the Hanoverian succession in the Treaty of Utrecht; but this was merely to placate public opinion. Their real sympathies lay with James, and so too did those of the Queen, who was James's half-sister. Oxford tried in vain to induce the Catholic James to change his religion, or, failing that, to promise to safeguard the rights of the Established Church. When James refused, the cautious Oxford was undecided over his next step; but before the Queen's death power had passed out of his hands into those of his ambitious colleague. Bolingbroke was all for boldness and action; he foresaw that the Hanoverian succession would ruin the Tory party, and he plotted to prevent it. On July 27, 1714, he persuaded the Queen to dismiss Oxford. Bolingbroke's scheme was to strengthen the Tory control over the country and then secure the return of the Stuarts; or, if that proved impossible and the Hanoverians were installed, to oblige them to continue the Tory government.

But fate intervened. Anne died on August 1, before Bolingbroke had even a week to arrange his plans. The Whigs had made elaborate preparations for the critical period following the Queen's death, and in their capacity of Privy Councillors they prevented the Tory ministers from having it all their own way. Messengers sped to Hanover, where the Electress Sophia had died two months before. They returned with her son, George, who became George I, King of Great Britain and Ireland. One of his first acts was to dismiss Bolingbroke, who fled to France for greater safety (September, 1714). One of the most critical periods in our history was over, and the Hanoverians, for the time being, at any rate, were safely installed on the throne.

QUESTIONS AND EXERCISES

1. Write an essay on the life of John Churchill, Duke of Marlborough.

2. Give an account of party strife under Queen Anne.

3. Write an essay on (a) the causes, (b) the terms, (c) the results of the Act of Union, 1707.

4. Write notes on: Dr Sacheverell, Dean Swift, Viscount Bolingbroke.

5. Summarize the main results of the War of the Spanish Succession. How far did they represent a loss to France and a gain to England?

6. Write an imaginary attack, from the Tory point of view, on the War of the Spanish Succession as it was being conducted after 1710.

CHAPTER XX

ECONOMIC AND SOCIAL LIFE UNDER THE STUARTS

(For a proper understanding of this chapter, frequent reference should be made back to Chapter IX.)

Mercantilism Supreme

MERCANTILISM, or the regulation of economic life by the state with a view to increasing the national power, found its fullest expression under the Stuarts. The regulation of apprenticeship and the fixing of wage-rates under the Elizabethan Statute of Apprentices continued throughout most of the period. Elizabeth's Poor Law was enforced, and its provisions in some ways were tightened. Monopolies were granted by the early Stuarts to encourage trade—and augment the royal income! Company-trading flourished till the Glorious Revolution.

The desire to obtain a favourable balance of trade, *i.e.*, an excess of exports over imports, influenced economic policy. Native industries were encouraged by the taxation of foreign imports. This was particularly true of corn-growing and cloth-manufacture. In Charles II's reign it was ordered that the dead should be buried in shrouds made of wool and no other material. While the export of raw wool was forbidden, to preserve supplies for the native industry, the export of corn was subsidized so as to encourage agriculture.

Mercantile ideas were applied to our growing possessions overseas as well as at home. Colonies were regarded as subordinate to the mother-country, for whose benefit their economic life was regulated. Manufactures, such as wool and iron, which might compete with those of the mother-country, were forbidden or strictly limited; but the production of useful raw materials, especially for shipbuilding, was encouraged. The colonies were also subject to the restrictions of the Navigation Laws. Thus grew up the old colonial system, an underlying cause of the later revolt of the American colonies. Ireland was treated as a colony, or even worse, for she had political and religious grievances in addition.

Mercantile ideas were not peculiar to England, but were held and practised by most countries at this period. Every empire was regarded by its mother-country as a source of profit. Colbert, for instance, under Louis XIV, regulated French industry and commerce as closely as any English mercantilist (see Chapter XV).

(A) Agriculture

A 'Golden Age'

The Stuart period was a time of steady progress and general prosperity in agriculture, with none of the upheavals that had marked the previous century. Enclosures, indeed, continued. The commoners of Wootton Bassett, in Wiltshire, petitioned Parliament under the Commonwealth against their lord of the manor, Sir Francis Englefield, who had attempted to enclose the common pasture and graze his own cattle thereon. But, in the words of the petitioners:

> the Lord in His mercy did send thunder and lightning from heaven, which did make the cattle of the said Francis Englefield to run so violent out of the said ground that at one time one of the beasts was killed therewith; and as soon as those cattle were gone forth it would presently be very calm and fair, and the cattle of the town would never stir but follow their feeding as at other times.

The Stuarts were more successful than the Tudors in checking enclosures, and with the balance restored between sheep-farming and corn-growing, enclosures produced less disturbance even where they did occur. In some districts enclosures accompanied the utilization of new land and were distinctly beneficial. Charles I himself subscribed money to the draining of the fens, which was successfully carried through by Dutch engineers under Vermuyden. New land in the Pennine district was also taken in for farming at this period. None the less, by 1700 about half the agricultural land of the country was still unenclosed, and in a broad strip down the middle of England open-field farming was still the rule.

The Stuart period was a 'golden age' for the small farmer. The free-holder found his fixed rent decreasingly burdensome with the falling value of money, and the copy-holder was more secure than in the previous century. The free-holder whose land was worth more than forty shillings a year could exercise the county vote for Parliament, and with the growing power of Parliament his own power and prestige increased. Many yeomen (by which was meant, strictly speaking, the free-holders, but which often included the better-off copy-holders) served in Cromwell's armies and played an important part in the struggle against the Crown.

The Emergence of the Squire

After the Restoration the social position of the lord of the manor began to undergo a subtle change. He was slowly being transformed into the squire of the eighteenth century, the petty dictator of his village. Travel or exile abroad broadened the outlook of the nobility and gave them an added sense of importance. The supremacy of Church and Parliament conspired to increase their power, for the landed interest was predominant in Parliament and often controlled appointments to Church livings. Parliament passed Corn Laws, placing import duties on foreign corn, and in 1689 agriculture was favoured by the Corn Bounty Act, which paid a bounty or sum of money to exporters of corn when the price fell below a certain level. When he held the office of Justice of the Peace the lord of the manor controlled the parish officers of his district (overseers, surveyors, and constable) and helped in the general government of his county. The essayist, Joseph Addison, has immortalized one of these squires in Sir Roger de Coverley, the 'hero' of the *Spectator* papers:

> As soon as the Sermon is finished, no Body presumes to stir till Sir Roger is gone out of the Church. The Knight walks down from his Seat in the Chancel between a double Row of his Tenants, that stand bowing to him on each side, and every now and then inquires how such an one's Wife, or Mother, or Son, or Father do, whom he does not see at Church; which is understood as a secret Reprimand to the Person that is absent.

A few Restoration squires, under the influence of continental ideas, introduced new methods on their estates, such as the cultivation of turnips and clover; but widespread improvements in farming did not take place till the eighteenth century.

MANOR HOUSE, LUSTLEIGH, DEVON

The present building was enlarged in the seventeenth century from the original structure erected in the early fourteenth century. The upper part of the porch was built in 1680, but the lower stone arch is of an earlier period. The fourteenth century hall occupied the whole of the house to the right of the porch.

(B) INDUSTRY

The Old-established Industries

The woollen-cloth industry continued as the most important of English industries and was fostered by Stuart statesmen. Although it was scattered in varying degrees throughout the whole country, its most important districts were still East Anglia, the south-west, and the West Riding. Wool was also increasingly used for the stocking-industry of Nottingham and Leicester.

The two next most important industries were coal-mining and iron-manufacture. Small pits were worked in many of the present-day coal-fields, but technical difficulties and the small demand for coal, both for household and industrial purposes, prevented their expansion. The only important coal-mining area was still the Tyneside, whence 'sea-coal' was shipped from Newcastle to London. The smelting of iron-ore was still done by means of charcoal, coal being unsuitable because its gases mixed with the metal to make it too brittle. But the supply of timber for use as charcoal was fast dwindling, and the iron-smelting industry was declining in the Weald and the Forest of Dean. England would have lost one of its most valuable industries had it not been for the discovery (just after the period covered by this volume) that coal could be used for smelting if it was first transformed into coke. The manufacture of iron goods was expanding, however, most of the pig-iron used for this purpose being imported from Sweden. Birmingham was the centre of the hardware-industry, and Sheffield of the cutlery-industry; in the seventeenth century the population of Sheffield more than doubled.

New Industries and Inventions

The earliest references to the cotton-industry occur towards the end of Elizabeth's reign and under James I. The new industry settled in the Lancashire district, where for a time it existed side by side with the older woollen-industry. Its progress under the Stuarts was slow but quite definite; supplies of raw cotton were obtained from Asia Minor by the merchants of the Levant Company. For a century or more it was faced with difficulties: the opposition of the woollen-industry, the competition of imported Indian calicoes, and the impossibility of making cotton thread strong enough for the warp, which led to the manufacture of mixed cloths, such as fustian, from linen and cotton. In 1700 the East India Company was forbidden by Parliament to import Indian printed calicoes. The intention was to protect the English woollen-industry; the chief result, however, was to give an impetus to the English cotton-industry by relieving it of foreign competition. But the tremendous expansion of the cotton-industry, which was to make cotton goods our most valuable single export in the nineteenth and twentieth centuries, did not come till the Industrial Revolution.

At the end of the seventeenth century English industry was once more enriched by many thousands of foreign immigrants—this time by the Huguenots who had fled from the persecutions of Louis XIV. They established or improved many industries, such as paper, linen, glass, and clocks. Most famous of all was the silk-industry, which was practically their creation and which grew up in the Spitalfields district of London and at Coventry and Macclesfield.

In 1705 a patent was taken out for a steam-engine by Thomas Newcomen, a Dartmouth blacksmith. Although expensive to run owing to the heavy consumption of fuel, the engine was very useful for pumping water out of tin- and coal-mines. Newcomen's engine held its own till it was improved by James Watt seventy years later.

Industrial Organization

The same variety of industrial organization existed under the Stuarts as we have noticed under the Tudors. Cottage-industries and crafts flourished in every village and were often pursued as a by-employment to agriculture. In the Sheffield and Birmingham districts small master cutlers and iron-workers made and marketed their own wares. In the West Riding the small independent clothier had not yet fallen a victim to the advance of capitalism.

None the less, capital was accumulating, and its owners were slowly spreading their tentacles over the nation's industry. Large-scale capital was necessary for working most of the coal-mines; but it was in the woollen-industry that capitalism was most advanced. The clothiers grew richer and more powerful, and thousands of workers scattered about the country in their own homes were sinking into the position of wage-slaves. These domestic workers still possessed the relative freedom of working at home, but their low rate of pay necessitated long working-hours and the employment of the women and children of the household. Disputes often occurred between clothier and worker concerning the amount of work done or the amount of raw material given out. Even in the north capital was advancing, albeit more slowly; witness the charming seventeenth-century 'halls' that the more prosperous clothiers of Lancashire and the West Riding built for their homes.

(C) TRADE AND BANKING

Company-trading continued

The trading-companies of Tudor times—the Merchant Adventurers, the Levant Company, the Eastland Company, and the East India Company—continued with varying fortunes under the Stuarts. In addition, new companies were founded.

In 1670 Charles II, prompted by his cousin, Prince Rupert, established the Hudson's Bay Company. Its object was to obtain a share in the valuable fur-trade, which otherwise would have fallen completely into the hands of the French. By the Treaty of Utrecht (1713) the rights of the company over the Hudson's Bay Territory were recognized by the French. The Hudson's Bay Company retained its privileges till 1869, and still carries on trade at the present day.

In 1672 Charles II granted a charter to the Royal African

Company, whose trade was based upon the inhuman traffic in human beings—the slave-trade. From Bristol ships set forth carrying cheap manufactured articles to west Africa. There captured negroes were obtained in exchange and transported across the Atlantic; the horrors of the 'middle passage' were so great that many negroes died before they reached their destination. Those who survived were sold in America, often for work on the valuable sugar-plantations, and the merchants returned home with colonial produce and fat profits in addition. In the eighteenth century Liverpool rivalled Bristol as a slave-port.

The East India Company

The greatest of all companies was the East India Company, founded on December 31, 1600. The company's sphere of activity was defined by its charter as all lands east of the Cape of Good Hope to the Straits of Magellan. At first the company tried to capture the trade of the Spice Islands, but this aroused the opposition of the Dutch, who, in 1623, massacred a number of English merchants at Amboyna. The East India Company, happily for its future history, soon diverted its main activities to India, where, in 1612, it had already built its first factory at Surat. The Mogul emperors of India later allowed other factories to be built. In 1639 Fort St George was built near the site of present-day Madras, and in 1642 settlements were made at the mouth of the Ganges near Calcutta. Charles II, as we have seen, obtained Bombay at his marriage and later rented it to the company.

The East India Company was subject to many criticisms in the seventeenth century, because it had to pay for its imports with precious metals, owing to the small demand for English products among the natives of India. In reply the company maintained that its imports were in demand and were supplied more cheaply than if they were taken by the overland route to the eastern Mediterranean and thence shipped to England. In 1621 it was shown that pepper, which cost 2d. a lb. in India, cost 2s. a lb. at Aleppo after going overland, but cost 1s. 8d. a lb. in England when brought by the East India Company's route. We have already seen how the company's imports of Indian calico were forbidden in 1700, to protect the English woollen-industry—but how this merely gave an impetus to the English cotton-industry! Despite the fact that from 1698 to 1708 a rival company was authorized, the original company triumphed and was instrumental in the eighteenth century in founding our Indian Empire.

The Navigation System

Although Navigation Acts to encourage English shipping had been passed at different times since 1381, it was not till the Stuart period that the navigation system took definite shape. The Navigation Act of 1651, passed by the Rump Parliament, laid down that all goods brought to England or her possessions must be carried in English ships or the ships of the country of origin. This was a direct blow at the Dutch, who made large profits by carrying goods from other countries to England. Other clauses injured the Dutch fishing-industry by prohibiting the import of fish in any but English ships; while the English coasting-trade was completely reserved to English ships. In 1660 the Navigation Act was repassed, with the important addition that certain enumerated articles from the colonies had first of all to be sent to England before any could be sold elsewhere. Among these enumerated articles were sugar (the product of the Barbados and Jamaica, and the most valuable of all colonial products) and tobacco (the chief export of Virginia).

The Navigation Acts were resented by the Dutch and led to the three Dutch Wars under the Commonwealth and Charles II (see Chapters XIV and XVI). During the next half-century English shipping increased tremendously, and the commercial importance of Holland declined. But these results were not entirely due to the Navigation Acts; England was no longer subject to civil strife, and Holland was exhausted by her long wars against Louis XIV. The American colonies and Ireland also resented their inclusion in the Navigation system. But while the colonies were subject to many restrictions, they also enjoyed certain advantages, and for a hundred years, moreover, widespread smuggling tempered the severity of the system and brought large profits to the venturesome.

The Growth of Banking

The conditions of internal trade underwent few changes during the seventeenth century. The navigable portions of some of the rivers were extended, and under Charles II the first Turnpike Act was passed in an attempt to improve the roads by allowing private companies to charge tolls. But little was effected in this direction for another century. Pack-horse trains, sometimes of thirty or forty horses, became more frequent; the post-horse and stage-coach systems were developed; droves of animals made their laborious journeys along the rough and muddy roads. A traveller might meet as many as a thousand geese or turkeys walking from Norfolk to their fate in London.

The seventeenth century's most valuable contribution to English trade and industry was the growth of an English banking-system. In the Middle Ages the Church had frowned upon the charging of interest, and the odious job of money-lending had been generally left to the Jews. After the Reformation the laws against interest were relaxed, and banking, which had originated in Italy, spread to Amsterdam and then to England. It began in England with the London goldsmiths, who had facilities for the storing of valuables—a practice much adopted by the wealthy during the troublous times of the Civil War. The goldsmiths gave their customers receipts for these valuables; these receipts were the first bank-notes, as they were a substitute for the valuables and could be passed from hand to hand as payment. Then the goldsmiths, realizing that their customers would not wish to withdraw all their money at once, began to lend some of it out; this offered opportunities for profit, for if the goldsmith paid his depositors 6 per cent. for storing their valuables with him, he could charge his borrowers 8 per cent. for the loans they took off him. Both Cromwell and Charles II borrowed money from the goldsmiths; but the 'merry monarch' was less honest than the regicide, for in 1672 Charles II refused to repay the capital of his loans (see p. 235). This 'Stop of the Exchequer' dealt a severe blow to banking but did not prevent its development. The convenient practice also grew up of depositors paying their debts by sending a note to their goldsmith asking him to transfer part of their deposits to their creditors; these private notes were the first cheques.

In 1694 the Bank of England was founded in circumstances explained in Chapter XVIII. It was the first joint-stock bank in our history, and owing to its large capital and its close connexion with the government, it soon became the leading bank in the country. In 1708 it was given the privilege of being the only joint-stock bank with the right of issuing notes. As the note-issue was then regarded as the most valuable part of banking, no other joint-stock banks were established for over a century. English banking grew up with a strong head but with weak members, for apart from the Bank of England, there were for long only numerous private banks, many well conducted, but many also with insufficient resources or regard for the rules of sound banking.

(D) THE POOR LAW

Elizabeth's Poor Law enforced and modified

The first two Stuarts tried honestly to relieve poverty by enforcing the provisions of Elizabeth's Poor Law, but after the Restoration Justices of the Peace and parish overseers were often allowed to grow slack and neglect their duties. The changed attitude was reflected in the famous Law of Settlement (1662), which allowed parishes to send new-comers with insufficient means back to their native parish (where they had the right of settlement) within forty days of their arrival. The excuse advanced was that poor people often moved from parishes where relief was small to those where it was more generously granted. The effect of the law was to prevent the poor and unemployed from moving about the country in search of employment, and the Law of Settlement came in for much hostile criticism on the part of later writers. It also led to many legal disputes between parish and parish, and overseers often seemed more intent on thrusting their poor upon other parishes than in attempting to relieve them.

About 1700 certain towns began to erect workhouses, where they could set the unemployed to work and test the genuineness of their destitution by a strict system of discipline. Bristol led the way in 1696, and by 1714 London and Norwich and several other large towns had followed its example.

(E) Social Life

The Development of Town Life

The Stuart period saw no great changes in the life of the countryside, but in the towns important advances were made, especially after the Restoration. Town life reached its highest development in London, though a few of the larger provincial towns, such as Norwich, Bristol, and York, or watering-places, such as Bath or Tunbridge Wells, whose popularity began about 1700, reproduced on a smaller scale many of the features of London life.

London was the economic and political capital of the country, and had long since overflowed the ancient city-boundaries. In its narrow cobbled streets could be seen every type and class of human society. Street-sellers shouted the virtues of their wares (our modern word 'coster-monger'

A LONDON BELLMAN

derives from the 'costard-mongers,' or apple-sellers, of the time); ballad-singers sang popular ditties or what passed as news; my lady's sedan-chair brushed the one-legged beggar just home from the wars or the fast-legged thief pursued by a shouting and tumultuous crowd; and when dusk fell and the dim street-lanterns were lit, the watchman could be heard shouting the hours of the night, and the late reveller hurried homeward and kept to the middle of the street for greater safety.

After the Restoration the court was gayer, and all sorts of amusements, such as card-playing, dancing, and horse-racing, flourished. The theatre was popular, and the opera was introduced from Italy. A new institution, the coffee-house, became fashionable at this period. Here men could

BOYS' SPORTS
From a book of 1659 A.D.

gather and, while they sipped the new beverage, could discuss politics, learn the latest news, conduct business—or perhaps just gossip. The House of Lloyd's, world-famous now for its insurance and its shipping-intelligence, began as a coffee-house. The ancestor of the modern newspaper

A SEDAN CHAIR

appeared at this time in the news-letter—a single sheet of paper giving information about coach time-tables, lost property, strange portents, and, above all, the latest political news. Pamphlets and periodicals, like Dean Swift's *Conduct of the Allies* and Addison and Steele's *Tatler* and *Spectator* were eagerly read and discussed wherever society foregathered, in the coffee-house, drawing-room, or the gardens that lined the river's embankment. Town life was just entering on perhaps the most interesting period of its history, the eighteenth century.

QUESTIONS AND EXERCISES

1. Write notes on the following industries under the Stuarts: coal, iron, cotton, silk.

2. Describe the domestic system as it existed in the woollen-industry. What were its advantages and disadvantages to worker and clothier?

3. Describe the main features of the trade of the following companies: East India, Royal African, Hudson's Bay.

4. Write an essay on the Navigation Acts.

5. Describe the main

K

INTERIOR OF A COFFEE-HOUSE

From a satirical print of the period. The momentous discussion between the two gentlemen standing seems to have produced disastrous consequences upon their neighbours.

features of (*a*) administration of the Poor Law, (*b*) banking under the Stuarts.

6. In what ways did the London of 1700 differ from the London of 1600?

CHAPTER XXI

LEARNING AND THE ARTS IN THE SIXTEENTH AND SEVENTEENTH CENTURIES

(A) LITERATURE

Early Tudor Prose

THE first half of the sixteenth century was an age of prose. Literature was stimulated by the development of the printing-press and the religious and social controversies of the time. The *Sermons* of Bishop Latimer, written in a vigorous and homely style, denounced the high living and the extortions of the wealthy classes. Sir Thomas More produced his *Utopia* in 1516—an account of an ideal state, written originally in Latin and not translated till after his death. He also wrote a *History of Richard III*. Among ecclesiastical writers we may notice Tyndale and Coverdale, whose translations of the Scriptures anticipated the Authorized Version of the following century, and Cranmer, whose work in producing the English Prayer Books under Edward VI rendered a valuable service to the development of English prose.

" The Spacious Days of the Great Elizabeth "

Although the Renaissance had produced the Oxford Reformers at the beginning of the Tudor period, it was not till the reign of Elizabeth that the full effects of the Renaissance were seen in England. The exploits of English sailors, the opening up of new lands, the defeat of Spain, the devotion of Englishmen to their Queen as the symbol of their national life—all these specifically English influences joined with the reawakening of the human mind and the renewed interest in man that characterized the Renaissance in general to make the reign of Elizabeth one of the most glorious in our history.

In prose Hakluyt collected together the exploits of English sailors in his *Principal Navigations, Voyages, and Discoveries of the English People*. Hooker's *Laws of Ecclesiastical Polity* justified the Elizabethan Church settlement by an appeal to our past history. The *Survey of London* by John Stow—a record of London's history over the past centuries—

YARD OF AN ELIZABETHAN INN
Showing the galleries.

demonstrated another aspect of the renewed interest in the nation's past.

But it was in the related realms of poetry and drama that the Elizabethan age excelled. England, it has been said, became "a nest of singing birds." Sir Philip Sidney, who was killed at the Battle of Zutphen in the Netherlands (see p. 103), developed the sonnet as a poetic medium and wrote in prose his essay on *The Defence of Poesy* and a romance called *Arcadia*. Edmund Spenser, who spent much of his life in Ireland, where he held an administrative post, used his enforced leisure to produce his *Faerie Queene*. In this long allegorical poem the praises of England are sung, and under a thinly veiled disguise Elizabeth herself often becomes the heroine of the poem. Spenser's imagery and versification have had such an abiding influence upon later poets that he has been called "the poet's poet."

The most significant literary fact of the age, however, was the development of the English drama. In the Middle Ages the gilds had provided amusement and instruction by their miracle-plays; but the gilds were decaying, and men were demanding more than the simple fare of the medieval pageant. They wanted plays which would give them the thrill of the adventurer into foreign parts, the joy of the historian in re-creating the past, or the delight of the satirist in exposing human weaknesses —in fact, plays about anything and everything relating to human life. Hence in the reign of Elizabeth there was a perfect spate

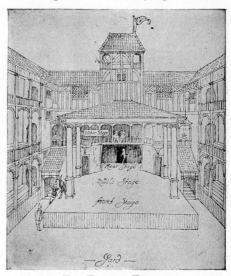

THE FORTUNE THEATRE

From a reconstruction made by Mr W. H. Godfrey for the *Picture Book of British History* (Cambridge University Press).

of play-writing, much of it mere rubbish, but some of it containing the greatest plays in our language. Hence, too, came the development of the theatre. At first bands of strolling players acted in the court-yards of inns, with the audience grouped in the surrounding galleries. But after about 1580 the first permanent theatres began to be built, including the 'Globe' theatre (1599), with which Shakespeare was connected. These early theatres, which had grown out of the inn court-yard, were very different from our modern elaborate buildings. The centre was open to the sky, the outer stage projected far into the 'pit' (so-called because it could be used for cock-fighting and bear-baiting), and galleries ran round three sides. As for the production, there was very little scenery, boys took the parts of female characters, and the players acted in 'modern dress' (the doublets, hose, ruffs, cloaks, bodices, and billowing skirts of the period).

WILLIAM SHAKESPEARE

From the copperplate engraved by Martin Droeshout as frontispiece to the First Folio Edition of Shakespeare's works in 1623.

Among Elizabethan dramatists may be mentioned Christopher Marlowe, the author of *Doctor Faustus* and *Edward II*; Beaumont and Fletcher; Ben Jonson, whose plays include *Every Man in his Humour*; and, of course, William Shakespeare, much of whose work overlaps into James I's reign.

William Shakespeare (1564–1616) was born at Stratford-on-Avon. As a young man he moved to London, became an actor, and was soon given the task of writing plays. In the 1590's his unrivalled contributions to our national literature began with his lighter comedies. Soon he was producing his historical plays, which revived the past of our own country and of Rome, and after 1600 he produced the famous tragedies *Hamlet*, *Macbeth*, *Othello*, and *King Lear*. On April 23, 1616 (his own birthday and St George's Day), England's greatest poet and dramatist passed away. Shakespeare drew freely upon classical literature and old English chronicles for his plots; but his delineation of character, his versification and above all his imagery make his work distinctively his own. His plays also illustrate the love of England and the pride and faith in human achievements that characterized his age. In *Richard II* the dying John of Gaunt thus describes his native land:

> This royal throne of kings, this sceptred isle,
> This earth of majesty, this seat of Mars,
> This other Eden, demi-paradise;
> This fortress, built by nature for herself,
> Against infection and the hand of war;
> This happy breed of men, this little world;
> This precious stone set in the silver sea,
> Which serves it in the office of a wall,
> Or as a moat defensive to a house,
> Against the envy of less happier lands;
> This blessèd plot, this earth, this realm, this England.

Early Stuart Literature

The outstanding literary figure of James I's reign was Sir Francis Bacon (1561–1626). Bacon was a true child of the Renaissance in his versatility and his detached, scientific outlook upon human affairs. His manifold interests are shown in his *Essays*, his *History of Henry VII*, his *Advancement of Learning*, and his *Novum Organum*. In 1611 appeared the Authorized Version of the Bible. With the growing practice of Bible-reading that accompanied the spread of Protestant and Puritan ideas, the Authorized Version soon had an unrivalled influence not only upon men's thoughts but also upon their language. The literary styles of John Bunyan in the seventeenth century and John Ruskin in the nineteenth century (to name only two later writers) are sufficient to show the influence of the Authorized Version upon our national literature.

In the middle of the seventeenth century many beautiful lyrics were written by Robert Herrick and others. The greatest poet of the age was the Puritan, John Milton, (1608–1674). Among his early works is the masque, *Comus*, a kind of play accompanied with singing and dancing; such productions were very popular at this time. In his most famous prose work, *Areopagitica*, Milton penned a noble defence of the freedom of the press. His majestic sonnets treat of many themes, including the Lord Protector, the massacre of Protestants in Savoy, and the blindness which afflicted the poet in later life. After the Restoration Milton devoted himself to his greatest work, his epic poem *Paradise Lost*, which deals with the fall of Satan from heaven and his temptation of man. It was followed by the less successful sequel, *Paradise Regained*. Milton's extraordinary knowledge of ancient and modern literature pervades these two works, while his Puritan disapproval of the frivolity of the Restoration period is shown in *Paradise Lost*, where he describes those

> luxurious cities, where the noise
> Of riot ascends above their loftiest towers,
> And injury and outrage; and, when night
> Darkens the streets, then wander forth the sons
> Of Belial, flown with insolence and wine.

Contemporary with Milton was the Puritan tinker, John Bunyan, who spent many years in Bedford Gaol after the Restoration for illegal preaching. Bunyan's masterpiece, *Pilgrim's Progress*, describes the journey of Christian from the City of Destruction and the many temptations and obstacles he had to overcome before he reached the Celestial City.

The Restoration and Queen Anne Period

Milton and Bunyan were far from typical of the Restoration period, when new influences appeared to give Restoration literature a distinctive character of its own. The nation became light-hearted, and so did its literature. The influence of Louis XIV's France was seen in the undue attention paid to the form in which thoughts were expressed. Wit and polish were more sought after than originality of thought, and Shakespeare was criticized for his breaches of the 'rules of good writing.' In poetry the heroic couplet became the commonest literary form, as in Pope's lines

> True wit is nature to advantage dressed,
> What oft was thought but ne'er so well expressed.

Social life at the time is portrayed in the diaries of John Evelyn and Samuel Pepys. The theatre, which had been closed by the Puritans, was reopened, and a new group of playwrights appeared to satisfy the broad taste of the Restoration playgoer. Among Restoration dramatists should be mentioned Congreve (the author of *The Way of the World*), Wycherley, and Farquhar. The statesman, Clarendon, contributed to literature his *History of the Great Rebellion*. In *Hudibras* the poet Samuel Butler satirized the Puritans, who, he alleged

> Compound for sins they are inclined to
> By damning those they have no mind to.

John Dryden (1631–1700) was the leading literary figure of the age. In his use of the heroic couplet and his mastery of wit and satire he is surpassed only by Pope in the next century. His masterpiece is his attack on Lord Shaftesbury and the Whigs contained in his *Absalom and Achitophel*.

Soon after the Glorious Revolution the Whig philosopher, John Locke, produced his *Essay on the Human Understanding* and his *Treatise on Civil Government*—books which justified the Revolution by preaching the necessity for intellectual liberty and maintaining that a government should hold power only so long as it performs its trust with justice and efficiency.

Queen Anne's reign was a period of intense literary activity, when many of the greatest of English prose-writers were living. Addison and Steele were contributing their essays to the *Tatler* and *Spectator*. Defoe was producing his hack-work for the political parties, and after Queen Anne's death he was to write his *Robinson Crusoe* and his *Journal of the Plague Year*. Dean Swift was influencing public opinion against the war by his *Conduct of the Allies* and placing obstacles in the way of his own clerical advancement by his *Tale of a Tub*, which offended the Queen's taste. In 1726 his best-known work, *Gulliver's Travels*, was published. Human activities cannot naturally be defined by reigns, and the reign of Queen Anne was only part of the larger

Augustan age of English literature—the period dominated by Alexander Pope, whose best work belongs to the reign of George I.

(B) MUSIC AND PAINTING

Elizabethan England was a land of music. Many of the old English folk-songs and country dances were written down at this time; instrumental and vocal music was popular, and many new pieces were composed. The ability to take one's share in part-singing or to play the viol or the virginal was regarded as an essential accomplishment. Among songs madrigals were very popular, and many beautiful Elizabethan madrigals are still sung. In barber's shops viols and lutes took the place of the modern newspaper, and the waiting customer would select his instrument, if he were so minded, and play an air upon its strings. Plays and masques provided opportunities for singing and instrumental music; many of Shakespeare's plays contain songs which are still often rendered in their Elizabethan setting. But it was Church music that gave the composer his best scope. The most famous Elizabethan composer was the organist, William Byrd (1538–1623), a pupil of Thomas Tallis, another organist. Both of these composed much Church music still in use. Byrd was closely followed by Orlando Gibbons (1583–1625), who composed many hymn-tunes and anthems and who died suddenly at Canterbury at Charles I's marriage service, for which he had composed the music. The greatest English composer in the seventeenth century was Henry Purcell (1658–1695), who, besides composing Church music, wrote much opera-music for the new form of entertainment that became popular after the Restoration. Thereafter English musical composition declined, and the revolutionary advances of the eighteenth century were made by the German composers, beginning with J. S. Bach and Handel.

In painting England for long remained a backward

country, although on the Continent important schools of painting succeeded one another. The Italian Renaissance school of the fifteenth and sixteenth centuries was followed by the Flemish and Dutch schools of the seventeenth century. But although England, over the course of two centuries, produced no outstanding native-born painter, she attracted to her shores important continental artists who made England their home. The German artist, Hans Holbein (1497–1543), painted numerous portraits of the leading figures of Henry VIII's reign. The Flemish painter, Vandyke (1599–1641), a pupil of Rubens, was made court painter by Charles I and was subsequently given an English knighthood. On his death he was succeeded by the German-born Sir Peter Lely, who, during the Commonwealth, portrayed Cromwell and, at the Restoration, was appointed Court painter to Charles II. Last in this succession of foreign-born artists was Sir Godfrey Kneller, another German, who remained court painter from Charles II to George I. Thereafter in Hogarth, Sir Joshua Reynolds, and many others England produced a school of painting of her own.

(C) ARCHITECTURE

From Gothic to Renaissance Styles

Henry VII's Chapel, Westminster Abbey, shows the transitional nature of early Tudor architecture. The building itself, with its flying buttresses, its ornamented pinnacles, its pointed windows, and its fan-tracery roof is unmistakably Gothic. The royal tomb inside, however, shows, in its Corinthian pilasters, the approach of the new Renaissance style.

The Renaissance style of architecture originated in Italy, where Gothic architecture had never taken deep root. It represented a return to the styles of ancient Rome and Greece, with, however (like many other aspects of the Renaissance), additional features which saved it from becoming a mere slavish imitation of the past. The classical Doric, Ionic, Corinthian, and Composite 'orders' were revived and widely used in the colonnades and rows of pilasters that distinguished the new style. The pediments which surmounted colonnades and porches were often filled with sculptures and ornamentation, often referring to subjects of classical mythology, in direct contrast to the Christian subjects in vogue in the Middle Ages. The pointed arch of the Gothic styles was now replaced by the semi-circular arch of ancient Rome, and tall, heavenward-pointing spires gave way to spacious and contented-looking domes. The Renaissance period has been called 'the golden age of accessories,' on account of the numerous special features, such as ornamental vases, festoons, fountains, balustrades, and monuments, that were often added to decorate the main building.

The most famous Renaissance building in the world is St Peter's at Rome. This was begun in 1506, took more than a hundred years to complete, and numbered among its architects such famous names as Bramante, Raphael, and Michelangelo.

Tudor Architecture: a Transitional Stage

The Renaissance style took a long time to reach England, and early Tudor architecture is either in the last of the Gothic styles (the perpendicular style) or else of a transitional nature. King's College Chapel, Cambridge—perhaps the best example of perpendicular Gothic in England—was completed by Henry VIII after having been begun by the Lancastrian Henry VI. Generally speaking, however, little ecclesiastical building took place under the Tudors; the Middle Ages had produced sufficient churches, and the temper of the Reformation period did not favour an increase. Instead, Tudor architects employed their talents on palaces, colleges, country houses, and mansions.

Early in Henry VIII's reign Wolsey built for himself

the magnificent palace at Hampton Court. This was constructed in narrow dark-red bricks laid together in what is called the 'English bond.' Massive gateways covered the entrances to the quadrangular courts, the walls of which were surmounted by battlements. Tall and curiously elaborate chimneys were used to produce a decorative effect.

COURTYARD OF MORETON OLD HALL, CONGLETON
An ornate example of Tudor architecture.
Photo Frith

Characteristic of the period also is the Great Hall, added by Henry VIII; its roof is of the hammer-beam type, and inside the hall can be seen the minstrels' gallery and the dais flanked by oriel windows. At St John's College, Cambridge (founded by Henry VII's mother, Lady Margaret Beaufort), and at Trinity College, Cambridge (founded by Henry VIII), can be seen other examples of Tudor red-brick architecture.

Elizabeth's reign is most remembered for its country mansions built for the growing class of successful merchants and enriched gentry of the time. These often exhibit both Gothic and Renaissance features, with the latter gradually predominating. These country houses were often built on an E-shaped plan, to allow more air and light than the former court-yard plan. Under Elizabeth, too, were erected many of the half-timbered houses characteristic of the Tudor period.

KIRBY HALL, NORTHAMPTON

Originally built in 1570, it was later added to by Inigo Jones. The central façade shows the influence of the sixteenth century Italian architect, Palladio.

Stuart Architecture: Inigo Jones and Sir Christopher Wren

After 1600 the full force of continental influences began to be felt. Inigo Jones (1573–1652) returned to England after studying the architecture of Italy, especially of the great Italian Renaissance architect, Palladio. In 1620 he built what may be regarded as the first purely Renaissance building of any importance in England, the Banqueting House, Whitehall.

With Sir Christopher Wren (1632–1723) English Renaissance architecture reached its highest point. Wren was an

Oxford mathematician and Professor of Astronomy, and with other scientists he helped to found the Royal Society. He forsook science for architecture, and after the Great Fire he was appointed surveyor-general of the royal works, with the task of rebuilding St Paul's.

Wren's St Paul's is one of the masterpieces of Renaissance architecture. Its lower façade consists of Corinthian columns, its upper façade of Composite columns, while the whole building is surmounted by a colonnaded drum supporting a magnificent dome which rises 365 feet above ground-level. The building took thirty-five years to erect (1675–1710). Wren's plans for rebuilding London with spacious streets were never carried out; but he was able to adorn the new London with about fifty churches, among which St Clement Danes and St Mary-le-Bow are the best known. Wren also completed

SIR CHRISTOPHER WREN
National Portrait Gallery.

Greenwich Hospital, the first plans for which had been made by Inigo Jones. Many Wren buildings can be seen in other parts of the country: at Oxford, the Tom Tower of Christchurch; at Cambridge, Pembroke Chapel and Trinity College Library. He also added extensively to Hampton Court Palace, which William III intended to remodel to rival Louis XIV's Palace at Versailles. At Hampton Court one can pass in a few seconds from the old-world red-brick courts of Wolsey to the dignified and symmetrical buildings of the Renaissance period built nearly two hundred years later. The Wren portions are built of lighter and wider bricks than the Tudor portions, and the bricks are set in the 'Flemish bond' common in Holland. Portland stone is used to face much of the brickwork. Balustrades, large rectangular windows, Corinthian pilasters, and pediments are typical Renaissance features. Inside can be seen wood-carvings by Grinling Gibbons (1648–1721), the most famous of English wood-carvers. Wren lies buried in the crypt of St Paul's with

ST PAUL'S CATHEDRAL
Photo Will F. Taylor

ST MARY-LE-BOW, CHEAPSIDE

This characteristic Wren steeple achieves the effect of a Gothic spire by the use of receding circles of columns.

the famous epitaph, *Si monumentum requiris, circumspice* ("If you seek his monument, look round you").

After Blenheim the government commissioned Sir John Vanbrugh to build a palace to be presented to the Duke of Marlborough. Hence arose another majestic Renaissance building, Blenheim Palace, in Oxfordshire. So extensive was it that the poet Pope suggested as an epitaph for Vanbrugh:

> Lie heavy on him, earth, for he
> Laid many a heavy load on thee.

The classical revival in architecture lasted throughout the eighteenth century and into the nineteenth century, by which time the neglected Gothic was once more revived.

(D) Science

English Men of Science in the Seventeenth Century

Modern science arose in the sixteenth century, and the greatest names were at first all foreign, such as Copernicus and Galileo (see pp. 17–18). The first Englishman affected by the new scientific outlook was Sir Francis Bacon, who, amid his other labours, found time to write the *Novum Organum*, advocating experiment and observation as the only sure bases of scientific progress. Bacon was too much occupied in politics and law to make any noteworthy discoveries himself, but, as he said of himself, he "rang the bell which called the other wits to work."

In 1614 a Scottish mathematician, John Napier, invented logarithms. In 1628 an English physician, William Harvey, published his discoveries on the circulation of the blood. Harvey was the most famous physician of his day and was with Charles I when the royal standard was raised at Nottingham in 1642.

During the Civil War several men of science formed a small society to discuss scientific ideas in peace and quiet. After the Restoration this developed into the Royal Society, still the most famous of English scientific bodies. In 1662 Charles II, who was himself interested in chemistry, granted it a charter. Its leading member was the Irishman, Robert Boyle, who discovered the law named after him concerning the relation between the volume and pressure of gases.

The most famous English scientist in the seventeenth century was Sir Isaac Newton (1642–1727). Newton studied at Trinity College, Cambridge, and in his twenties was made Professor of Mathematics in the university. In 1687 he published his *Principia* giving an account of many of his discoveries. He contributed much to the mathematical theory of the calculus, and was the first to enunciate clearly the Laws of Motion and of Gravitation that lay at the basis of all later mechanics and astronomy. In 1703 Newton was elected President of the Royal Society. With characteristic modesty he stated that if he had been able to see a little farther than most men it was because he could stand on the shoulders of the giants who had preceded him. But he himself was a giant among giants, and his shoulders have proved invaluable to all later investigators, including the present-day Jewish scientist, Einstein, who has modified some of Newton's conclusions.

QUESTIONS AND EXERCISES

1. Show briefly how the spirit of the Renaissance affected (a) literature, (b) architecture, (c) science.

2. Write an essay on "The Spacious Days of the Great Elizabeth."

3. Write notes on the following buildings: St Peter's, Rome; Henry VII's Chapel, Westminster; Hampton Court Palace; the Banqueting House, Whitehall; St Paul's Cathedral; Blenheim Palace.

4. Write briefly about the work of (a) William Shakespeare, (b) John Milton, (c) Sir Christopher Wren, (d) Sir Isaac Newton.

5. With what do you associate the following: Sir Francis Bacon, William Harvey, Inigo Jones, Robert Boyle, John Bunyan, Henry Purcell?

APPENDIX I

INDEX TO BOOKS AND AUTHORS RELATING TO BRITISH HISTORY

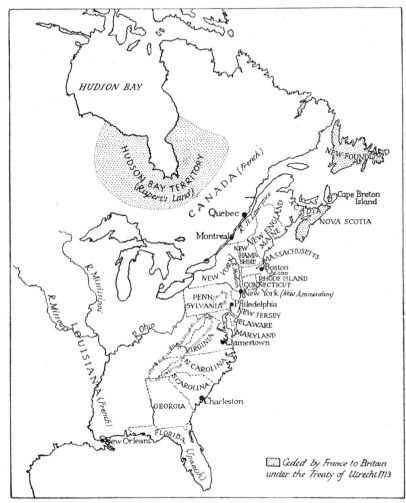

HUDSON BAY

HUDSON BAY TERRITORY
(Rupert's Land)

NEW-FOUNDLAND

CANADA (French)

Cape Breton
Island

Quebec

St Lawrence

ACADIA

NOVA SCOTIA

Montreal

NEW ENGLAND

MAINE

NEW
HAMP-
SHIRE

MASSACHUSETTS

NEW YORK

Boston

Hudson

RHODE ISLAND

CONNECTICUT

New York (New Amsterdam)

R. Mississippi

R. Missouri

LOUISIANA (French)

R. Ohio

PENN-
SYLVANIA

Philadelphia

NEW JERSEY

DELAWARE

MARYLAND

Jamestown

VIRGINIA

N. CAROLINA

S. CAROLINA

GEORGIA

Charleston

FLORIDA

New Orleans

(Spanish)

Ceded by France to Britain
under the Treaty of Utrecht 1713.

EUROPEAN COLONIZATION IN NORTH AMERICA

APPENDIX II

DATE-SUMMARY OF ENGLISH COLONIZATION IN NORTH AMERICA

1583 Failure of Gilbert's attempt to colonize Newfoundland (p. 103).

1585 Failure of Raleigh's attempt to colonize Virginia (p. 103).

1607 Virginia colonized (p. 163).

1620 Pilgrim Fathers (p. 163).

1620–1640 (about) Puritans emigrate to found New England states (p. 173).

1633 Maryland founded for Roman Catholics (p. 173).

1663 Carolina colonized (p. 244).

1667 Treaty of Breda gives England New Amsterdam or New York (pp. 230 and 244).

1670 Hudson's Bay Company established (pp. 244 and 290).

1681 Pennsylvania founded by the Quaker, William Penn (p. 244).

1713 Treaty of Utrecht: England obtains Hudson's Bay Territory, Newfoundland, and Nova Scotia (p. 281).

1732 Georgia founded (p. 245).

	MONARCH	ENGLAND	SCOTLAND & IRELAND	OTHER COUNTRIES
	HENRY VII (1485–1509)	1487 Lambert Simnel 1492–1497 Perkin Warbeck 1496 Intercursus Magnus	1494 Poynings' Law	1492 Columbus 1498 Vasco da Gama
1500		1505 Charter to Merchant Adventurers	1503 marriage of Margaret and James IV	
1510	HENRY VIII (1509–1547)	1510 execution of Empson and Dudley 1515 Wolsey Chancellor 1516 Utopia 1517 Commissioners on Enclosures	1513 Flodden Field	1513 Battle of Spurs 1516 Erasmus' New Testament 1517 Luther's attack 1519–1522 Magellan
1520		1528 divorce proceedings begin		1520 Field of Cloth of Gold 1521 Diet of Worms 1525 Pavia 1527 Rome captured by Charles V
1530		1530 death of Wolsey 1533 Cranmer Archbishop 1534 Act of Supremacy 1535 More and Fisher executed 1536 & 1539 monasteries dissolved 1536 Pilgrimage of Grace 1539 Act of Six Articles	1534–1535 Revolt of Geraldines	1536 Calvin's *Institutes*
1540		1540 execution of Thomas Cromwell	1542 Solway Moss	1540 Society of Jesus 1540–1564 Calvin at Geneva 1543 death of Copernicus
	EDWARD VI (1547–1553)	1547 Somerset Protector 1549 First Prayer Book; Ket's Rebellion; fall of Somerset	1547 Pinkie	1545–1563 Council of Trent

III

CHARTS

TUDORS

	Monarch	England	Scotland & Ireland	Other Countries
1550		1552 Second Prayer Book		
	Mary (1553–1558)	1553 Lady Jane Grey 1554 Spanish marriage; reconciliation with Rome		1553 Willoughby and Chancellor
		1556 Cranmer burn.		1555 Peace of Augsburg
	Elizabeth (1558–1603)	1559 Elizabeth's Religious settlement	1505–1572 John Knox	1558 England loses Calais
1560			1560 Treaty of Edinburgh 1561 Mary Stuart in Scotland	
		1563 Statute of Apprentices	1565 Mary marries Darnley 1567 murder of Darnley 1568 Mary in England	
		1569 Rebellion of Northern Earls		
1570		1570 Elizabeth excommunicated 1571 Ridolfi Plot		
				1571 Lepanto 1572 Sea-beggars at Brille; St Bartholomew 1577–1580 Drake's voyage round world
1580		1580 Jesuit mission 1583 Throgmorton Plot	1580 Spanish troops at Smerwick	1584 William of Orange murdered 1585 Leicester in Netherlands; attempt to colonize Virginia
		1586 Babington Plot 1587 Mary Stuart executed 1588 Armada		
1590		1591 'The Revenge'		1590 Ivry
		1598 death of Burghley	1598 Tyrone's victory at Yellow Ford	1598 Edict of Nantes

	Monarch	England	Scotland & Ireland	Other Countries
1600		1600 East India Company 1601 Poor Law	1602 Mountjoy reconquers Ireland	
	James I (1603–1625)	1604 Hampton Court Conference 1605 Gunpowder Plot 1606 Bate's case	1607 Plantation of Ulster	1607 Virginia colonized
1610		1611 Authorized Version 1612 death of Cecil 1613 marriage of Elizabeth and Elector Palatine 1616 death of Shakespeare 1618 execution of Raleigh		1609 Dutch truce 1618–1648 Thirty Years War
1620		1621 Bacon impeached; Commons' Protestation		1620 Pilgrim Fathers 1623 massacre at Amboyna 1624–1642 Richelieu 1625 Grotius
	Charles I (1625–1649)	1627 Five Knights' case 1628 Petition of Right; murder of Buckingham 1629–1640 Eleven Years' Tyranny		1627–1628 siege of La Rochelle
1630		1633 Laud Archbishop of Canterbury 1637 Prynne, Burton Bastwick; Hampden' case	1633 Wentworth in Ireland 1637 new Prayer Book in Scotland 1639 1s Bishops' War	1632 death of Gustavus Adolphus
1640		1640–1642 Long Parliament's Reforms 1641 execution of Strafford 1642–1646 1st Civil War 1644 Marston Moor 1645 Naseby 1648 2nd Civil War: Preston 1649 execution of Charles I	1640 2nd Bishops' War 1641 Irish Rebellion 1643 Solemn League and Covenant 1645 Philiphaugh 1649 Drogheda and Wexford captured	1642 death of Galileo 1648 Peace of Westphalia
1650	Common-wealth (1649–1660)	1651 Worcester; Navigation Act 1652–1654 1st Dutch War 1653 Instrument of Government 1655 Major-Generals	1650 Dunbar; Monk in Scotland	1655 Jamaica captured

320

STUARTS

	MONARCH	ENGLAND	SCOTLAND & IRELAND	OTHER COUNTRIES
1660		1657 Humble Petition and Advice 1658 death of Cromwell		1657 Blake at Santa Cruz
	CHARLES II (1660–1685)	1660 Restoration 1661–1665 Clarendon Code 1665–1667 2nd Dutch War 1665 Plague 1666 Fire 1667 fall of Clarendon 1667–1673 Cabal		1661–1683 Colbert's reforms in France 1667–1668 War of Devolution 1668 Triple Alliance
1670		1670 Treaty of Dover 1672 Declaration of Indulgence 1672–1674 3rd Dutch War 1673 Test Act. 1673–1678 Danby 1678 Popish Plot 1679–1681 Exclusion Question 1679 Habeas Corpus Act	1679 murder of Archbishop Sharp; Bothwell Bridge	1672–1678 Louis XIV's Dutch War
1680	JAMES II (1685–1688)	1681–1685 Personal Rule of Charles II 1685 Monmouth's Rebellion 1686 Hales' case 1687 1st Declaration of Indulgence 1688 2nd Declaration of Indulgence		1685 Edict of Nantes revoked
	WILLIAM III (1689–1702)	1689 Bill of Rights; Toleration Act	1689 Killiecrankie; Londonderry	1689–1697 War of League of Augsburg
1690			1690 Battle of the Boyne 1691 Treaty of Limerick 1692 Glencoe	1690 Beachy Head 1692 La Hogue
		1693 National Debt 1694 Bank of England; Triennial Act 1696 Whig Junto	1696–1698 Darien Scheme	1697 Treaty of Ryswick 1698–1699 Partition Treaties
1700				1700 death of Charles II of Spain
	ANNE (1702–1714)	1701 Act of Settlement 1702–1710 Godolphin's ministry		1702–1713 War of Spanish Succession 1704 Blenheim; Gibraltar
			1707 Act of Union with Scotland	
1710		1710 Sacheverell; fall of Whigs		
		1714 failure of Bolingbroke's Plot		1713 Treaty of Utrecht

INDEX